6.

D0408362

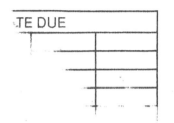

.TE DUE

THE BEAST
THE EUNUCH
AND THE
GLASS-EYED
CHILD

ALSO BY RON POWERS

The Newscasters: The News Business as Show Business

Face Value *(a novel)*

Toot-Toot-Tootsie, Good-Bye *(a novel)*

Super Tube: The Rise of Television Sports

White Town Drowsing: Journeys to Hannibal

RON POWERS

THE BEAST
THE EUNUCH
AND THE
GLASS-EYED
CHILD

Television in the '80s

HARCOURT

BRACE

JOVANOVICH

San Diego   New York   London

Library of Congress Cataloging-in-Publication Data
Powers, Ron.
The beast, the eunuch and the glass-eyed child:
television in the eighties/Ron Powers.—1st ed.
p. cm.
ISBN 0-15-111251-7
1. Television broadcasting—United States. I. Title.
PN1992.3.U5P69   1990
791.45'0973—dc20   90-4446

Designed by Michael Farmer
Printed in the United States of America
First edition
A B C D E

Acknowledgments

These essays originally appeared as columns in *GQ* magazine. I am doubly indebted to *GQ*'s resourceful editor-in-chief, Arthur Cooper—first for his conviction that a topic as quicksilver as television programming could be fitted into a monthly format, and second for his gallant carte-blanche tolerance of my disputatious voice. As for my working liaison at *GQ*, the precocious managing editor Eliot Kaplan, he has transcended the inherently irritating properties of being both young *and* irrefutable. He is a writer's editor, and thus a kind of scarce public resource. Considering that, I forgive him for being well-groomed.

Contents

FIRST FLICKER   xv

I THE INDUSTRY   1

SORRY, FAWN, YOUR 15 MINUTES ARE UP   7

THE COOL, DARK TELEGENIUS OF ROBERT PITTMAN   21

THE AGONY OF DECEIT   40

LAWYERS, GUNS AND MONEY   47

TWAIN WRECK   55

BROADCAST OOZE   62

                                                                   xi

IVAN THE TELEGENIC   70

OUT, OUT, DAMNED SPOT   76

BILL COSBY MEETS THE MAYFLOWER MADAM   83

II   PLAYERS   89

IT CAME FROM NEW JERSEY   95

REAL (SICK) PEOPLE   105

THE VOYEUR   113

THE MOST DANGEROUS MAN IN TELEVISION IS . . .   119

JOE "THE LIVING LEGEND" FRANKLIN IS A VERY
    LOVELY GUY. WE'VE GOT PROOF!   126

THE APPRENTICESHIP OF SHELLEY LONG AND KITTY FELDE.
    KITTY *Who?*   134

NORMAN MARK GETS THE LAST NYAH-HAH-HAH-
    HAH-HAH   140

WHERE THERE'S A WILL, THERE'S A MOYERS   151

III   PROGRAMS   160

SUNDAY MOURNING   165

L.A. Law: D.O.A.   175

SORRY, MAURY   183

THE MALE EUNUCH   191

OMIGOD, WHAT HATH HOLLY WROUGHT?   199

TRIVIAL PURSUITS   206

THE POPCORN PUGILISTS   213

Thin of the Night   220

The Beastie Girls   227

The Last Human Being on Saturday Morning   235

"But Daddy, Try to Grok the Story Line"   242

The Last Angry Mouse   248

IV   LAUGHS   257

When the Laughter Was Real   263

The Last Angry Man   269

Mother Knows Best   276

A Most Uncommon Common Man   283

Dabney Coleman, World's Greatest, Uii, Jerk   290

V   NEWS, WEATHER AND SPORTS   297

Dan Rather Loses the Frequency   305

Womb with Ado   313

Shock of the News   320

. . . And Now, a Nanosecond for the News   327

The Boob Tube   334

The Right's Tough   341

Hurricane Willard and Other Blowhards   349

Love That Bob   355

The Seat of Power   362

Afterglow   369

First Flicker

I used to wonder—once, for instance, as I stared at a rouged woman eating alone in a cafeteria, decked out in a pillbox hat, a lace veil and padded shoulders—what it might be like to become suspended, half-consciously, in a pluperfect state, a sealed capsule of age: specifically, that age when we are, in the words of the poet Linda Pastan, most typically ourselves.

(I probably need to specify that this sighting occurred after pillbox hats and padded shoulders went out of fashion, but before they came back in again; or rather, before "fashion" itself ceased being something that came and went, and yielded instead, like everything else in American time, to endless re-combination.)

I have since come to know what that suspended state is like. Still a few fall seasons short of my jubilee, I am aware that as contrasted to my society, and certainly to my fitful and oft-abandoned profession—television criticism—I am increasingly an anomaly, an artifact: I am old enough to retain a cultural memory *anterior to television.*

It is within that cultural memory that I feel most typically myself.

And most estranged from this work of evaluating television.

Television programmers of the "videofluent" era tend to regard my generation of critics—a dwindling herd, to be sure, like caribou or liberal Democrats—with a kind of anthropological bemusement.

We don't get it. We have the inexplicable inclination to compare television to *something else*—some netherworld that might be described, for want of a more specific label, as That-Which-Is-Not-Television.

As nearly everyone knows, there is no longer any such place.

Not that we caribou had been denied fair warning. It was as early as 1974—about two distinct geological ages ago, in the video epoch—that a shrewd audiovisual theorist named Tony Schwartz proclaimed, in *The Responsive Chord*, the death of history outside the widening sphere of TV. History was obsolete, suggested Schwartz—along with Truth, as Truth was presently understood. Both had been replaced by what Schwartz called "a state of resonance."

By "state of resonance" Schwartz meant this: that the electronic communicator has departed from all traditional ways of imparting information or referring to a coded record of the past. The process is reversed: The point now is to trigger the release of visual memories that TV watchers have stored up— by saturating the viewers with more visual images.

Watching television, then, evokes a memory of television. Thus television becomes its own referent, its own test, its own standard for measuring validity.

Schwartz stated it in the form of a maxim:

"In communicating at electronic speed, we no longer direct

information *into* an audience . . . but try to *evoke* stored information out of them, in a patterned way."

So much for History. But the resonance process neutralizes Truth in the same stroke. "Truth, as a social value," Schwartz announced, "is a product of print. . . . The question of Truth is largely irrelevant when dealing with electronic media content."

The essays in this collection amount to a view of post-Schwartzean, mainstream television in the 1980s from the vantage point, as it were, of the lady in the pillbox hat. (For reasons of masculine vanity I wish it had been a bozo in Damon Runyon pinstripes that I'd spotted there in the cafeteria— but an image is an image.)

They are "occasional" pieces—selections from a monthly magazine column—and therefore serendipitous in their various choice of topic. What unifies them, I think (not that "unity" is such a big deal these days), is my ongoing attempt to isolate and examine the vast manifestations of Schwartz's prophecy—the deaths of Truth and History—as they fissioned through the cosmos of television in that decade.

It was the Eighties in which American television peeled itself away from its remaining adherences to external norms, scales and restraints, and asserted itself as a primary, generative force in the culture. In its brokering of three Presidential elections (not to mention countless other political campaigns); in its transformation of news and information; in its desanctifying of the Protestant liturgy; in its usurpation of text as the basis of education in many public schools; in its unrestrained celebration of majoritarian, corporatist values; in its merging with the technologies of data storage and of surveillance; in its radical destabilization of typographic culture; and in its invention of a pervasive, *sui generis* idiom—the decontextualized idiom of MTV—television in the Eighties finally fulfilled the worst nightmares of a half century: It devoured its host culture.

Not at all coincidentally, the Eighties marked the decade in which television criticism shifted, to some extent, from a distanced, adversarial locus (the locus of typographic logic, proof, refutation, context and sense of history) to the autovalidating locus of the emerging video culture itself.

This shift was true not only in criticism that appeared in newspapers and magazines. For about 40 years there endured a prickly tradition of literary skepticism toward television—from E. B. White in the late 1930s through George Orwell, and Anthony Burgess, and Norman Mailer, and on through Jerzy Kosinski, with his quintessential video-voyeur Chance Gardiner, of *Being There*, published in 1971.

And then that tradition fell silent for a few years. In its vacuum Andy Warhol welcomed the medium into the sacristy of Art. When television re-emerged as a referent in literary writing in the early 1980s it occupied a curiously *accepted* status at worst in the work of the new, toneless minimalists. A little later on, with the emergence of the subtoneless Bret Easton Ellis and Tama Janowitz— incarnations, in a certain sense, of Chance Gardiner— TV was enshrined, without irony, at the center of the cosmos.

There remain a few powerful and independent voices of daily and weekly TV criticism in this country. In fact, television criticism in certain important ways is more informed, more politically aware and more eloquent than at any time in the medium's history (or antihistory). The surviving skeptics of periodical journalism can take advantage of the growing stature of television studies in academia, with its rich and growing body of analysis, interpretation and dissent.

The problem is, however, that these voices do not define the great conversation about video as it affects the consciousness of most Americans. The permeating voices of TV criticism in the 1980s have been those of writers employed by daily national newspapers and weekly magazines that are themselves compromised by a perceived need to merge their identities with television's.

Only in that perspective is it possible to explain the transcendently asinine observation of the TV critic for *USA Today* (an observation examined in a bit more detail inside these pages) that if Bill Moyers really wanted to get it *right* about the condition of black people in America, he would stop interviewing unwed mothers and their estranged sexual partners in the slums of Newark, and tune in instead to *The Cosby Show*.

This critic's flight from rational coherence, by the way, is a ghastly validation of the most frightening indictment against video by its academic critics: That as it seeps ever more deeply into the root system of our consciousness, it attacks our capacity to differentiate between reality and the representation of reality. Stephen Donadio, a professor of American literature at Middlebury College, has argued that represented experience (as seen on the video screen) is rapidly replacing direct experience as the defining sensibility in American life. Echoing Walker Percy's earlier observation about the movies, Donadio suggests that television *certifies* what it shows (and, by implication, decertifies what it does not show).

This certifying of represented experience may account, in part, for the macabre escalation of moral anesthesia that surfaced throughout the American culture in the 1980s, an anesthesia that showed up in many varied ways. The movies, heavily conditioned by television, offer a handy example. It's an example that, inexplicably to me at least, has gone generally unstressed among regular reviewers and critics.

I am referring to the acute rise of graphically rendered sadism, prolonged violence and attenuated suffering—most peculiarly, in movies that are not primarily *about* sadism, violence and suffering. (*Who Framed Roger Rabbit* and *Batman*, two recent movies that caught the attention of children the world over, each contained scenes of maiming and disfigurement that would have been unthinkable as recently as 15 years ago.) It is at least plausible to raise the question of a link between this new cinematic bloodthirstiness, and the tone of corrosive jocularity that impels much of this bloodthirstiness, and its lethal replication in the nation's streets, city parks, school playgrounds, workplaces, highways and homes.

But then, of course, one of the tenets of the video culture, as articulated by its emerging generation of programmers, is that *there are no links*. It's all—ebb and flow. That at least is central to the philosophy of Robert Pittman, the mastermind of MTV, whose thoughts on the irrelevance of moral authority are examined somewhat further inside.

REWIND.

I was born two years after television itself—at least after its American birth inside the World of Tomorrow pavilion at the 1939 World's Fair. My hometown, Hannibal, Missouri, on the banks of the Mississippi River, was literary ground: Samuel Clemens had lived there as a boy a century before.

I lived in Hannibal for 17 years, long enough to form an expectation of the world defined by an allegiance to the land, to one's relatives and neighbors, to useful work, to the seasons and their celebrations, to a kind of civic *stream* of agreements, duties, worship rituals, myths, moral codes. (How enlightened those moral codes were, or the myths and the worship rituals, is of course another story.) For the first 16 of those 17 years I never saw a television set; and television would remain at the periphery of my life for the next 10.

My first memory of electronic media involves my grandfather's lap, an easy chair and a console radio. I sat there listening with him to the words, as he dialed through the rich static of American radio air. I was fascinated that when he turned the radio switch off, the voices would linger for a few seconds as the tubes cooled and the orange glow behind the glass dialing plate faded.

My grandparents bought the first TV set in my extended family—an Emerson, as the resonances of American history would have it—when I was in high school. In order to watch TV, my parents, my brother and sister and I would have to get into my father's Nash and drive the nighttime length of

Hannibal, then up to the crest of Union Street Hill, to the house where my waiting grandfather, in his white shirt and suspenders, would usher us into his living room and, with a little formal bend at the waist, turn on the volume knob.

My grandmother thought that Fred and Ethel Mertz were man and wife in real life. My Baptist grandfather would say, of a trapeze artist on Sealtest Super Circus: "She ain't hard to look at." None of us could figure out why the basketball games we saw took 10 minutes or more to finish when the game clock showed 2:45.

But the TV set was never more than a curiosity for me. Words were what seemed to matter. Words linked things. Words had linked Samuel Clemens with his great place in the world, and in history. I decided that I would write words, too. I imitated Clemens. I became a newspaperman. Eventually I found my way to Chicago.

"The magic of words still remains for me," wrote one of Chicago's grandest old-time newspapermen, Ben Hecht. "I prefer them to ideas." It was a love of words, not a taste for ideas, that drew me to writing a television column for *The Chicago Sun-Times* in 1970. Chicago newspapering was a word-loving game then, and I wanted in. I wanted a column, any column, and the TV beat was what happened to be available. I got it. I did not own a television set. (I went knocking on the doors of my friends, asking to watch, say, *Me and the Chimp*, in the way one might ask to borrow a cup of sugar.) After a while the managing editor ended the standoff and requisitioned me a set. But it seemed almost incidental, somehow. The point was words. Chicago newspapering was still like that in those days.

As was the world. In 1970 the video cosmos was still cooling down from its postwar Big Bang of about 25 years before. Half as old as it is now, that cosmos was still about twice as identifiably . . . *other*. Television was still over *there*. People sat over *here* and watched it, and then at some point they crossed the intervening distance and switched off the set and reinvolved themselves in what was still quaintly known as the "real world."

Television was like the movies, then—or so people thought— in that it was this separate, discrete universe of entertainment. A diversion from Life Itself.

It hadn't yet become Life Itself. Not quite.

FAST FORWARD.

Some candor is required here: I've tried a few times, over the years since then, to stop writing about television altogether. To get away— put real distance between myself and It. "Attempting to find in motion what was lost in space," as Tom's weirdly apt soliloquy in Tennessee Williams's *The Glass Menagerie* has it. I have never been able to develop, or rationalize, that winsome, rueful, can't-live-with-it, can't live-without-it affection that some critics find it necessary to profess, and may actually feel. Ask me what my favorite program is and you're likely to get a blank stare. It isn't intellectualism, it isn't elitism. I'm simply like the lady in the pillbox hat. Pluperfect. I just want to express what is most typically myself.

Okay. That, and I tend to think of television as the goddamned American Id made manifest, an image that terrifies me more than a little.

And yet I've never been able to stray very far. As Tom confesses a few lines later, "I tried to leave you behind me, but I am more faithful than I intended to be." (Tom, of course, is addressing his absent sister Laura; I don't even want to think about the post-Freudian implications in *that* analogy.) I've come back for all the usual obsessive, love-hate reasons—convenience, necessity, prurience, sentiment, guilt—but always with the underlying conviction that grew in me during those lambwhite days at *The Chicago Sun-Times* twenty years ago:

That television, for better or for worse, is a subject that matters, perhaps *the* unifying and inevitable subject of our time, besides the warming and poisoning of the planet itself. And that its baleful signals, as inimical as they seem to be to narrative expression, must be engaged and resolved through words—bold, assertive, adroit, insouciant *words*; words as representatives of the most ancient and primary human expressive impulse, arrayed against what is newest and most artificial.

REWIND.

Not long ago I moved with my family from New York to our present home in Vermont, where the white disks of satellite dishes are still partly obscured by foliage, and at least one family we know personally doesn't own a set. In packing the dusty detritus from our basement, the stashed memorabilia of a quarter century, I came across two scrapbooks from my *Sun-Times* days—bulging old Dickensian ledgers, yellow-paged and burgundy-bound, of the kind that managing editors used to pass out so that reporters could paste up and store their work: the floppy disks of their time.

In these scrapbooks were some of my first TV columns. There was my grinning, clean-shaven, yokel face in the photo cut at the top of each, a hall-of-mirrors regression into my youth. It started to come back: how I had waited at my city-room desk every late afternoon, with a pair of scissors and a glue pot— waited for the green-bordered Three Star Final to come up still warm from the web-perfecting presses downstairs, at water level with the Chicago River on the outside wall, and then ripped one open and scissored out my column and jigsawed it into the scrapbook.

Nixon was President. The Vietnam War was on, and the antiwar movement was still in the streets—Kent State happened that spring. The United States had landed a man on the moon. The world seemed at once terribly risky and luminous with possibility. I was a by-lined columnist for a Chicago newspaper. I was working alongside incredibly talented writers, poets- and essayists- and novelists-manqué, in an enclave of literary journalism that still traced its lineage to Sandburg and Hecht and MacArthur and Lardner. The fact that I was writing about television was less important to me than the fact that I was *writing*—television, after all, was but one discrete precinct of a bursting world.

But I was *writing*—improvising and polishing what I hoped would someday be a literary voice, and sending it out into the city every late afternoon in *Sun-Times* delivery trucks, to join the big argument. The pleasure I felt at this was almost illicit. It did not occur to me that things would change much beyond the way they were then—we had landed a man on the moon. I was using a dial telephone and a manual typewriter, and I was writing sassy, playful columns, and I could not know that within a few years half the newspapers in town would be dead, casualties of the medium I was writing about, nor that within a few more years my own paper— me long gone— would be seized and lobotomized by an Australian media baron in the process of transforming much of American publishing into an imitation of television's hyperkinetic rush.

How inevitable, in hindsight, that he would eventually acquire *TV Guide*.

Nor could I know then (although I started to know it, or sense it, before long) that television was starting to move, inexorably, from over *there* to over *here*.

PAUSE.

I haven't looked at those old columns of mine more than once or twice since I'd glued them in, and not at all for more than a decade. Now I switch on an overhead light and sit down on the bottom step of the stairs of the latest house I am leaving, and begin to read.

PLAYBACK.

Two waves of recognition wash over me in quick succession. The first is anxiety: how little I knew then, how really *little*, about the television industry.

The second wave is pure delight. I remember how god-damn much *fun* it was. Having a column in Chicago, with my picture at the top of it. Polishing that style. Showing off a little.

I scan columns as if they were old snapshots, finding the occasional image that makes me grin. Here I am, reporting on a group interview with a new soap-opera starlet: "I wasn't this far from Diana van der Vlis. I could have gotten up and taken two steps and touched her on the panache."

Not too shabby. And here I am grousing about an early touch of the networks' election-night competitive obsession (a symptom that has since blossomed into an exit-polling frenzy that threatens the very integrity of the electoral process): "If the quality of someone's life was improved by the fact that he heard Adlai Stevenson III declared winner at 6:43 P.M. on NBC, rather than at 6:51 on CBS, then I'm happy for him. And I feel nothing but compassion and charity for the benighted souls who spent seven minutes of their lives in ignorance of this fact because they chose to watch CBS."

That's telling 'em. And there I am plunging bravely into trenchant sociopolitical inquiry: "What TV do the radicals watch when the radicals watch TV? The radicals watch the very same stuff that is watched by you and me. . . ."

Ah, well. That was then. Half of television's lifetime ago. *Playboy After Dark* was still in syndication. Red Skelton was on. And the Ty-D-Bol man, in his little outboard motorboat. And Marjorie Lord. And, of course, Nixon. Could the world ever have had that much *ago*-ness?

PAUSE.

Where did the time go? And how did television get from *over there* to *here*? And how come I'm still writing about it?

Beats me. All I know is that it feels a lot different, like floating in a zero-gravity chamber, trying to write *about* a medium that has neutralized—swallowed—the distance between itself and anything else, including critical perspective. (I'm not being entirely figurative here. For five years in the mid-1980s I did criticism *of* television *on* television, a pleasant but ultimately dizzying adventure in metaphysics: What if I began to answer myself? Or demand that I try and see things from *my* perspective? Toward the end I began sitting in my small office at CBS for long hours with the door locked, staring at the white walls, waiting for somebody to cross the distance and switch me on.)

I believe in the redemptive power of the written word. But I recognize how vainglorious this word-hopeful belief might seem. We have grown radically separated from words and their promise of transcendence in this century—not entirely thanks to television, let it be acknowledged. The loss of faith in the past after two world wars and the rise of totalitarian police-states, the bureaucratization of evil, the replacement of the Hero in literature with the case history (and then the replacement of the case history with the text itself as subject)—these and other numbing, collective trends and forces had virtually assured the decline of language and its replacement by an increasingly blank, indifferently fraudulent electronic montage.

"The whole tendency of modern prose is away from concreteness," wrote George Orwell in 1946, perceiving, in his essay "Politics and the English Language," that the advent of vast, technocratic political bureaucracies had resulted in a new use for language: an instrument for concealing or preventing thought. Orwell was exactly right—and already too late: The age of the *nonverbal* lie had already begun to dawn.

More recently, there has evolved an even more ingenious new application for language, particularly written language: its conversion into a kind of freeze-dried subgenre of television.

Terror-stricken with the prospect of flash extinction, newspapers, magazines, even book publishers in the past 15 years have taken great pains to assure a generation of nonreaders that their prose is as unproselike as possible—that is, anti-narrative, free from context and internal cohesion, self-referencing, unburdened by moral weight. This trend has chipped a lot of the, oh, *cartouche*, let us say, from the sarcophagus of literary journalism, and it has presented some interesting identity problems even among those critics who have bought (or sold) into the new order. Bill Moyers, meet Bill Cosby.

I suggested earlier that much of the vital center of television criticism has shifted, over the past decade, from newspaper columnists to professional scholars, psychologists and social scientists. This shift has not been without its rewards. Specialists such as Ben Bagdikian, Todd Gitlin, Neil Postman, Pat Aufderheide, Mark Crispin Miller, Kathryn Montgomery and Peggy Charren (of the noble Action for Children's Television) have kept alive an indispensable tradition of political, ethical and behaviorist accounting of television's presence in the culture. Even a short survey of their recent propositions would have to include the following:

that as big corporations keep buying up TV and radio stations (not to mention newspapers), competitive diversity is quickly being replaced by a suffocating tyranny of the middle, silencing disputation and dissent;

that TV commercials for luxury cars and other high-status products portray the American consumer as a kind of lone-wolf survivor in an alien landscape, reinforcing an already corrosive sense of alienation in America;

that advertising and the behaviorist sciences continue to refine their tactic of enlisting the consumer in his own seduction and debasement;

that the still-recent video revolution has overwhelmed the 500-year-old typographic tradition, annihilating its ancient capacity to induce disciplined thought, the skills of logic and the habit of refutation. What the video era offers as a replacement is entertainment as a requisite for any exchange of ideas (an early symptom of culture death);

that MTV (almost certainly the defining video idiom of the

1980s) has become an antiauthoritarian "primary experience" (supplanting experience in the empirical world) for a white, suburban generation;

that the interests of child viewers, once partly safeguarded, at least, by licensing agreements, have been brutally ground under by the growing legitimization of corporate greed.

Whether one agrees with them or not, these are significant propositions. And yet the debate over them is carried out in increasingly narrow circles of people who are generally predisposed to these sorts of concerns—in a word, specialists. Meanwhile, the larger public, even as it is virtually being thrust forward from one communications epoch to another, only has access to such debates as what's Hot and what's Not.

This collection of essays about television is not offered with the grand delusion that it will do one hell of a lot of good vis-à-vis the grotesqueries I've just outlined, or even a lot of useful harm. I don't expect it, for instance, to reverse recent history (or antihistory, as the case may be) and restore the world to any pristine pre–vid-saturated Eden.

What then?

A couple of modest things, I hope. Perhaps it will provide a little pleasure. Words, you know. Beyond that, my wish here is the same as it is with anything I have yet written, or hope to write: to share "serious" ideas—however playfully couched—with general readers.

PLAYBACK.

The fact that these essays were originally columns in a large-circulation magazine pleases me. I am by temperament and personal history a journalist and a generalist. I am also an unreconstructable midwesterner (and thus inevitably an outsider), a sojourning witness like my fellow townsman Mark Twain and, like my literary idol James Agee, an excitable advocate of the concerns that concern me.

Record.

Television concerns me. ("For nowadays the world is lit by lightning," says Tennessee Williams's Tom, ruefully preparing to ease himself out of the picture once more.) I have tried to make my concerns plain, and as unencumbered by pretense as is possible. "Above all else, don't think of it as Art," admonished Agee; and, apropos these essays, I agree: don't.

I don't even know much about Art.

But I do know what I don't like.

— Middlebury, Vermont
December 1989

I

The Industry

American television is not "about" entertainment. It is not "about" news, or sports, or music, or Oprah Winfrey's quest to pry an engagement ring out of Steadman. Strictly speaking, it is not even "about" advertising (although now we're getting warm).

American television is about corporate arrogation and corporate will. Its message, a subtextual whisper through most of its brief history, has been that its flickering cathode ray screen is the true locus of reality.

In the 1980s—the decade of American television's radical rebirth—that whisper swelled into a roar.

The Television Industry's great accomplishment in the 1980s was to elevate TV spectatorship to an exalted status: the defining sensory experience of American life. The aim of this exaltation was to eliminate what remained of the critical, evaluating distance between the audience and the screen, a distance that still marginally interfered with the ongoing creation and gratification of consumer desires. The media scholar Mark Crispin Miller has described the success of this accomplishment in the following way: "TV has almost purified itself, aspiring to a spectacle that can remind us of no prior or extrinsic vision."

And how has The Industry managed that near-purification? By no less a stroke than the manufacturing of its own "reality field," a field at once more vivid and less ominous (at least on the surface of the screen) than the diminished reality of the empirical world.

Television in the 1980s was in many ways an endless recombination of reality, an infinite, gorgeous merge of shadow and light. News merged with entertainment; entertainment merged with religion; religion merged with politics; political reporting merged with political advertising; advertising merged with celebrityhood; celebrities merged with public figures; public figures merged into docudrama; docudrama merged with exploitation; exploitation merged with children's programs; children's programs merged with rock and roll; rock and roll merged with public-affairs talk shows; talk shows merged with tabloid journalism; tabloid journalism merged with dramatic recreations of actual events; dramatic recreations merged with Connie Chung. A terrible beauty was born.

This merging took on an institutional, as well as a thematic aspect. TV in the 1980s saw corporate interests overtly merge with the interests of political parties, even those of the Presidency itself—as, for instance, when leading corporate advertising executives volunteered their services in the 1984 re-election campaign of Ronald Reagan; and when network news divisions cut the cloth of their Presidential coverage to suit that year's public-opinion polls. (CBS News Washington correspondent Lesley Stahl has publicly stated that her superiors gave her strict instructions to modify the adversarial tone of her reports on the Reagan Administration, and even went

4

so far as to edit traces of toughness from her finished reports. With surreal equanimity—surreal, at least, by the standards of a vanished era—Stahl has continued to work for the network whose calumnies she exposed, and that network has continued to pay her salary.)

And it continues: after the ascendancy of President Bush, at least one local-station anchorman (Ernie Anastos, WCBS in New York) got himself taped, in an on-air promotional clip, strolling and smiling in lockstep with a strolling, smiling Vice-President Quayle.

These and other symptoms of top-heavy power alliances between corporate and statist interests did little to alleviate American commercial television's rapidly crystallizing image as shaper and arbiter of "reality," not to mention instrument of social orthodoxy and control.

This trend of reshaping the terms of reality seems likely to influence the content and character of American television into the twenty-first century.

Most of the pieces in this section deal, in one way or another, with The Industry as it synthesized and packaged its new "reality" in the 80s.

"Sorry, Fawn, Your 15 Minutes Are Up," written two years ago, examines television's role in blurring the distinctions between celebrityhood and substance in American culture.

At the time I wrote it, there seemed to be emerging a hopeful countertrend to all the fawning: the growing cachet of small, independent movie studios that were turning out radiant films with unknown actors and actresses, films that seriously engaged the folklore and the politics and the social history of this country. It was not to be. In the intervening months, most of these independents were either forced into bankruptcy or acquired by the corporate "majors," as the giant studios entered their present, accelerating global growth-spurt. Folklore, politics and social history have given way to Eddie Murphy— a product of television, as it happens.

I have included one profile of an individual in this section—

5

"The Cool, Dark Telegenius of Robert Pittman"—because in certain ways, Robert Pittman *is* The Industry as it enters the 1990s. As the architect of MTV, Pittman (The Glass-Eyed Child of the title) created a video environment of pure illusion. A child of the medium himself, he provided a generation of television babies (not to mention many of their parents) with a perpetual television womb.

I wrote "Ivan the Telegenic" in 1984, while Soviet Premier Chernenko was still alive, and well before Gorby and Raisa had become the David and Maddie of world domination. But Gorbachev's tour-de-force refinement of the Soviet media image only confirms the seeds of what I spotted back then. Call it the Marx Factor effect.

"The Agony of Deceit" follows the retooling of reality into the political realm, and examines the rise of TV's contribution to democratic dialogue—the Nonverbal Lie. "Lawyers, Guns and Money" offers a glimpse of The Industry celebrating its many victories in reality-engineering, and plotting many more, at its annual trade convention (NATPE) in Houston.

"Twain Wreck" and "Broadcast Ooze" offer two examples of television's effects on book publishing: its strategies for promotion and its emerging, colder sensibilities in nonfictional themes.

Sorry, Fawn,
Your 15 Minutes Are Up

And you too Ollie and Bernie and Ivan and Eddie and
Spuds. A few thoughts on the perils of fame in a
disposable culture

It is the 1980s, and we are in the world of "We Are the World"
and Olliemania and I Got a Peek at the Pope and What Will
Vanna Wear Tonight? (and Christina De Lorean Is Dressing
for Acquittal) and The Twenty-five Most Intriguing People
(What Will Vanessa Not Wear Tonight?) and oh, is Woody
really not eating at Elaine's? and "What a nice toilet," Halston
said, and "In the future," said Andy, "everyone will be . . ."
". . . more famous than Jesus Christ," screamed the Beatles
from history, and oh, God, Martin's directed Michael's latest
and "Hug," said Phyllis, and I Ran Into Tammy at the Mall
and look this way, Mr. Gotti (the crime lord as *New York*
magcover), and we love ya too, Bernhard and Ivan and Sydney Biddle and . . .

Oh, look: Why can't we all just face up to it?

Why can't we just . . . shove the whole mucilaginous mass to one side? And heave ourselves off the couch that has been our pop-cult cocoon lo this anesthetized decade and a half? And somehow get on with our lives—with our national life?

Why can't somebody just say it out loud?

Isn't everyone about . . . bloody . . . well . . . screaming . . . BORED SICK . . . *of celebrities?*

I mean, look at them. All these 1980s celebrifaces. They're no longer off at a distance, constrained within a grid. They're closing in, in a metronomic sequence of little pops and quivers; there is a sense of them adhering to one's fingers, one's lap, one's upholstery. . . .

THEY'RE EVERYWHERE!

Look! Eddie and Bo and Dolly and Phil and Di and Fergie and Max and Emilio and Whitney and Glenn and Pia and Spuds and Jessica and Willard and Tina and Magic and Joan and Bruce and Cybill and Billy and *yaddada, yaddada, yaddada, yaddada.* It's impossible; the celebrifaces lose distinction; they occlude into one horrible agglutinated hive, as in one of those camera pullbacks from a lithographic plane. But what is this image, this graphic, that the aggregate dots suggest?

It looks a hell of a lot like a . . . popcorn kernel.

Bingo. This decade's celebrity onslaught is like nothing so much as the inside of a giant amok Warhol popcorn popper: The celebrinuggets as popping pips, ceaselessly set aquiver by some new blastogenesis.

Can't stop eatin' 'em!

Ah, but such atrophied, such spavined little pips. You thought the Seventies were overpopped? Silly goose. Look. Here's one squishing her way over the top of the rim, nylons twisted, makeup askew. Nudged along by her little William Morris kernel. It's Fawn! Fawn is going into TV journalism, it says here. Says so in "Liz Smith."

Remember Fawn? Fawn is one of the summer class of '87; that's the summer they stopped adding the Wesson oil. Magna cum overbearing on the Contragate hearings. Last summer, she couldn't stand journalists; now she almost are one. ("That's all the news for tonight that I care to report—*sirrr!*")

Fawn and Jessica and Donna and Tammy Faye. What a soggy quartet. What an appalling desecration of their subgenre, the Suffering Siren. (And all four sirens busy as bees, efficient as Herbalife saleswomen, reinvesting the capital of their catastrophes.) What a comedown from the grand distress those old goddesses of grocery-line grief used to lay out. Jackie! Liz! Patty Hearst! Sunglasses! Seclusion! Ari! Submachine guns! *Transcendent* tack!

Now . . . ?

Now we have lumpish Jessica ("I Am Not a Bimbo") flaunting for a fee her far-flung fundamentals in the puerile pages of *Playboy*. While Donna of the unfocused stare peddles her pants ("No Excuses!"), and Tammy Faye bleeds great godly gouts of green eyeshadow into the recording studios of No-Fault Rapture.

Kernels. Pips. Let's face it—jokes. Grotesque passing curiosities; viscid images to consume absentmindedly as they flit through our fast-edit consciousness, without passion or compassion, surely without joy. And therefore quite close to the essence of what celebrityhood has become in the late 1980s.

And what has it become? Banal. Mendacious. Separated from the merits of performance. An expression of television's omnivorous need for the next image; a feeding system for *Entertainment Tonight* and the morning network news shows. The last refuge of the scoundrel, the criminal, the corporate capitalist, the jingoist, the spoiled child, the whore. A false vindication of unformed talent, of attitude as creative act. A protected arena for the manipulations of the imperial publicist and the agent-cum-editor (as the adversarial distance vanishes between the celebrity subculture and the press that covers it).

Celebrityhood in the 1980s has become Sean Penn slapping photographers and Bernhard Goetz opening fire on the subway. It has become the accused sex killer Robert Chambers as

9

cover boy and the rape faker Cathleen Webb as queen of the morning talk shows. It has become mogul Lee Iacocca and Madam Sydney Biddle Barrows, whose life stories were presented to a grateful nation by the same ghostwriter. It has become the retrograde comedy of Eddie Murphy and Joan Rivers and the puerilities of Howie Mandel. It has become the unspeakable televangelists and all the coke-snorting ballplayers given standing ovations on their return from court and all the pornographers of cinematic suffering as enacted by Schwarzenegger and Stallone and Norris. It has become the Fat Boys in music, and in literature it has become Bret Easton Ellis and Tama Janowitz. It has become Vanna White. And Michael J. Fox. Briefly, it became Oliver North.

It has become, in short, a vision of America as defined by the political-economic vulgarities of Ronald Reagan and the artistic neutralities of Andy Warhol—a truly Sartrean slum that reveals no exit, only unlimited access.

It has become the dregs of the sinecure for an age without heroes.

Americans have been prone to adoration from the outset. The first touring rock star to ring our bell was Charles Dickens; his U.S. lecture appearances in the 1860s helped his hit singles— *Bleak House, A Tale of Two Cities*—go platinum. Crowds went nuts for him; they saw him onstage and then jammed the docks to mob the schooner bearing the latest serialized installment of his next novel. (In a New York audience one night was the young Sam Clemens, who went on to become our own white-costumed writing-and-performing king.)

The movies brought Valentino—boffo funeral—and Fairbanks and Chaplin and Garbo. Then came the radio stars of the Thirties and the fanzine movie idols of the Forties and Fifties—Sinatra and Gable and Wayne . . . oh, my! And M. M. And then the record industry, backed up by television and Ed Sullivan, took over to open up some fairly major undetected chambers of fame lust: Elvis and then the Fab Four.

But nothing like this. Nothing like this present transition from fame as performance to fame as state of being, as mere presence.

How, then, did it become what it has become?

The image of the giant amok popcorn popper is useful here.

The popper started getting assembled in the mid-1970s (let's fix the year at 1974) for a perfectly plausible reason: to accommodate the greatest single efflorescence of pop-cultural entertainment in American history.

America was just then starting to peel itself free from the maw of its most socially divisive and traumatic epoch since Reconstruction. The previous fifteen years had witnessed the civil-rights struggle, the war in Vietnam, the assassinations of three American statesmen and the disgrace of a sitting president.

With the resignation of Richard Nixon and the imminent withdrawal from Southeast Asia, the nation happily . . . belched! America declared, in effect, "It's Miller time!" Public-opinion polls began to register a shock wave of release from social consciousness, a libidinous plunge into private pleasures.

BOOGIE! (*All night long!*) And the foundries of mass media (which had been tooling up progressively for half a century) were primed to provide . . . the apparatus.

It began in the print sector: a spontaneous combustion of an agreement that *people*, not "issues" or "ideas" or anything that raised the dread specter of *polemics*, were to be the new coin of exchange. Newspaper gossip columnists took on a new preeminence; gossip itself replaced the New Journalism as the new journalism. Mere Murdochry was loosed upon the nation. In 1974, Rupert heaved from down under, first to claim *The San Antonio Express-News* and later to launch the national tabloid *Star* in competition with the *Enquirer*—thus turning the supermarket checkout lanes of America into elongated libraries of the licentious.

A whole debouchment of women produced books detailing their affairs with former presidents. "The public act most characteristic of the seventies," wrote Ron Rosenbaum in 1975, "is the Pious Snitch." The great bulk of all snitchees, it need hardly be noted, were celebrities.

In 1974, Time Inc. institutionalized—and vanillaized—America's resurgent fascination for snitchery by introducing *People*, the proto-newsmagazine of the post-social culture. *People*'s principal content was actually its cover, and editor Richard Stolley revolutionized magazine-cover design in the Western world by making *People*'s cover a weekly statement (or well-calculated guess) about the shifting hierarchies of celebrityhood. Stolley's cover mantra went as follows: "Young is better than Old *ooohm* Pretty is better than Ugly *ooohm* Rich is better than Poor *ooohm* TV is better than Music *ooohm* Music is better than Movies *ooohm* Movies are better than Sports *ooohm* Anything is better than Politics."

Two years later, television kicked in with its role in the symbiosis. An ABC cop-fantasy series, *Charlie's Angels*, introduced the living embodiment of Stolley's mantra. In the space of a few summer months in 1977, Farah Fawcett-Majors gritted her pearly teeth from the cover of not only *People* but also *Vogue*, *McCall's*, *Good Housekeeping*, *New Dawn*, *Ladies' Home Journal*, *Woman's Day*, *Photoplay*, *TV Guide*, *Los Angeles Magazine*, *Gossip World*, *TV Greats* and her own magazine, *Farrah*, in which she revealed her chocolate-chip cookie recipe. Along with Dr. Joyce Brothers and Patty "Call Me *Tanya*" Hearst, she became perhaps the defining icon of Seventies celebrityhood.

Viewed from the perspective of ten years, Farrah Fawcett was the Muse incarnate. Hell, she memorized lines. In 1987, something approaching her famous hairdo once again graced *People*'s cover—but this time it adorned the secretarial scalp of Jessica Hahn, who had earned the privilege by her tremendous feats of being hit on by some evangelical suits and then dropping her drawers for *Playboy*.

By the end of the Seventies, the Age of Farrah was already

giving way to the Age of Jessica. The popper was blazing. Celebrities poured out. Barry White. Billy Carter. The Bay City Rollers. Mister Whipple. In 1977, Elvis Presley died, and in the national tantrum of mourning that ensued, several previously anonymous performers carved out successful careers as *Elvis imitators*. Celebrityhood, it seemed, had not only learned to cheat death, it had somehow floated free from the living personas of the human beings it celebrated. It began to seem almost like some ambient cloud, or a virus—benign, to be sure—that invested itself in the deserving and the undeserving alike.

John Irving caught it, and Clifford Irving too.

But it wasn't a virus, of course. It was discharge from the popper, and the popper was being tended by people who knew what they were doing. The momentum of marketing was on their side. Post-political people wanted celebrities. And if there were not enough real ones to shake into the pan, then a little synthetic mix would have to be added. Who'd care?

In April 1982, *People* spotlighted the Vietnamese boat people—Third World refugees as this week's pop-cult elect. A month earlier, the magazine had gushed over the rugged good looks of Roberto "Major Bob" D'Aubuisson, who was the suspected leader of Salvadoran death squads. That same year, the Gannett Company introduced a national daily lollipop called *USA TODAY*, which managed to turn the United States of America itself into a celebrity. The television networks began to generate entertainment built around a mix of established celebrity hosts and ordinary folks willing to caricature their lives in the mode of celebrities (*Real People* on NBC, *That's Incredible!* on ABC).

Entertainment Tonight, which had its premiere in 1981, partly restored the tinfoil diadem of celebrityhood to its rightful context of Hollywood glitz, but it accomplished something more important. The satellite-delivered syndicated program translated *People*'s celebro-journalism iconography to the TV screen—anchormen, anchorwomen, anchorhair, anchorknees. But these weren't wary, skeptical, even ironic, journalists—they were stars, as pink and primped and shellacked as the bonbons they covered, and just as in love with the life. *E.T.* in turn became an irresistible model for the morning network shows and the local evening news-chat shows, celebs as news subjects, but nonadversarial news subjects. Into this widening vacuum of editorial sovereignty, the publicists and the agents wedged themselves a little further—setting terms, stipulating conditions. It was all so glittery, and so much fun.

This flattening out of distinctions between talent (however marginal) and mere *display* (or chic evil, in the case of D'Aubuisson) had its dark legitimizer in the world of art. From the labyrinths of SoHo, the former illustrator–silk-screener–moviemaker Andy Warhol was consolidating his most significant legacy: his permissive extension of the celebrity rubric (he called them "superstars") to cover *just about anyone*, regardless of talent, merit, achievement. "Everyone will be famous," he decreed, and the fashion crowd gasped, "Thank God!" This was a telling, pivotal assault on the distinctions between creativity and commerce, between the profound and the poseur, between the masterpiece and the mass market.

Warhol's magazine, *Interview,* enshrined the celebrity stream of consciousness as cultural artifact and lent a high-toned validation to all the mass-market sycophancy. Warhol's lifelong genuflection to surface (and his attendant horror of substance) had drawn him by the mid-Seventies to a career of celebrity addiction as performance art; his life was a twenty-four-hour TV screen, broadcasting the single bulletin that fame is self-defining, ubiquitous, arbitrary. Warhol's embrace of the media-charged fashion world unleashed a great torrential whirlwind of pure vacuousness into the spheres of rock and advertising and literature: The spiritual starvelings of *Bright Lights, Big City* and *Slaves of New York* are Warhol's children, as are the attitudinizing androids of MTV.

But if Andy Warhol was the decade's aesthetic demiurge, its sociopolitical dynamics—greed and aggression—were provided by the movie-star president.

It was left to the Ronald Reagan administration to convert the social phobias and fatigue of the early post–Vietnam-Watergate era into an active declaration of personal avarice. No accident that in the season of Reagan's inauguration, J. R. Ewing and his *Dallas* cronies became the most-watched characters in prime-time television. No accident that the most cravenly ingenious new idea in TV syndication of the early Eighties was *Lifestyles of the Rich and Famous*—host Robin Leach intuiting correctly that power and money, not show-biz glamour, made up the new bedrock of mass-cult fantasies.

No accident that the decade's emerging comic superstars— Joan Rivers, Eddie Murphy, John Belushi—practiced the comedy of arrogance, of orifice, of contempt, of consumption, and lived life-styles of bejeweled and bemansioned opulence, until (in Belushi's case) the glut proved fatal. They were just being funny in the new way, the Republican, free-market, Barbara Bush "We Go Rich" way.

No accident that Stallone and Schwarzenegger stood tall in the box office, that Iacocca and Biddle Barrows became twin symbols of celebribusiness, that John De Lorean and Ivan Boesky glittered on the criminal edge of business or that Goetz and Chambers became the avatars of New Wave urban mayhem.

This infestation of pop by neoconservative values and attitudes wasn't limited to the celebrities themselves, however. In fact, the most significant dosing did not even affect the celebs directly. It hit the people who covered them: the reporters and correspondents, the editors and producers, the publishers and network vice-presidents.

The 1980s saw a general collapse of the necessary distance between show-business stars and the press (print and electronic) that covered them.

People and *Entertainment Tonight*, as mentioned above, were the prototypes. But the new softness soon spread like runny cottage cheese through the precincts of mass journalism, fed by a variety of internal, competitive needs.

Newspapers, warned by their consultants that they were "perceived" as stodgy and pompous by their TV-glitzed readers, began to "humanize" their bylined writers in much the same way that local-news stations "humanized" their correspondents. One humanizing ploy was to affect a chumminess with celebs, the resident columnist as confidant of the famous. ("Johnny Carson phoned up the other day to tell me . . .")

With the advent of *USA TODAY* and its "Life" section (and its standing order from publisher Al Neuharth to frame every possible story in television terms), this chumminess became institutionalized—celebrities as confidants of *us*. The mind-set took its toll on the sensibilities of *USA TODAY* staffers. When CBS telecast its searing 1985 documentary about broken black families in New Jersey's urban ghettos, the paper's television critic, Monica Collins, sniffed imbecilicly that correspondent Bill Moyers—the "doyen of downers"—would do well to check out the Black Family as interpreted by Bill Cosby on NBC.

Time and *Newsweek* rushed into the sycophancy sweepstakes, slapping celebs on their covers, vying ponderously to be first to proclaim new show-business royalty and trends. *New York* magazine, expressing owner Rupert Murdoch's distinct vision, staked out the macabre, police-blotter edge of the new celebrityhood. The magazine dealt lovingly in cover stories of fashionable suicides, murders, sex scandals and the sweet rot of decadent style. Typical was a July 22, 1985, cover celebrating the return to society (the release from prison) of Studio 54 founders Steve Rubell and Ian Schrager:

> On the third night, the waitresses were serving champagne with aplomb and the bartenders were jumping at the sight of a famous face. Steve took Halston and Baby

Jane Holzer on a tour of the club. He started with Kenny
Scharf's basement lounges.

"What a nice toilet," Halston said.

Into this gorgeous new target of opportunity streamed the press
agents and the publicists—the new editors.

Just as "The Deal" had, in Joan Didion's memorable formulation, become the new art form in Hollywood, so did
Control become the new art form in print and TV news. Aware
that their famous clients had soared in market value as com-
modities in a never-ending auction for access, the publicists
grew absolutely brazen in their lust for editorial power.

With Robert De Niro and Bob Dylan turning reclusiveness
into a new show-biz badge of aristocracy, with Vanessa Red-
grave staring stonily at the floor during interviews not to her
taste, the press began to appreciate the godfatherly powers of
the publicists. The publicists grandly condescended to make
some offers the press couldn't refuse.

They demanded text approval. Quote approval. Photo approval. (Michael Jackson, it's said, tried to buy up all the pictures of himself from all the photographers in the world.) They
demanded approval of the writer or correspondent assigned
to do the necessary fawning. They set limits on what sorts of
questions would be asked.

And to a shocking extent, more than a few magazines and
television shows knuckled under. "They're like gangsters," said
one magazine editor of the people she was dealing with.

To be sure, there were wonderful mavericks within the cowed
celebripress—witty and thoughtful writers who refused to
genuflect. Nora Ephron, George Trow, Robert Ward, Lewis
Grossberger (writing on the exact moment Sylvester Stallone
realized he was an asshole), Roy Blount Jr., Joyce Wadler, a
fellow, name of Buschel, at a popular men's fashion magazine, a few others. Their pieces flared like tracer bullets in the

17

darkness. They picked off a few of those popping kernels, these folks, they did.

But the popper, this amok apparatus, pops on. And a paradox emerges from the goo: that of a culture cramming itself almost compulsively with the great buttery avalanche of names, faces, brief lives flickering in the cathode glare; yet with a curious, brain-dead roteness, a hooded sense of probing, probing for the next celebri*hit*, the next celebri*high*. The next personality as morselcrunch.

The prognosis? Not especially good. As we've seen, television is the central dynamic cog in the popping process, and television has an intrinsic voraciousness for the next image. The same, unfortunately, must now be said for much of the popular print media. Print is a natural referent to the past. It is *record* incorporate; it is our cultural linchpin for the management of knowledge, for our very sense of collective optimism. But print has not been managed as print, over the past dozen years or so; it has been managed (with exceptions) as a colonial property of broadcasting. The shattered idiom of Gannett and Time Inc. and the Washington Post Company (*Newsweek*) and Murdoch's News America Holdings and their many, many fellow capitulators is scarcely typographic; it is bastardized video, a wholly owned subsidiary of teleculture.

Teleculture has no capacity for memory, for retention, for transmitting any sense of orderly, contextual flow from the past. It recalls and suggests only memories of itself. It has an imperative only to be fed. As it consumes and disgorges its interchangeable celebrikernels into an increasingly anesthetized society, it trivializes, deadens the awareness of history. And that is the real legacy of the celebrity glut of the Eighties: its abolishment of a textured, communal—and moral—sense of the past, from which an optimistic vision of the future must proceed.

Can anybody here make a case that our present pop-cultural idols transmit any emotion that can be remotely linked to *optimism*? Is there any star, any group that can approach the aura of delight generated by (to take a relatively recent example) the Beatles? The Who? Sting? Twisted Sister? Schwarzenegger? Penn? Bill Cosby? John McEnroe? Joan Collins? Don Johnson? Brigitte Nielsen? Adrian Lyne? The Los Angeles Raiders? Bob Guccione? Mayor Clint Eastwood?

Why can't somebody just say it? These are grim, hard, cold, joyless people—to judge at least by their public accomplishments—as are most of the other personalities cited in this screed. Among the mass of them they could not generate three kilowatts of grace, or generosity, or gallantry, or laughter from the heart, or conspicuous compassion, or humility, or insight, or—well—celebration, as that term was once understood.

Maybe television is not the whole problem. Maybe we've had it too easy lately. Maybe it will take, perversely, a resurgence of hard times to reawaken the country's collective grit and restore its ancient need for heroes. (If so, the October 19 Wall Street collapse was day one of the new era.)

Happily, the old proletarian scale of things is in fact beginning to stir once again—in the movies, of all pop forms, which is where our twentieth-century star system began. The big-studio system, with its wasted millions and its cynical pandering to the teen-slob market, is finally crumbling under its own decadence. Young independent filmmakers such as the gloriously humane John Sayles (*Matewan*) and Jonathan Demme (*Something Wild*) and David Lynch (*Blue Velvet*) and Robert Townsend (*Hollywood Shuffle*) and Tim Hunter (*River's Edge*) are turning out "small" movies with complex adult themes and characters, and they are reaching appreciative audiences.

And let us take heart from the mercilessly satiric new anti-celebrity magazine, *Spy*. Puckishly edited by E. Graydon Carter and Kurt Andersen, it is the only publication to feed on the vacuous pretensions of celebs and their lap-dog chroniclers as fervidly as *People*, say, feeds the hopper.

Could these few hopeful straws be the advance trickle of a new kind of fuel for the popper? Might the realities of a new economy promote a new preference for discipline over dissi-pation and thus accelerate the trend?

One optimistically hopes so. In the meantime, however, a slightly more realistic note to all those publicists and agents whose clients were *not* mentioned as examples of the current low state of celebrityhood: Please contact me through *GQ* magazine. I'm sure we can work something out.

THE COOL, DARK TELEGENIUS OF ROBERT PITTMAN

The man who brought you MTV and Morton Downey Jr. has tapped into a culture's soul, if not his own

Child of Television. Bodeful title. It has been applied, at various times, to nearly every young programmer born into the video era. It is meant to suggest an extraordinary intuitive grasp of the medium's inner dynamics, possibilities—its Weltanschauung.

To the best of my knowledge, Television has spawned only one child, a son. His name is Bob Pittman. He may yet prove to be the medium's father as well.

Childhood is a fascinating motif among television executives. Walk into almost any of their offices and you enter a temple to lost childhood. Amid the memos and the Maalox, sprigs of kid winsomeness poke through like landscaping in a mall. The catcher's mitts. The filched traffic signs. The candy stash. The rock posters. The little figurines from Disney World.

Rosebud Central! The trinkets seem to tinkle, "I may come on like a bastard, but what a *tyke* I am at heart."

Bob Pittman's office at Quantum Media in New York City is shadowed and nearly featureless, except for a terrifying piece of prophetic art that dominates one wall. It is a painting, by David Deutsch, of a male figure gazing out serenely at a lyric landscape. The jarring element in the composition is the figure's head. It is a television set.

"Somewhat appropriate," acknowledges Bob Pittman dryly.

Bob Pittman's childhood was interrupted, altered, the first time around. But that's all right. He is redesigning American television—and, to a large extent, American popular culture—so that we can all experience it on his terms this time.

His conventional childhood ended at age 6, when he was thrown from a horse during a family Thanksgiving gathering in Mississippi. His parents—his father is a Methodist minister—looked on helplessly from behind a window. He lost his right eye. The doctors gave him a glass one.

He watched television and absorbed a kind of education for ten years. Then he came out of the small-town South, gaunt, with a beard and a hippie ponytail, to take hold of broadcasting. The year was 1971. His first stop was a Milwaukee radio station.

He was 17 when he began programming music for a station in Detroit. He was 18 when he took a Pittsburgh station from nowhere to the leading teenage draw in the market. He was 20 when he went to Chicago in 1974 and masterminded one of the legendary radio turnarounds in broadcast history. He was 27 when he invented MTV and introduced America to its new defining popular-culture sensibility, that of the Antiauthoritarian Child.

He was 33 when he created *The Morton Downey Jr. Show* (The Antiauthoritarian Child as adult; public affairs as MTV); when his firm, Quantum Media, attempted to take over the J. Walter Thompson advertising company; and when he started to be mentioned as a possible future president of CBS.

He was 34 when he devised an action-adventure format (his cinema verité of Newark cops, *The Street*) that broke down the authoritarian "proscenium" barrier of television drama and allowed the child-viewer into the epicenter of the action. (His only setback so far, the show was dropped from syndication after last year's screenwriters' strike stopped the supply of scripts.) The same year, he also joined the steering committee of an American presidential candidate.

Bob Pittman is 35 now. He has yet to finish college. But apparently he has decided it is time to do something with his life. A few weeks ago, he began exploring a new partnership with an old collaborator, the legendary advertising maverick George Lois. Their combined vision is a political-advertising firm. Their first goal will be to elect a mayor of New York. Then they will look for serious work.

One of Lois's most famous advertising campaigns was "I WANT MY MAYPO," which he later adapted for client Bob Pittman as "I WANT MY MTV."

The signs suggest this is the onset of Pittman's next logical enterprise: to redesign American electoral politics. In the image of the Antiauthoritarian Child.

"Television prob'ly showed me more of the world than my parents did," Bob Pittman says in his office. "I can't get enough of television. I accept it."

The remark is pure Pittman: an innocuous-seeming observation, uttered in an innocuous soft drawl—a throwaway line, on the surface, until you begin to prod at it a little and grasp that it is, in fact, a fiercely compressed and apocalyptic little piece of haiku, a glimpse as deep into Pittman's inner cosmos as it may be possible to penetrate.

It is this aura of serene mysticism—an almost childlike simplicity and absence of guile—that has consolidated his reputation within the industry as a genius of the medium, perhaps its prophet. Greater than Arledge, greater than Silverman, a more transitional force than anyone, perhaps, since Paley. It

23

is Pittman and Quantum that are considered the cutting edge of television as it will be defined in the early twenty-first century.

"They said to me, when I started MTV, 'You're violating the contract you have with the viewers,' " he murmurs softly. "They said, 'People want a beginning, a middle and an end to their television.' And I said, 'There *is* no beginning, middle and end. It's all ebb and flow.' "

He sits in his office beneath the brooding canvas, almost an extension of it—his face expressionless, awaiting questions. It is hard to find the southern child in him, the minister's son. The hippie denim has long since given way to elegant Italian weaves; the ponytail yielded to a razored coif. A trace of his roots survives in his posture: knees splayed apart, ankles pressed together, hands clasped in his lap—the pose of a gentleman caller on a front porch on a Sunday afternoon.

But the surviving eye is not the eye of a man clutching jonquils. It is scanning private frequencies. Bob Pittman has been called aloof, arrogant. Perhaps he is only thinking about something else. In any event, his preternatural surface blandness recalls another childlike sojourner from obscure places: Warhol, whose pop-cult legacy—visual hypersaturation cut with moral numbness—has become the identifying content of Pittman's new video forms. (Warhol starred, for a time, in his own program on MTV.)

"I do attitude-based programming," Bob Pittman says in his dreamy southern voice. "It's all attitude. The attitude is: Nothing is sacred. We're all having a rilly good time. We're all in on something everybody else doesn't get. We're special 'cause we're keeping everybody else out."

Whatever else Bob Pittman may or may not achieve in his life, he has done this: He has deconstructed American television and, via that accomplishment, much of the American popular culture, and not a little of the American political process. His MTV, the first truly original application of the cable-TV revolution, did more than liberate itself from the look and the meaning of orthodox television. It liberated television it-self from derived, orthodox meaning. The meaning of time, for instance, or narrative. Or paradox. Or necessity, cause and effect. Or of the sacred (the symbols of Judeo-Christian wor-ship) or of the profane (Nazi regalia). Or of authority, as rep-resented by schoolteachers, policemen, clergy. And parents.

"This is a non-narrative generation," says Pittman. "You communicate to them via sense-impressions. There are two groups of people in this world: those who grew up with tele-vision and those who didn't grow up with sense-impres-sions."

In this vacuum of narrative obligation, music videos in-stalled the aesthetic of the perpetual child: the self as star of the universe, appetite as the locus of endeavor, consumption as art, advertising as education, the grotesque as amusement, defiance as moral vision.

Arriving as it did in 1981, at the outset of a sociopolitical transformation based on greed and assertion, MTV gave defi-nition to a new self-concept in American life. MTV's idiom of feckless, pointless montage—its ebb and flow—replicated it-self in the culture like a computer virus: in movies; in adver-tising; in mainstream television drama (and television news); in fashion; in newspapers, magazines and book publishing; in history itself (someone turned the Vietnam War into a music video). It even transformed the style and content of political campaigning on television—and thus the style and content of political candidates.

MTV was the LSD of the Reagan Revolution.

Bob Pittman explains it more cryptically. "The key to MTV, from day one," he says "was our logo. We had a logo that changed colors and shapes and positions. That goes against the grain of what logos are supposed to do. But what we wanted it to do was tell our audience that MTV was change."

Message received.

Pittman left MTV at the beginning of 1987 to become presi-dent and chief executive officer of Quantum Media, Inc., a firm half-owned by MCA. One of his first acts was to yank out of obscurity a fringe entertainer and Chicago talk-radio man, Morton Downey Jr., and plant his act on the New Jersey superstation WWOR, also an MCA entity.

"We invented the kind of show that Mort does before we found Mort," Pittman says. (Indeed, at one time G. Gordon Liddy was looked at as a possible host.) "We wanted a certain trashing of the boundaries of politeness in television. We wanted an antiauthority figure. When we called Mort to invite him to audition, his first words to our guy were 'Lissen, you sonovabitch, I don't do auditions for anyone!' Then he hung up. I said, 'That's our guy.' "

The fiftyish Downey quickly became a national synonym for grossness by behaving, in essence, like an MTV cartoon version of the Acceptable Adult: strutting, chain-smoking, a mouth-off artist and a gang-protected bully—that is to say, like an antiauthoritarian child. Downey triggered a rush of imitation similar to that of MTV itself. Within a year Geraldo Rivera (who had begun *his* new talk show imitating Phil Donahue) got his nose famously busted in an onstage brawl.

"Everyone trashes Mort," Pittman says, betraying not the slightest trace of anxiety over that fact. "To a great degree, you've got a herd mentality there. No one goes below the surface to analyze why Mort is working."

And what is below the surface? Bob Pittman shrugs.

"This generation doesn't respond well to authority figures," he says softly. "They don't respond to critics, for instance. My parents might go to a movie and say it wasn't a good movie because some critic said it wasn't. Kids don't think that way. What we're discovering is that the younger generation does not like the pontificating style of traditional authority figures."

Pittman reflects for a moment and then adds, with a slight smile, "That's why Ronald Reagan was so popular. He wasn't cut-and-dried. He cracked jokes about stuff. He said people were idiotic when they were. Toward the end of his campaign, George Bush began to embrace some of that. George Bush became a little like Morton Downey.

"Mort, I think," he says, "is the wave of the future in television." When I ask whether Mort is the future in politics as well—this was before the news broke regarding George Lois and a political-advertising firm—Pittman chuckles, as if I were making a joke.

Bob Pittman has a habit—almost a tic—in interviews of citing his parents as points of contrast to his present world. "That works well for my parents, but not for us," he was quoted as saying recently, explaining why Downey did not interview civilized professors instead of, say, protofascist demagogues. "My parents are used to finishing one train of thought before starting another. I can carry on two conversations while I'm reading my mail," he confided in print. "Television prob'ly showed me more of the world than my parents did" is how he put it to me.

I decided to go and visit the parents of Television's Child.

The stop signs in Brookhaven, Mississippi, are right out in the middle of the neighborhood intersections—four to an intersection, fastened to the sides of a barrel-shaped stand. An old railroad line runs along the town's spine; cars have to stop when the freight comes through. Sycamore and magnolia trees still drip their foliage over the sidewalks in late autumn. And now comes the frame where Twisted Sister leaps into this deceptive idyll: The high school directly adjoins a cemetery.

Brookhaven is where Bob Pittman and his older brother, Tom, went to high school. I stopped there first and talked to Thomas E. Sasser. Twenty years ago, the red-haired, boyish Tommy Sasser was Bob Pittman's chemistry teacher.

"I guess the most memorable thing I have about Bob," Sasser told me, grinning a sociable grin, "is the first time I ever had to paddle him. He was a junior. Tenth-grade or a junior,

I'm not sure. It was probably my second or third year here. He had a glass ah. And the first lick I hit him with a paddle, he popped that glass ah out. There I was, a young teacher. I thought I had knocked his ah out. Scared me to death."

(Bob Pittman chuckles when I ask him about this later. "Prob'ly apocryphal," he murmurs. "But I did used to put a straight pin through an eraser of a pencil and tap my eye with it until the teacher noticed I was sticking a pin in my eye.")

Pittman's parents now live in Jackson, fifty-five miles north of Brookhaven, where they returned after the boys graduated from high school. Warren Pittman has served in the Methodist ministry for forty years.

Lanita Pittman was not at home when I went to see them— she was baby-sitting for the Tom Pittmans up in Tupelo—so Warren greeted me alone at the door of their beige-colored house, a modest but immaculate bungalow with shutters and a flower bed in the front yard. It was a rainy Sunday, after church. Warren Pittman wore a dignified starched white shirt, a gray-and-burgundy tie, Sansabelt gray slacks and laced-up cordovan wing tips that gleamed like polished hardwood.

"A typical kid," the father responded carefully when I asked about Bob as a boy. "As far as going, you know, farther than just a typical kid, you know, I wouldn't say that he was any more than typical in this, that and the other."

Any particular images?

Warren Pittman reflected. "Bob was a night kid," he said. "Tom would get up early. Bob hated to get up early. But he'd stay up half the night."

What would he do?

"Study. Watch TV. Or if he was in photography, maybe work in the darkroom, and all these sort of things. Oh, he was in a little band, too, one time. That was one of the things he went through for a while. Several of 'em in the Brookhaven band."

("I think back to the Sixties,' Bob Pittman tells me quietly in

New York. "I sat in my room with a red light bulb on, listening to Doors records. My parents thought it was corrupting. But rock and roll is just the music of people making the transition from childhood to adulthood.")

Did Bob's accident result in any sort of personality change? I asked his father.

Warren Pittman thought about that. "It's hard to tell, at that young age; it's really hard to tell. I would say, offhand, not necessarily. But . . ." He let the thought trail off.

"I think one of the defining things about Bob was the accident where he lost his eye." The speaker is Tom Pittman, Bob's older brother by three years. I met him the following day in Tupelo, about three hours north of Jackson. Tom is editor of *The Tupelo Daily Journal.* Like his father, he is an ordained Methodist minister—a warm and thoughtful man who might be Bob's twin, except for the patches of gray beginning to appear in his thick dark head of hair.

"Bob's reaction to that accident was to try to prove that he could be just as good, or do anything that anybody else could do with two eyes," said Tom. "I think it made him competitive and show that he didn't have to be handicapped."

Tom recalled one other shaping influence on himself and his brother: As a Methodist minister's sons, they were always moving. "We were always the newcomers," he said. "Monticello, Centreville, Forest Hill, Hattiesburg, Forest, Jackson, Brookhaven. Bob was always the youngest kid in his class. The youngest kid, and late-growing. And a newcomer, with one eye.

"That's all a big disadvantage—but it also gives you some vantage point on society. When you're an outsider, you can see people more clearly in some ways. You listen. You pay attention. You figure out where the power is, who the leaders are. What their values are. Bob did that. He learned very early in life to live by his wits. How to get along with kids so they wouldn't beat him up. How to have some identity apart from that formed by being the strongest, the fastest, the best-football-player kind of identity."

("I tend not to be interested in what other people are doing," Bob Pittman insists when I ask him about his competition among the newer television programmers. "I tend not to play competitive sports. I tend to be interested in consumers. In politics. In what's going on with people's morals.")

The small, handicapped outsider, the perpetual newcomer, took refuge in his records, his hobbies—and in watching television. Tom Pittman remembered that before they moved to Brookhaven—before Bob was 10—Jackson, Mississippi, was the site of an experiment in a new and generally unheralded form of TV.

"We grew up with *cable* TV," he said. "Gosh, we had that in elementary school. That's because we were so rural. In Hattiesburg, they erected a huge antenna to pick up distant signals. You know, later, when HBO started, it got tested simultaneously in two places—West Palm Beach and Jackson, Mississippi. So Mississippi has always been in the forefront of cable TV."

And so the child Bob was among the first to experience television as the present generation experiences it: as self-edited montage, as interruption of sequence, of narrative, of context—the viewer as (watch . . . *click* . . . watch . . . *click* . . . watch . . . *click* . . .) the authoritarian. The very mode that became the identified look of Bob Pittman's cable breakthrough, MTV, with its seductive appeal to the very kinds of kids Bob Pittman could never really join: the strong, the fast, the best-football-player types—the anti-intellectual, anti-authoritarian children.

Recalling Warren Pittman's assurance that his younger son was "just a typical kid," I asked Tom whether he thought his own childhood aspirations were any different from his brother's.

"Bob always wanted to be rich and famous," Tom responded without a beat of hesitation. "That was clear. He wanted to be rich and famous."

How did Tom know?

"Well, he said so."

Pittman's entry into broadcasting was apparently as circumstantial, as casually intuitive, as any of his other boyhood hobbies. Like several of his classmates, he did a little part-time DJ-ing on the local FM station, WCHJ. The next thing anyone knew, he was in Jackson. Then Milwaukee. Then Detroit. Then Pittsburgh, where he joined forces with an older and perhaps only marginally less shrewd version of himself, Charlie Warner.

"He's a small-town boy that has an incredible brain," says Warner. "It's just one of those rare things that comes along— somebody that was born with a big bucket. He has one of those very rare minds that is both analytical and creative."

Warner is now a faculty member at the University of Missouri School of Journalism. Through the 1970s, he was an outrageously successful—and successfully outrageous—manager of radio stations in Pittsburgh, Chicago and New York. At each stop, Pittman was his program director and protégé. Charlie Warner may know Bob Pittman better than anyone.

"When he came to work for me at WPEZ in Pittsburgh, he was 18," Warner recalls. "It was 1972. He had a long beard, long hair—but he was very mature, even then. *I don't think he ever had a childhood.* He was a grown-up program director, just like he is now. Very controlled.

"And even then, he knew how to win. He knew more about ratings than anybody at the station. He knew that in radio, you don't program to people—*you program to people with ratings books.* If you're gonna give away a thousand dollars in one call-in, you do it on a Wednesday, because that's when people fill in their ratings books.

"He took that station from zero to a leader in the market."

When Charlie Warner was rewarded in 1974 with the general managership of a failing NBC-owned radio station in Chicago, he made sure to take his prize protégé along with him.

The result was the Miracle of WMAQ. It took Bob Pittman exactly one ratings period to bring the station from twenty-second in the market to third. His formula was country-western music and cash-giveaway telephone promotions: endless local television commercials in which an extremely fat woman shrieked, "WMAQ'S GONNA MAKE ME RICH!!!" followed by a show of dollar bills and a graphic showing the station's telephone number. Local critics began to write columns to the effect that WMAQ was buying a listenership. Meanwhile, "MAKE ME RICH!!!" calls to the station reached such a volume that at certain hours of the day it was impossible to dial into the area's *entire telephone exchange*.

"He didn't even *like* country music," says Warner. "He *hated* it. Nobody else in the world knew that. I knew it. But he knew what to do. He was an execution *freak*."

An example of Pittman's execution style involved a disc jockey at the station named Ellie Hellman. "The name was sort of nowhere," says Warner. "Bob asked her what name she'd *like* to be. She said she liked Bob Dylan. Bob said, 'Okay, you be Ellie Dylan.' Bob took her and trained her, as a mentor. She became one of the first big-time DJs in country music."

In 1977, Warner, Pittman and Ellie Dylan all went skipping down the yellow brick road to Oz: to New York and the NBC flagship station, WNBC. Their mission: replicate their fabulous adventure at WMAQ. The task proved far more formidable; radio competition in New York was tougher, more sophisticated than it was in Chicago.

Using a contemporary-hits format, Pittman tried to make a star of Ellie Dylan, with whom he was, by then, romantically involved. But within a few months it was apparent that Dylan's soft, southern nighttime voice was unequal to the strident daylight demands of the Apple.

Charlie Warner recalls the denouement: "I called him into

my office and said, 'Bob, it's not working in the morning.' He said, 'I know.' I said, 'I'm gonna fire Ellie today. I will do it. I will go over to her house and fire her.' He said, 'Thank you.' And I went and did it."

Pittman's distraction vis-à-vis Ellie Dylan was an aberration. His prodigious objectivity had never before yielded to emotion. ("Bob is always in total control," says Charlie Warner. "I've never heard him express great emotion, either sadness or joy. Always complete and total control.") It is not likely to yield again. He is settled now. A few years ago, he met a chic young fashion editor named Sandy Hill on an airplane. It was mutual compatibility at first sight. Sandy, now Mrs. Bob Pittman, recalled the encounter for me via cellular telephone from her limo en route to Kennedy not long ago.

"I was thrilled with my across-the-aisle mate," she briefed me. "I gathered my strategy together as to how to talk to him. I did what I always do: I started to read a magazine. I had every title under the sun in my bag. I thought I'd better not take out certain magazines. If I took out *House & Garden*, he'd think I was married. If I took out *Cosmo*, he'd think I was a Cosmo girl. I took out *The New Yorker*, 'cause that says a lot about a person. I was looking at the jokes and laughing self-consciously. He turned to me and said, 'You must be reading *The New Yorker*.'"

I asked Sandy if she could remember exactly what it was about Bob that caught her fancy.

"I just thought he was so cute." she said. "He had great style, he was extremely handsome. And we had the same haircut."

Pittman romanced her with roses for a month. "I had what looked like a funeral home" was the way Sandy affectionately put it. A couple months after that they were married. They now have a rustic house in Connecticut, a Cessna 340 that Bob flies as a hobby and a helicopter for Sandy. "I'm not much interested in flying fixed-wing," she explained.

They also have a child, a 5-year-old son named Robert

Thomas—Bo. This of course makes Pittman the very sort of creature lampooned so successfully on MTV and by Morton Downey Jr.: a parent. An authority figure.

But Bob Pittman has spared Bo from authoritarianism as surely as he is sparing the generation that consumes his brand of television: So far, the child has backpacked in the Grand Tetons, skied in Aspen and logged a half hour of flight instruction in the family helicopter.

It was Charlie Warner who finally steered Pittman into his natural destiny, television.

Among Warner's New York media pals was John Lack, then a young executive with Warner Amex. Charlie Warner helped persuade Lack to hire Pittman as program director for a fledgling cable competitor to HBO and Showtime called the Movie Channel. Lack had some other vague concepts floating around the office as well—an all-game channel, an all-music channel. . . .

"I went over to Bob's office one day," Warner recalls. "This was early 1981, I guess. And he showed me some music videos that the record companies had sent over." Warner's comment was worthy of Neville Chamberlain himself:

"I said, 'That's great—but aren't people gonna get tired of watching 'em?'

"But I'd forgotten the hallmark of Bob Pittman. *Execution.* The real secret of MTV's secret was the way Bob *created the image.* He said, 'The one thing we want to communicate to our audience is, we don't look like the networks!' "

"John Lack had already had the idea of a cable channel devoted entirely to music," Pittman says. "But even though John is a brilliant guy, he was thinking in conventional-television terms. He envisioned a whole series of *programs.* What I brought to it was the whole concept of what is a music channel."

Ebb and flow.

It must be reported that not all of the MTV insiders bought

the image, the perception, of Bob Pittman, champion of the antiauthoritarian child.

"What struck me," says one longtime MTV staffer, "was his complete callousness toward the consumer of the product. Bob was sort of a chameleon in a way. He chose a field—rock and roll—to make his fortune. Rock and roll attracts a lot of people who are star-struck, fame-struck and hip-struck, if that's a word. Bob hid behind the trappings of hip to exploit the consumer in a way as thoroughgoing as any show-business person has ever done."

Asked to elaborate, this staffer says, "I don't think Bob had any feel for the music whatever" (an echo of Charlie Warner's "He didn't even *like* country music. He *hated* it").

"But," the staffer goes on, "he knows the young and adolescent mind. He knows it is very easily led. It's very turned off by adult figures, but if you can look hip, you can pick every penny out of their pockets."

How has MTV done that?

"Look at the idea—a station that runs commercials [the videos, as promos for performing groups] twenty-four hours a day. The choice of artists was always dictated by who was willing to provide videos. Bob said, 'Everything we do, we do for nothing.' And the outlandish contests, the giveaways. A weekend with Van Halen. Get to be Bruce Springsteen's roadie. Be in a David Bowie movie." (Echoes, all, of "WMAQ'S GONNA MAKE ME RICH!!!")

"Genius?" says this insider. "I don't think of him as a genius. Every production-value decision he has ever made is based on budget; then he tries to pass it off as aesthetics. Hey, he's a real Eighties guy, Pittman. A real Reagan rock and roller. A guy in a suit and a Learjet."

Well, to be fair, not exactly. A Cessna.

Since Television's Child never hesitates to cite his parents as points of contrast to the culture he is helping to create, I was eager to learn whether they—and his brother—see his work as a contrast to their own culture and values.

In Jackson, I asked the Methodist minister Warren Pittman whether the social and moral messages transmitted over his son's brainchild cable system ever troubled him. Warren Pittman shifted in his chair. "I—as far as I'm concerned, the jury's still out on how much impact, and values, that MTV really . . . it may reinforce certain values. It probably reinforces more than it establishes values." He thought some more. "I don't see it as a corrupter of values, things of that sort.

"How *impressed* I am with it is a good question, you know."

The next day, in Tupelo, I posed the same question to Tom Pittman—who had told me he'd chosen to remain in Mississippi "because I felt like I was equipped to make life better in this place."

"It's a *medium*" was Tom's careful answer. "Bob created, in essence, a new *medium*, by combining some preexisting elements. And then the way that medium's used, I mean, you know, that's another decision. Whereas to create a new medium is a morally neutral act, I'd say. What kind of content you put on that medium would be the ethical question, I'd say."

That the content of MTV has raised moral and ethical questions is one of the better-known pop-cultural facts of the decade. One of the most vociferous opponents of certain rock albums and videos, based on their sexual and antisocial content, has been Tipper Gore, the wife of Senator Albert Gore, who campaigned last year for the Democratic presidential nomination. Ms. Gore endured a great deal of hostility, not to say public ridicule, from the firmament of MTV stars and their defenders as she pressed her case.

Yet when the New York steering committee for Senator Gore's campaign was announced last summer, one name on it was that of Bob Pittman. I ask Pittman whether he would care to unravel that particular paradox.

"I understand what Tipper is saying," he replies. "I understand her feelings. I think she's wrong."

And now Bob Pittman is in the process of forming a political-advertising apparatus that might advance candidates, such as Tipper Gore's husband (Pittman and George Lois are both Democrats), through an application of the very techniques he perfected on MTV.

"None of the current political advertising is geared for my generation of viewers," Pittman acknowledges when I ask him about this. "It has no credibility. They don't understand how to create an image with a whole attitude."

In the 57-year-old Lois—an aggressive and often profane Madison Avenue warrior—Pittman feels he has the consummate ally. Lois has created campaign ads for many politicians over the years, including Robert Kennedy in the Sixties, and he has a long history with Pittman and MTV.

"We understand how to communicate in this day and age, using the options available," says Pittman. "Look at George Bush. Here's a man who used the tools. George Lois and I have worked together a long time. I used him for almost everything. He'll come up with a great ad for you."

Just all sorts of things are cooking at Quantum Media. Children—real children, Bo-sized ones—are to be the next beneficiaries of its special vision. The company has produced two episodes of a kids' game show "with a high-tech new look," says Pittman. A pilot is also in the works with Fox Television. There is a series commitment with CBS, which has also bought a special from Quantum.

Pittman is silent on the details of every project that has not yet aired—with one exception: a home-video feature that he mentions in the context of what he calls "social trends." The subject of the home video is golf.

"Golf is a major growth sport," he says, his voice taking on some animation. "We've come across a man with a plan. He's looked at the physiology of the body as it relates to golf. The

37

body doesn't produce power in the ways that have been tra-ditionally assumed. [I half-expect him to add "by my par-ents."] He's developed a new system for teaching golf, and we're producing a home video on that."

A home video on golf. It seems a peculiar passion for the man who has built an empire reshaping American culture in the image of the unleashed, antiauthoritarian child. (Pittman himself does not play golf.) But when you begin to add it up, so did country-western music. So did rock and roll. So—for a softspoken son of a southern minister—did Morton Downey Jr. So did the candidacy of Albert Gore. So does the partner-ship with George Lois.

One of the most consistent and noticeable features about Bob Pittman (aside from his extraordinary intelligence) hap-pens also to be an overarching characteristic of television it-self: an utter absence of a consciousness of paradox.

The video consciousness is a consciousness of *the moment*— isolated from past and future, disconnected from cause and effect. And absolved, therefore, from such tedious linear con-siderations as paradox. Or irony. Or consistency, logic, coher-ence, memory. Or moral accountability.

It's just ebb and flow.

These are among the traits that behaviorists and social crit-ics are beginning to identify as central to the personality being shaped by the onrushing environment of a video culture. These are the traits of that creature of the right-brain hemisphere, Analogic Man: intuitive, nonlinguistic, image-sensitive, but disinvolved from sequential reasoning, linear logic, context, narrative—artifacts, all, of downcast Digital Man, the debased and dustbinned creature of the left-brain hemisphere. Of typography.

"I've never lost anyone any money," says the Child of Tele-vision in his office, beneath the portrait of the man with a TV set for a head.

Not the most ringing of epitaphs, perhaps. But this is an age of logos, not epitaphs. Barely anyone remembers epitaphs anymore. Or axioms, or proverbs—such as the one relating to who shall rule, in the land of the blind.

The Agony
of Deceit

*In politics, commercials, even sitcoms, it's
the truth that's uncouth. The fib is fab*

The other night, I was watching a little television, and *It's
Garry Shandling's Show* came on Fox, and Garry walked out on
the set that was designed to look exactly like his living room,
or somebody's living room, and he spread his arms toward
the studio audience and said, in that deadpan way of his,
"Welcome to my home!"

See. And the studio audience just went, I mean, *nuts*, because the joke was, of course, that it wasn't Garry Shandling's
home at all; it was a goddamn *television studio*, and obviously
Garry was putting on the whole phony tradition where stars
pretend that a television-studio set is actually their home. Or
some tradition like that.

See. And then I got this, like, totally postmodern-concept

flash: *What if there wasn't a studio audience at all?* What if Garry was putting reality through another warp, pretending to let this nonexistent TV studio audience in on his nonlivingroom TV joke? Because *some* postproduction was definitely happening there; the audience was laughing in real time at a shtick that was obviously videotaped and edited; real-time laughter at slomo gags. . . . But then at the end of the show they flashed this *postcard* that said where you could write for tickets to attend a taping of *It's Garry Shandling's Show.* . . .

And that's when it hit me. Bang. Ton of bricks.

The 1988 political campaign hasn't ended.

Actually it never began, either, exactly. It was just sort of *there*, like all of television is just sort of there, solid-state, permutating, waiting to be perceived. Or misperceived.

Anybody here remember the 1988 political campaign? George Bush and Michael Dukakis? For the presidency? Of the United States? The Olympics were the lead-in? Yeah, *that* one! Okay. Remember how everybody was going nuts about the distortions, the crooked TV commercials, the rigged photo ops, the hoked-up negatives, the trivializing, the exaggerations, the all-round bunco and flimflammery that went on? (Hey. Really. Was that George Bush or was that *Garry Shandling* up there in front of Boston Harborrrrr?)

Remember how some expert got quoted in *The New York Times* as saying that the Bush advisers believed they could distort with impunity? Remember how the *Times* itself stated flatly on Halloween that "the next President will have been chosen in a campaign dominated as never before by television"?

Remember that spigot of sneakery, that fountain of phoniness? Well, excuse me, I think somebody forgot to turn it off. It's still running. In fact, it was running before Willie Horton was ever a gleam in Roger Ailes's beady little eye. The real lesson of campaign '88 should have been that campaign '88 was no aberration. It was very much in the mainstream of what television is about as we have come to understand and accept it in the 1980s. And what is television about? It is about the technocratic neutralization and circumvention of truth. What else is new?

Government With the Consent of the Governed has been replaced by Conning With the Consent of the Conned. But that's only a sideshow, a footnote. (Who the hell cares about *governing* anymore?) The bigger picture is this: falsity, deception, the chimerical, the patently fraudulent—these have become the routine, the accepted (hell, the *preferred*) modes of communication here in the Land of the Free. (Preferred by the consumers, as well as the programmers, by the way.) The Collaborative Lie is everywhere. It's Telemerica's newest contribution to the family of man. It's our first truly indigenous art form since jazz.

The Bush political commercials were a bald-faced, contemptible and gross perversion of the "real" world? Hey—"In modern America, *nothing is real anymore*." That is the conclusion of pop-cultural critic Joel Achenbach, writing in *Utne Reader* after an excursion through such neo-Wonderland manifestations as Pepperidge Farm's Machine Designed to Make Cookies That Look as Though They Were Made by Hand. ("Then," wrote the incredulous Achenbach, "they admit the hoax right there on the bag. They *brag* about it. They say, yo, these cookies only *look* as though someone made them by hand.")

"The technology of falsehood has greatly outdistanced the progress of our judgment," wrote Achenbach; and he then took note of an eerie cultural submission to it all: "From this mess has arisen a strange sort of *comfort* with artifice and falsehood. There may be an actual preference for the unreal. . . ."

And just in case there might be some surviving mutant out there in consumerland, someone with enough brain cells still firing to attempt a few critical distinctions, the media-masters of metafiction have one more strategy to activate: irony. Citing the industry's acknowledged need "to get the viewer to like the advertising" (and so to resist zapping it on his VCR playback), critic Mark Crispin Miller noted that the hippest TV commercials nowadays seek to *flatter* the viewers' supposed enlightenment "by reflecting back his/her own automatic skepticism toward TV." A beer spot placed inside *Saturday Night Live*, for instance, may be so artfully preposterous in its depiction of consumer lust that it is in effect whispering to its wised-up audience, "Sure, this is what we do. Funny, huh?"

The Bartles & Jaymes commercials are downscale versions of the same thing. They mock their own phony real-folks pitch to real folks. Nobody complains. The Joe Isuzu spots are, of course, classic illustrations of the strategy. Everyone sort of knows that automobile commercials con the consumer; they camouflage the product's competitive defects and exaggerate its virtues—not to *mention* their Big Lie, their sanitizing of the hellscape in which American cars are driven, or nudged. "Joe Isuzu" flaunts the fibbing.

Television entertainment is onto the game. David Letterman has conjured up the meta–talk show, a format that is at once authentic and self-spoofing. *Moonlighting* is constantly parodying its own production problems. Then there are *Max Headroom* and, more recently, *Murphy Brown* and *Studio 5B*—all network shows that cannibalize network news, gleefully validating every paranoid fantasy about TV newspeople as liars, thought-control totalitarians or penny-ante fibbing fools. Nobody seems to care. Why should they? In modern America, nothing is real anymore.

But—look. Let's be honest. The issue here is not really "lying" as lying has traditionally been understood. (Don't worry, there's still plenty of good old-fashioned lying going on—it's just so recherché these days.) The issue here is the neutralization of truth.

Television neutralizes truth. Renders it irrelevant. This isn't just me being a shameless flatterer. It's a matter of codified theory. It was stated as a proposition fully fifteen years ago by the video scholar and commercial maker Tony Schwartz in his book, *The Responsive Chord*.

"In communicating at electronic speed," wrote Schwartz, "we no longer direct information into an audience . . . but try to evoke stored information out of them, in a patterned way." What he meant was that television makes people want to *collaborate* with it—getting the eye and brain to cooperate in the chore of "finishing" complete pictures out of ever-shifting masses of dots on the screen. This is a radically different level of engagement than, say, reading lines of type on a page. The mind can decode those static symbols in a detached, coolly analytical and critical way.

Schwartz's thundering conclusion:

"Truth, as a social value, is a product of print. *The question of truth is largely irrelevant when dealing with electronic media content.*" (My italics.)

Yo, George Bush! To apply Schwartz's ideas to campaign '88: What is the "truth" (or its opposite) of Willie Horton's menacing, and racially suggestive, black face glaring out from the screen as the announcer intones, "Weekend prison passes. Dukakis on crime"? What is the "truth" (or its opposite) of candidate Bush standing in front of Boston Harbor and visually associating his opponent with its polluted waters?

These are not "lies" in the sense of logical propositions that one could challenge or refute by citing a text with contrary claims. They are not texts at all. Each is a self-enclosed, self-defined little universe of atomized visual data. A self-generated myth. Evoking stored information out of us, in a patterned way.

Land sakes, how times have changed.

"In our time, political speech and writing are largely the defense of the indefensible. . . . Thus political language has to consist largely of euphemism, question-begging and sheer cloudy vagueness. . . . Such phraseology is needed if one wants to name things without calling up mental pictures of them."

George Orwell published that argument forty-four years ago at the heart of his "Politics and the English Language." Orwell was among the first social thinkers to recognize that twentieth-century state bureaucracies had learned to camouflage their intentions not by overtly lying so much as by relieving language of its specific meaning. Orwell had another big insight: that the best way to relieve language of meaning was to drain it of its imagery—its capacity to call up mental pictures.

He offered some examples: "Defenseless villages are bombarded from the air, the inhabitants driven out into the countryside, the cattle machine-gunned . . . this is called *pacification.*"

Orwell's criticisms were valid. They still are. *Within their purview.* His confident remedies—concrete, clear, jargon-free prose—are also appropriate. *Within their purview.*

But Orwell's purview was printed thought, as generated (mostly) by state bureaucracies. Sadly, this prophet who three years later was to stun the world with the image of Big Brother on a television screen, did not think to confront the central question of the Television Age: *What if the deception is presented as a mental picture, prepackaged and stocked with images?* What are the confident remedies then?

And remedies there must be. Whether we choose to call it "lying" or whether we sanctify it as a new and necessary residue of technology, the social dangers are the same as they have always been.

Those dangers were well outlined by the philosopher Sissela Bok twelve years ago in *Lying: Moral Choice in Public and Private Life*—a book that was not (it somehow seems necessary to point out) prompted by the influence of television.

Ms. Bok made no bones about the seriousness of her topic: "Deceit and violence—these are the two forms of deliberate assault on human beings." And she added, rather prophetically as it turns out: "Imagine a society, no matter how ideal in other respects, where word and gesture could never be counted on . . . [such] a society, whose members were unable to distinguish truthful messages from deceptive ones, would collapse."

Until some modern-day Orwell comes along to offer us a means for repairing the video-driven neutralization of truth, we can amuse ourselves by imagining the scale and the terms of that collapse. (Are the fault lines below Los Angeles dangerous or aren't they? Is the greenhouse effect going to sundry our children like so many Italian plum tomatoes or isn't it? Is that shield going to work or not?)

In the meantime, we can expect campaign '88 to keep on running. It will not matter that the next George Bush is telling tele-lies about the next Boston Harbor. That was the case last fall. What's scary is that we may not be able to tell, or care, that the next George Bush is really Garry Shandling.

Lawyers, Guns
and Money

*Greed meets the pioneer spirit in Houston, as a
convention of programmers proves that crime does pay*

"MAN AGAINST SHAWK! IN A BLUDDY TANK! Won't
matter the outcome! It'll be the *oyl*-timate event!"

Every big American convention seems to produce its own
prophet, its spiritual spokesman: Jesse Jackson for the Democrats, Dan Quayle for the Republicans and for the twenty-sixth
renewal of the NATPE International Program Conference in
Houston earlier this year, Robin Leach—rich, famous and
life-styling it around the Teletrib booth on the floor of the
George R. Brown Convention Center, regaling the hordes of
passersby with his vision.

"Man against shawk! To the finish! Doesn't matter who wins!
Oyl-timate telly-vision event," Leach kept crying. The idea
seemed to suffuse him with pleasure. Social criticism! Slashing

47

irony! Was *that* how the blokes did it? It was so easy, and such fun! He was wearing a light-blue (hell, let's face it, a *robin's-egg* blue) double-breasted suit, and he appeared to be sipping champagne, and he offered his naughty prognostication, with a little toast, to all who caught his eye.

"Man against shawk! . . ."

Some of the sleek-coated passersby slowed a little, flexed their dorsal fins and gazed speculatively at Leach—not the sort of gazes one sees directed at a maniac roaring operatic arias on the sidewalk at 57th and Broadway in Manhattan, say, but the sort that suggest quick calculations of formatting, host, projected audience share.

NATPE stands for National Association of Television Program Executives. At Houston, that seemed to be about all it stood for. Seventy-five hundred of the nation's new mandarin class of commercial-video high rollers had converged to turn the Brown Center, for a few gossamer days, into Gomorrah-by-the-Gulf—a lubricious temple to the New Television, the deregulated, Republicanized, free-market television of porno-crime, tablotrash and gladiatorial combat, set to an MTV beat. Little decanters of jelly beans were arranged on buffet tables in display booths all around the floor, sacramental offerings to the Great Liberator.

The conventioneers were uneasily insouciant, a sure sign of frayed nerves beneath the glitzy surface. "If Beethoven and Mozart came back to earth today," a slick young mandarin brayed at a network news crew, "they couldn't work in our industry!"

The false bravado in the George Brown Center will leave its unlovely residue on American television screens in a few months. The fall season, which used to be the three major networks' private little block party, will be defined this autumn largely by alternatives to network fare: most tellingly, by first-run syndication. This fall, the syndication alternatives will be partly rooted in American nightmare.

NATPE is a syndicator's bazaar. Syndication is currently enduring the backlash of its own recent success. For years, "syndicated" meant "off-network," and NATPE was the place where local-station buyers went bargain hunting for hit network series that had finished their runs and were being recycled by their production studios as filler for the late afternoon, the wee hours or—in the case of unaffiliated stations—in competition with network prime time. (Does the name Hawkeye Pierce ring a bell?)

Then syndication shed its cocoon. In the early 1980s, Paramount—a dominant but foundering supplier of network programs—began generating syndication product for *first run*. Its breakthrough hit was *Entertainment Tonight*, the nightly satellite-delivered package of same-day entertainment reportage and features. This was a bold new strike at the networks' oligarchy. The marketplace had performed the rare feat of acting in everyone's favor: profitability for the suppliers (Paramount topped $1 billion in revenues by 1984, a tenfold increase since 1973) and diversity (topical miniseries and sophisticated TV movies on Operation Primetime) for the viewers. First-run syndication seemed about to usher in an artistic as well as a financial Utopia.

But commercial television had been provided with an almost supernatural shield against true diversity; the shield is called greed. As early as 1987 the promise had gone sour: A pattern of overpricing the top-rated hits, a tendency to exploit federal deregulation with commercial clutter and a new glut of buck-hungry program suppliers had drained first-run syndication of its variety, its sense of risk, its confidence. The average ratings of syndicated shows began to drop. Profitability fell. And the vicious cycle kicked in: programs stripped bare of innovation, political consciousness, complexity; a gathering rush toward the epicenter of American narcissism, fixation, masochistic reverence.

By January 1989, at Houston, that epicenter had clearly revealed itself: crime.

49

Crime—the emerging pornography of the century's last decade—ran through the NATPE booths and stalls like a homecoming theme, like love's old sweet song. The buyers and sellers had a whole positive type of attitude-posture regarding crime. It was a crime kind of convention. Everyone was dressing Crime—the male executives in shiny black double-breasted suits, the females in tailored black mini-dresses, black spike heels, black hose.

No wonder. "Crime" was preestablished as the password into the national id. Americans were obsessed with crime. Their fixation with it had moved beyond terror into a kind of macabre crush, a morbid mooning. The opinion polls were unambiguous. "Fear of crime pervades the nation," the Gallup Organization announced recently, noting that nearly half of all Americans were afraid to walk in their own neighborhoods at night—and a *tenth* felt the heebiejeebies behind their own locked doors.

There was only one possible conclusion: Crime was "exploitable" (an assertion that appeared in more than one sales pitch at NATPE). And not make-believe crime either; *real* crime, docucrime. Crime had just got a president elected! Crime was as respectable as motherhood! Thematically speaking, crime was safer than Sex! (Crime shows, unlike skin shows, raised no inconvenient questions about why Mom 'n' Pop Primetime were peeking: Why, to see justice done, of course!) Fear of crime had long since corrupted the country's resistance to its own pop-cult bestialization—twenty crimson years of movie bloodletting, from *The Wild Bunch* to *Robocop*, were testament to that. Now it was time for television, newly liberated from its "public interest" straitjacket, to get in on the rake.

As indeed it had been! Weren't *America's Most Wanted* and *Unsolved Mysteries* among the few big packaging innovations of the last few seasons? Wasn't Maury Povich, with his crime-soaked *A Current Affair*, turning into the Geraldo Rivera of the

Eighties—even as Geraldo was turing into Morton Downey Jr. (all three gentlemen recent NATPE success stories)? Didn't *The Houston Post* report, midway through the convention (the timing couldn't have been more perfect), that the owners of a blighted apartment complex were demolishing it building by building rather than having the police continually try to rid it of drug dealers? Hey!

The conventioneers, the Mugs 'n' Molls, strutted 'n' gawked. Crime savoir faire! When they weren't queuing up a city block or so to have their pictures taken with the cast of *Designing Women* or of *Married . . . With Children,* the buyers could stroll past the Qintex Entertainment booth, where the publicity kits for *Crime Diaries* ("A true-fact cop show with a new twist . . . Cops in Love!") assured them. "YOU CAN'T FIGHT CRIME. CRIME IS HERE TO STAY. MYSTERY, MURDER, BLACKMAIL, PASSION, DECEIT, JEALOUSY, LUST. . . . AND IT'S ALL REAL!" Or they could pause before the LBS Communications booth to consider *Manhunt,* "television's most important new crime investigation series" ("HIGHER CASH REWARDS . . . MORE VIEWER INVOLVEMENT . . . LOCAL POLICE TIE-INS").

There was the ITC Domestic Television booth, hawking *Secrets and Mysteries* ("THOUSANDS HAVE DIED TO BRING YOU THIS SHOW"). And there was the Paramount exhibit—it had actually come to this for Paramount—where materials for *Tabloid* affirmed, "The American appetite for 'hot,' 'sensational,' 'exploitable' material is . . . insatiable." *Tabloid,* the Paramount publicity kit promised, "will be a daily dose of sensational crimes, international scandal and titillating gossip.

Children are, of course, a part of crime, and children were not forgotten at NATPE. *America's Search for Missing Children,* from M&M Syndications, offered the eye-catching slogan "Some people take children for granted . . . others just take them." And over at the Ascot Syndication booth, the promotional pitch for *Has Anybody Seen My Child* discreetly assured that the format had found a way around the "skittishness . . . of advertisers" toward " 'crime-viewer involvement' shows." (The solution? This program will reenact the last few moments *before* a child's abduction.)

The displays, the huckstering, took on a kind of inadvertent dark topicality. The Muller Media booth was flogging a pair of syndicated movie packages, each with organizing graphics: "LETHAL WEAPONS" (a smoking pistol pointed at the observer) and "TOP GUNS" (two crossed handguns, one a semiautomatic). They triggered, as it were, memories of recent news reports that hospital trauma centers in American cities are at the point of structural collapse, overloaded with Vietnam-style casualties from the semiautomatic-weapons drug wars that rage in the streets.

Meanwhile, the sulfurously costumed cast members of two new proto–street gang entertainments roamed the aisles, pecs and buttocks twitching, staging impromptu displays of muscled hostility for the Mugs 'n' Molls. They were the *American Gladiators* ("the quintessential fusion of classic Roman games and futuristic athletic battles . . . finely-tuned bodies, 'new age' armor . . .") and the cast of *RollerGames* ("They're rough, they're tough, they're rotten"). These fantasy goonclowns summoned up the latest educational news from New York: An actual street gang—its name, the Decepticons, inspired by a cartoon—has struck such dread into the city that parents have kept children home from school on days of rumored "invasions."

And then there was Ike Pappas.

In a way, the whole debased logic of NATPE, and the whole spurious legitimacy of the crime shows it will send onto the American airwaves this fall, depends on Ike Pappas. Pappas was the prize exhibit at the Orion booth—he was there, live, in person; big, beefy, black-suited, *legitimate* Ike Pappas, a genuine god from the glory years of CBS News. A short dossier is in order for those who came of age a little after Pappa's prime.

Pappas covered every presidential campaign since John F. Kennedy's in 1960. He watched Jack Ruby shoot Kennedy's assassin, Lee Harvey Oswald, in Dallas. He covered the civil-rights movement in the South. He covered the great political trial of that era, the conspiracy case of the Chicago Seven. He covered coups in Greece and he covered hot spots in the Middle East and he covered Vietnam.

Ike Pappas was as legitimate as it got in television news. He once played himself in a movie. He even became a footnote in literature—satirized, for his humid and somewhat overripe on-camera style, as "Ike Ironic," in Philip Roth's *Our Gang*.

Then Ike Pappas made a serious professional mistake. He grew a little old, and a little hefty, and a little expensive in his accumulated years of service. Remember the layoff scene in *Broadcast News*? That's what happened to Ike Pappas. But Pappas is a proud man, fierce and dignified. He refused to accept that he was washed up. He turned himself into a corporation—Ike, Inc.—and put himself on the open market. Orion Syndication came shopping.

This fall, Ike Pappas will be seen in first-run syndication as the star of Orion's *Crimewatch Tonight*. Last January, in Houston, he was strolling around the Orion booth, shaking buyers' hands and just being Ike Pappas. Nearby were attacks of publicity kits explaining the marketing advantages of purchasing *Crimewatch Tonight*. "TERRORIZE A TIME PERIOD" suggested the graphics on the Orion kits. "MURDER YOUR COMPETITION . . . PROFIT FROM ORGANIZED CRIME . . . CRIME PAYS! AND PAYS!"

I sat down with Pappas for a brief conversation. It was a little awkward. Pappas is one of my heroes in the television news business; we'd both worked for the same network; but this was the first time I had ever met him. Pappas is a big, broad-shouldered man with a big, honest Greek face, black-haired and powerful-looking, but formal in the manner of all the great old CBS hands. I think we both felt conscious of being out of place.

We talked about his career at CBS and about the changes there, and then I finally brought up the subject of *Crimewatch Tonight*. He said some corporately correct things about the

53

program, and I took notes, but the conversation was uncomfortable and terse, and when I got back home and looked over the notes, just one remark of Pappas's leapt out at me, for what it said and for what it didn't say.

"I know that people are going to say that this is tabloid television," Ike Pappas told me, and then he paused, and then he said, a little wanly, "There is tabloid, and there's tabloid."

Before I left the Orion booth I had previewed a sample reel of *Crimewatch Tonight*. There was Ike Pappas, standing in front of what looked like a back-lot mockup of some seedy precinct headquarters, introducing a segment about the national scourge of beautiful young American models disappearing into the sin-traps of European luxury. . . .

There is tabloid, and there's tabloid. There is loss of vision, and there's NATPE. There's moral numbness, and there are the American communications corporations who will drag themselves and the whole scared, groping society down to any level of abasement—PROFIT FROM ORGANIZED CRIME!—for the purpose of getting a vehicle on first-run syndication.

Talk about your crime.

TWAIN WRECK

How Cyndi the trilling anchor deep-sixed me, and other confessions along the author-interview trail

I am a human puddle of authorial ooze, poured like some disposable talk-show guest (precisely the case) into the concave toadstool of a molded-plastic seat at the Minneapolis airport. Paper clips bind my French cuffs together. A split along the seam of my right Loafer sole grins up at me like some lewd instep Muppet. On my right index finger throbs the purple swelling of a jagged scar where, the previous night in Detroit, a tugged hotel corkscrew (molded plastic) burst apart in my fist. Moments ago I barely escaped federal arrest and prosecution after a snarling match with a luggage inspector, who had wanted to know—in a stunning imitation of Garrison Keillor's Minnesot'n dialect—why I'd vouchsafed him a small package of plastic instead of letting it slide under the X-ray machine.

"It's an audio cassette," I had hissed, fixing him with my best homicidal grin. "I didn't want it *erassssed.*"

"Wou'nt a-bin erased," this worthy had the temerity to rejoin, and biliously.

"And now it won't be erased *for sure,*" I commented, in tones that caused his ears to ripple like wheat sheaves along the sides of his head.

I am on the last fractured leg of an author's promotional tour, bound for home. And my thoughts are of Cyndi the Friendly Anchorwoman. Of whom (not her real name) more after these messages.

There was a time, and not too long ago, when a torrid romance sizzled between that Blue Angel, television, and the Emil Jannings–like fuddy-duddies of the literary world. Mailer on Cavett! Vidal on Carson! Germaine Greer on Griffin! Vidal and Buckley at each other's throats! Vidal versus Mailer—and look, isn't that Rod McKuen? No, it's John Dean! What the hell, it's an *author*! Heavy!

Why, it was going to be a regular Alliance for Progress, this unlikely fusion of the printed word and the cathode image that began to take hold in the early 1970s. How vast a wasteland could television be as long as it sold books? And what books, what authors! The entire dramatis personae of the counterculture-Vietnam-Watergate era, it seemed, had rushed offstage to a waiting bank of typewriters. And now they were marching from studio to shining studio: bound galleys firmly in hand, a few well-rehearsed bons mots firmly in mind—planted there, quite often, by the cottage industry of editors-cum-video-coaches that had sprung up to gratify the medium's more vulgarian imperatives.

It was a time of miracles and rumors of miracles. Any starry-eyed scrivener in elbow patches had a shot at converting his catharses to cash by hitting the makeup-and-swivel-chair circuit. A nobody stacked some copies of his new psychobabble book in the back of his station wagon and rolled out on the road, talking his way onto the local-city talk shows, acting as his own booking agent. That man was Wayne W. Dyer, and his book was *Your Erroneous Zones,* a monster of the late 1970s. Another unknown, Robert Haas, took his diet book on *Donahue* along with the tennis star Martina Navratilova, who pronounced the magic words: "This book changed my life." The book—*Eat to Win*—went through an entire printing that day. The video-based book tour had entered American pop mythology.

It had to end.

I am hustling down the long corridor of a St. Louis television studio in the tow of Cyndi the Friendly Anchorwoman. Cyndi (not her real name; her real name is Debi) has personally clattered out to meet me and guide me back toward the news set. I say "clattered" because Cyndi is wearing some very serious high heels, and she is setting a pace suitable to a nuclear evacuation.

As we chug along, Cyndi cheerfully informs me that (a) the scheduled time allotment for my book interview, four minutes, has been cut back to *two* minutes, and that (b) she would like to devote half of that time to a general discussion of the state of American mass media. "We'd like for yew to put on your media critic's hat" is the way she puts it, winningly.

Stifling an urge to remark that I would like to pull my media critic's hat firmly down over Cyndi's Memphis-debutante earlobes, I improvise an appeal to her moral sense: This visit was arranged and *financed,* I point out to her (it is a *long* corridor), by my publisher. It would be misleading to pretend that I am on the news show as a topical "newsmaker" guest, since my book is about the effects of 1985's Mark Twain sesquicentennial on my hometown of Hannibal, Missouri.

Cyndi's response—we have by now clattered and careered onto the news set, a curved anchor desk in front of a hand-painted trompe l'oeil rendering of the St. Louis skyline—is pure situational ethics: "Jes' tell'em," she trills, happily batting her eyes, "it was *mah* fault."

The newscast begins, and I see at once why my interview time has been slashed in half. It is one of those four-alarm local-news days in St. Louis: The station has found it necessary to cover, among other key breaking stories, the previous night's premiere of Joan Rivers's talk show and the results of a *People*-magazine poll on the twenty sexiest men in America.

Hello, sweetheart, get me rewrite—oh, the hell with it. Get me two on the aisle.

Just a nanosecond before the red light of the camera flashes to signal the start of our live interview, Cyndi leans forward, beaming, to administer the ritual coup de grace. "Ah have to *confess*," she confides enthusiastically, "Ah jes' haven't had a *sey*-cond to look at yoah bewk!"

After the interview, she wonders if I will autograph her copy, supplied to her, gratis, by the publisher.

It did not take long to comprehend that Cyndi's machinations (oh, let's give credit where it's due; the machinations of her executive producer) were hardly a fluke along the latter-day TV author-interview trail. Back in New York for some scheduled book chat on Cable News Network's afternoon show *Take Two*, I received a call at my home on the eve of my appearance. A producer, her voice thick with eleventh-hour hypertension, asked if I'd consent to spend a portion of the interview discussing television's effect on the congressional elections. (She may have used the phrase "media critic's cap.")

I pointed out that the elections would take place the day after the interview. Right, she said; well, of course she meant the effect of *negative political TV ads* on the elections. Or the electorate. Whatever. I sighed something sullenly assenting, and we rang off.

Hours later, she was back on the line. Would it be okay if we *began* the interview on the topic of the elections and *then* turned—"segued," she might even have said—to the inconvenient matter of my book?

Now *my* voice was thick with hypertension. Feeling helpless with anger yet stubbornly defiant, I tried the same appeal to fair play with this woman that I'd used to utterly no avail with good old Cyndi.

Look, I said, it *won't* be okay. I accept the realities of quid pro quo in TV author interviews, but I sensed that the CNN quid was about to engulf my quo. That is, the original premise of the interview would be reduced to the status of an afterthought. My own consent to be a handy actor in the network's "newsmaker" agenda would severely blunt the emphasis on my book, which had brought me to CNN's attention in the first place.

I made all of this explicitly clear. Imagine my mirth, my astonishment, my joke's-on-me look of discombobulation, as I sat in the CNN interview chair the following day, listening to the announcer billboard my upcoming live interview, "Media expert Ron Powers discusses the effects of those *negative political ads . . . ,*" and watching a montage of those ads roll as an intro to my segment.

Not to put too fine a point on it, I felt violated. But I also felt that I had begun to understand something essential: the new dynamic that exists between authors and television programmers in an age that is witnessing video's full flight from any vestige of narrative, reflection or sequential thought—from any lingering frame of reference that is not an ironic, a facetious, a fleeting, an explicitly *video* frame of reference.

I began to realize that I was one of the lucky ones. That is, I was the sort of author for whom television could find a *pretext* for allowing on the air. (*New York Times* columnist Tom Wicker was similarly "lucky" a couple of years ago: The author of a 700-page, labor-of-love historical novel about the Civil War, *Unto This Hour,* Wicker was invited on TV talk show after TV talk show—to chat about that mess in Washington.) God help the poor biographer, first novelist or serious nonfiction writer who *doesn't* possess the kind of calling card that will allow him or her to flatter the imperial medium's notions of itself in exchange for a few seconds to explain what might have taken a year, or five, to create, with little expectation of Tina Turner–level rewards.

The love affair is over. Too hot not to cool down. Television is in the midst of purging itself of its recent infatuation with writers and the written word. There still exist TV shows that welcome authors and "sell" books—*Donahue*, most notably; the *Today* show, with its relative friendliness toward novelists; the syndicated *Hour Magazine*, if you happen to have written a commercial, "high-concept" book.

Beyond those oases, the long trail is mighty bare these days. The good local-city "magazine" shows, the lifeline of any author's TV tour, have mostly shut down or constricted their formats, the victims of a recent glut of high-gloss national chat shows, from Oprah Winfrey to Sally Jessy Raphael. Gone are Carol Randolph's show in Washington, D.C., *L.A. Today, Good Morning Detroit*. Cleveland's legendary *The Morning Exchange* continues to flourish—but Philadelphia? Boston? The entire *South*? Forget it, unless your idea of an author is John ("Hey! I Just Wrote Another Book!") Madden.

The news isn't all bad, however. Television's withdrawal from the world of writers has perhaps even been a blessing, in that it has shifted the burden to the medium historically best equipped to enhance the written word: radio. For authors who are willing to scale down their video vanity and settle for a "blue highways" route across the American airwaves, some richly rewarding enclaves lie in wait: Boone and Erickson at WCCO in Minneapolis; the indefatigable Larry King at his Mutual Broadcasting redoubt outside Washington; Roy Leonard and Milt Rosenberg at WGN in Chicago; Michael Jackson and Owen Spann on ABC Talk Radio. These radiomen are, by temperament, devotees of narrative flow—and thus of good conversation about the art of narrative flow. Many of them have actually troubled to read the text at hand, a gesture that can make a miraculous difference in the structure and nuance of a conversation about a book. Best of all, they have *time*— great gobs of it, parceled out in wonderful gusts of give-and-take, and never you mind about the commercial breaks.

That cassette, which I rescued from potential erasure at the Minneapolis airport? It was a treasure, an heirloom: the recording of a transcendent hour I spent in the generous and passionate aura of Studs Terkel in Chicago, perhaps the most sublime author interviewer in the history of broadcasting. (It is hardly beside the point that Terkel is an author of some legendary stature himself.)

For his interview with me (as for his interview with any author lucky enough to secure a booking on his syndicated show), Terkel approached the microphone with a cigar and a copy of the book, which had been annotated on virtually every page, with several sections marked for reading aloud. What was more, he had foraged in his station's considerable music library (the station is Chicago's fine-arts FM giant, WFMT) for music appropriate to the mood of certain sections, music he then played at the appropriate intervals.

What resulted was a writer's dream: not so much question-and-answer as lovingly improvised variations on a theme; a finished narrative in itself, controlled from first to last by Terkel's instinctive wish to shape the conversation along the curves and rhythms of the book.

For that kind of redeeming moment, I'll wear a thousand hats for a thousand Cyndis. Not her real name.

Broadcast Ooze

Our impassioned critic engages two new biographies of Jessica Savitch, TV news' original Golden Girl. They are not glittering prizes

Why is it that television—unlike the movies, say, or organized crime—has called forth such an arid, such a *desolate* body of literature?

Important books? Sure, there have been plenty. Incisive criticism? Without question. Useful polemics, necessary moral passion? Step this way.

But think about it: Can you recall the last book about TV that actually *lifted your spirits*? That awakened the imagination? Affirmed a sense of possibility? Limned a heroic or even an exemplary life? Looked back with affection? Lampooned with wicked wile and wit?

Can you recall a TV book—and perhaps this is getting close to the nub of it—that merely displayed a love of written English? One that aspired to a style of minimal finesse and sufficient delight to justify the inherent exaltedness of being a book?

All right—there are Michael J. Arlen's works. Arlen is television's Baudelaire. Arlen reached down from Valhalla to touch and transfigure television's tawdry terrain with his ennobling sensibilities and the tonal grace of his sentences.

But Arlen's three "television" books are collections of essays aimed at an anointed readership (of *The New Yorker*), and, at any rate, he has not published *anything* on the topic of television in seven years. Apparently Arlen has accepted his own lament that meaningful television criticism is nearly impossible, given the medium's grounding in the meretricious, the second-rate—and given that this grounding *is deliberate.*

That is not a completely frivolous point. But in Arlen's absence, the vid-lit (sorry) nightscape is lately a blasted heath indeed. False grandeur and sneering irony, giving way to the grudge-nursing tell-all of network exiles, the Former Reagan Aide School of Civic Vision . . . books whose very pages seem sterilized of charm, hope, life, by the proximate parching glare of the cathode tube.

But, wait—that was the *benevolent* phase.
Now they've pried open the grave of Jessica Savitch.

She died young and famous and miserable in 1983, a ghastly pratfall of a death, her companion's rented station wagon flipping off a stone wall into the Delaware Canal in an October rainstorm and burying them both, plus a dog, upside down in the mud. ("Savitch's eyes were still open," notes one of her biographers scrupulously.)

June 1988 brought the release of the first book, *Almost Golden: Jessica Savitch and the Selling of Television News,* by Gwenda Blair (Simon and Schuster). Next month comes the second, *Golden Girl: The Story of Jessica Savitch,* by Alanna Nash (E. P. Dutton).

If the two current studies, to use a neutral word, of her life are remotely reliable, she endured an absolutely hellacious thirty-six years of existence: lacerated with ambition to claw her way to a network-television anchor desk, pathologically numb to the pleasures of the goal achieved; a hard-bitten, hysterical, ruthless, sadomasochistic, cocaine-addicted, twice-married, thrice-aborted, anorectic, lonely basket case of limited intellectual scope, negligible journalistic talents and non-existent copywriting technique who nonetheless looked like a million bucks when the camera was on. (She "projected vulnerability and authority," notes the other biographer insightfully.)

This is not Virginia Woolf we are talking about here. Nor is it convincing to pretend that Jessica Savitch left much of a trace, for good or ill, on the oft-scarred ledger of television news. In a more genteel age—the sacking of Troy somehow comes to mind—the tacitly appropriate literary response to Jessica Savitch's unfortunate life would have been . . . silence.

But, hell, man, these are the 1980s, the Age of Go for It, an era in which the famously dead (Dorothy Stratten, Elvis, the *Titanic*, Capote, Capone) are properly viewed as entrepreneurial resources. And so it is simply a matter of market inevitability—call it a function of supply-side economics—that Jessica Savitch's eternal sleep be disturbed, burst in on; that she be hauled out, propped up (eyes still open, one assumes) and flogged posthumously past the fleeting American gape in two (2!) hardcover incarnations, trailing the shreds of her mortal privacy like tatters from a winding-sheet. The sensibilities of her relatives, lovers, few friends and unsuspecting former fans be damned: No one ever said the best-seller racket was pretty.

Both books trace the broad outlines of Savitch's sad trail: middle-class girlhood in Kennett Square, Pennsylvania; the early loss of her beloved father; the family's retrenchment in Atlantic City; Jessica's teenage fascination with radio broadcasting; her education at Ithaca College; her television debut in Houston; the phenomenal years of stardom at KYW in Philadelphia; the ascension in 1977 to NBC News, Washington; her weekend-anchoring breakthrough; her coronation by *Newsweek* as the "Golden Girl" of TV news; her two disastrous marriages (the first ended after a year in divorce, the second even quicker in the suicide of her husband, Dr. Donald Payne); her emotional deterioration; her after-dinner death alongside the newspaper executive Martin Fischbein.

But broad outlines don't get you chatted up on *Good Morning America;* they don't earn a "Sizzling!" bouquet from Liz Smith. Broad outlines don't get the property optioned (one is already braced for Holly Hunter in a blonde wig). What's required here is a little defilement. A little sordidness. A morbid smorgasbord of the subject's abjectness. It is a requirement that causes neither author the slightest momentary tremor of hesitation.

And yet this grim enterprise is not without its subtle etiquette. The etiquette calls for the property in question—the venture, the *book*—to be invested with a Higher Purpose (higher, in this case, than ghoulish gossip).

Gwenda Blair's Higher Purpose fairly quivers with social-watchdog urgency: Jessica Savitch's pitiful saga is either a cause or an effect (maybe both!) of no less an atrocity than . . . "the Selling of Television News!" (Not *Television News*! Is there no cultural treasure that is safe from their bottomless perfidy?)

Alanna Nash, on the other hand, is after something more, you know, personally meaningful. She's after psychohistory. Her "quest for the answers to the Savitch enigma began as a journey of self-exploration," you see. She was 36 when she started research for her book, she confides to us—*the age Jessica was when she died*! "Was there actually a personality profile of the journalist in general, and the broadcast journalist, in particular? Did Jessica seek fame as a panacea for a host of psychological ills?" Is there to be no atonement in this life for non sequiturs? Never mind. Go for It!

The liner notes to Blair's tome identify her as the writer of a regular column on ethics for *Mademoiselle*. So we pay respectful attention as Ms. Blair begins her narrative with an on-

65

air incident that occurred a few weeks before Ms. Savitch's death: The anchorwoman, in some distress, is flubbing her lines during a live sixty-second transmission of *NBC News Digest*. The moment is freighted with history, like the shooting of Archduke Franz Ferdinand in 1914:

> At two minutes to nine in the evening, and again at two minutes to ten, Jessica Savitch did not simply deliver the news; in the minds of millions of Americans, Savitch *was* the news. And when she broke down, what those millions saw was not the breakdown of an individual woman, but the breakdown of the *news*—or, rather, the collapse of the elaborate, expensive and mostly invisible machinery which maintained it . . . alarm bells rang throughout NBC and, subsequently, in the larger world outside.

Remember where you were when those alarm bells rang out? By this scale of consequence, Dan Rather's six-minute walkabout just four years later should have caused the planet earth to veer dingdonging out of orbit.

But no matter. This passage has a strategic purpose: It sets up Ms. Blair's bona fides. It serves as her search warrant. If Jessica Savitch, don't you see, was this seminal figure in broadcast journalism—a sort of Murrow with a red dress on— then aren't the minutiae of her life, however unfortunately lurid, matters of compelling public interest?

You betcha! *Sizzling* public interest! And thus, ennobled by historic *necessity*, Gwenda Blair joins Alanna Nash in responding selflessly to the duty at hand: dishing it.

So we get the early tantrums ("Savitch started to think her shit didn't stink," a KYW reporter informs Blair), the late tantrums, and we learn (Blair again) that some of the guys at NBC called her "Plastic Cunt." We get pages upon pages of cuts and bruises incurred during Savitch's long and bloody affair with the outlaw-style news director Ron Kershaw—a highly available source for both books, it should be noted. (Nash: "This time, she did not try to provoke him with kicking or punching. . . . Her words were slow and deliberate. 'Do it,' she said softly.")

We get the time Jessica threw up on her tan suede pantsuit before a job interview in Houston. (Nash, consistently the superior reporter, has her vomiting five times.) We chuckle over the time a good-ol'-boy KHOU cameraman introduced her to her first "floater" (a "rotting, maggot-filled corpse," Blair helpfully explains).

We get abortion (the ever-alert Nash counts three, Blair one), we get weed, we get cocaine, we get more tantrums. ("Who do I have to fuck to get out of here?" Blair posits Savitch as possibly screaming during one famous dustup at KYW.) We learn thirdhand from a maid that during her marriage to Donald Payne, "Savitch was having the best sex in her entire life." (Blair neglects somehow to report on her favorite position, but in Nash's book we're allowed to infer that it was on top.) A few lines later we learn of the rumors that Payne was gay. Then we get Payne's suicide by hanging from a dog leash. (Blair: ". . . Payne's tongue was hanging out and bloated, his eyes were popping out of his face, his body had no color, and his hands were swollen." Nash has Savitch trying to free the knots with a broom. "But as she began batting the leash, he twisted around to face her. Both eyes had hemorrhaged.")

In the mood for more? Nash scores with a suicide try. Blair reports on the "lurid" rumors of Savitch's lesbian leanings. We have both biographers to thank for undressing Savitch for us in her last, pathetic years. Blair, via a "friend's" description: "She had this horrible anorectic body and her skin looked terrible, with these sores that wouldn't heal." Nash, through a friend who "had to help her on and off the toilet," draws attention to Savitch's "ulcerated sores," her "skin abscesses," "the kind of pustules a person gets with malnutrition." And it is through Blair that we hear a broadcast colleague analyze the nuances of Savitch's remarkable hold on her viewers: She had "men all over the country creaming in their pants."

By this time the attentive reader might have surmised that Gwenda Blair, in particular, and even comparative to the desolate genre of books about television, writes like a pig; but that conclusion would be only partly true. In the interest of fairness, I must report that there are long—I daresay *preternaturally* long—digressions in *Almost Golden* where Blair writes like a tortoise, of the genus found on the Galapagos Islands; the type that lives for 190 years.

These are the sections in which Blair plods back to her Higher Purpose—the Selling of Television News. Here, Blair is grimly, doctorally flat and dense with sober-sounding detail, pages of it, vertical anvils of typography in which she identifies and then quotes *everyone in the history of television news*—an incandescently boring and interchangeable lineage of wunderkinds and fast-trackers, it turns out, and a group singularly addicted to fecal imagery in their conversation. But does she shape this appalling mass of insider detail into a coherent context for her portrayals of Jessica the Megabitch, or a coherent context for *anything*?

It's hard to say. I remember actually plunging into one of those paragraphs, now and then—"In mid-1975, Joe C. Harris was transferred to Westinghouse headquarters in New York"—and then awakening several hours later with a cottony mouth, the shadows lengthening on my study wall. The political philosopher Hannah Arendt made a famous case for the banality of evil; *Almost Golden* may be establishing something equally brilliant concerning the evil of banality. It's beyond me. If someone held a gun to my head and I had to choose, I'd opt for Gwenda Blair's dirty parts.

Alanna Nash, by merciful contrast, is a more discerning reporter, a more intelligent synthesizer and a less insipid writer than Blair (who isn't?). Still, her prose lacks a voice distinctive enough to heighten, or make universal, the dreadful story she has chosen to tell. To her credit, she has the moral imagination to feel affected by the dark dissolution of Savitch. And yet, *Golden Girl* still fails to justify the laying open of all those wretched privacies, including Savitch's own.

As mentioned, Nash frames her book in the conceit of psychohistory. This means ceding her own authorial intuition at several key instances to the diffuse rhetoric of anonymous psychiatrists. It also means a stylistically damaging overreliance on psychobabble; weary buzzwords such as "threatened" and "vulnerable" turn up with annoying frequency. It also means that her inquiry into Savitch's life, hemmed in as it is by therapeutic cant, will never penetrate into the useful ground that Gwenda Blair, however hollowly, at least promises in her subtitle—a kind of public or cultural-political significance. Her Savitch will remain imprisoned forever in the enfeebled formulas of narcissism, a Dorian Gray anti-image of a golden cover girl.

Perhaps both Blair and Nash would have profited (though surely not financially) from meditating on the words of an NBC correspondent named Bill Schechner, recalling for Blair his reaction to Savitch's *NBC News Digest* fiasco:

"It was something I didn't want to see. I didn't like it. It was something I wasn't *entitled* to see—a devastating private moment, and none of my business."

Exactly so.

Ivan the Telegenic

Bad enough they have the bomb, but now, by God, Soviet media smoothies like Vladimir Pozner have discovered the blow dryer

The thing about television is that sooner or later, everybody figures out how to use it.

But *everybody*. California used-car salesmen in the Fifties. Christian evangelists and Students for a Democratic Society in the Sixties. Billy Carter and half the population of Tehran in the Seventies.

And now, in the Eighties, it's the Russians; the Russians are suddenly just *scrumptious* on the American tube.

You laugh, running dog of reactionism? Pah! When was the last time you looked closely at a Soviet spokesman on a net-work-news interview? Not lately, if your image is of a Khrush-chevian demi-Mongolian glowering inscrutably under thatched eyebrows, his *couture* by Ivan the Terrible, exhorting us with translated maxims about toaster production in Bratsk while keeping cadence with a shoe clutched in one fist.

No more. Today's media Russian tends to resemble, well, Alan Thicke. He is upscale. He is vernacular. He knows from Ted and Lesley. He is not unaware of the proper width of a lapel. He may arrange a "photo opportunity" involving Premier Chernenko or even throw a press conference—as the Soviets did last year, hoping to fine-tune a few global perceptions after one of their fighter planes gunned down that Korean airliner.

And above all, our contemporary media Russian has a keen sense of America's own ambivalence regarding television and its packaging of images—which he is quite glib at exploiting when an opening presents itself.

Consider this exchange last spring between Lesley Stahl, moderator of CBS's *Face the Nation*, and one of her guests, Georgi A. Arbatov, a Soviet Central Committee apparatchik and a familiar face on the swivel-chair-and-earphone circuit. The program aired shortly after the Soviet Union withdrew from the 1984 Summer Olympics.

STAHL: You know, people in this country now believe the Soviets are trying to hurt Ronald Reagan's reelection chances.

ARBATOV: Well, you know, you are very good in show business and public relations, so you can persuade your people in a lot of things, but this is just not true.

Now, accusing the U.S. television-news establishment of "show business" is not exactly a revolutionary tactic. But to hear these phrases—"show business," "public relations"— uttered with such casual knowingness by a descendant of Lenin's Cheka and Stalin's genocidal social engineering . . . well, it lies like an icy finger upon the spine. *They've already got the bomb; my God, have they cracked our subliminal-persuasion vocabulary as well?*

Apparently they have. Arbatov may be one smooth-talking media Russkie, but he is by no means the ultimate weapon in the Soviets' expanding telecommunications arsenal. That particular honor falls to a tasty number named Vladimir Pozner.

You may have caught Pozner on ABC's *Nightline,* where he has appeared, via satellite, from the USSR (he is a commentator for Radio Moscow) with only slightly less frequency than Don Rickles drops in on Johnny Carson. It has gotten to the point of being strictly "Vlad, this" and "Ted, that," ("Vlad, you and I have been talking together on and off over the past four years or so. . . . How do you assess the current relations between the United States and the Soviet Union?" "Ted, I would assess them as being bad, worse than at any time four years ago, and prob'ly being lower than at any time since, uh, the end of World War II.")

It's the *prob'ly* that leaps out of this rejoinder, disorienting the American ear by virtue of its extreme colloquiality. Foreigners—especially Eastern-bloc foreigners—rarely drop those hard consonants. It's like watching Ivan the Bear's lips move but hearing Norman Podhoretz's voice—except that this Pozner is hardly Ivan the Bear.

Long-jawed and neatly barbered at 50 (one suspects there is a blow-dryer concealed somewhere in his Moscow duplex, but one wouldn't want to risk an international incident to find out), Pozner favors crisp business suits of medium grays and beiges—the lapels never stray a quarter inch from current designer fashion—and friendly ties. If Russian tanks should ever rumble through the streets of Anytown, USA, Vladimir Pozner is the *chuzhoi* you'd want pounding at your door. In the land of hammers and sickles, Vlad is Mr. Goodwrench.

Or seems to be. This illusion is the key to Pozner's effectiveness, and therefore to his visibility as a symbol of the Soviet Union's emerging media image: *a bunch of nice guys.* (The Russians have not factored women into the equation yet; it's just as well—they might come up with Phyllis Schlafly.)

In terms of this recent design, Pozner is a gold mine. The American accent—the "prob'ly"—is not learned. It is real. Vladimir Pozner was a bona fide American high-school student in the late Forties—Stuyvesant High School in Manhattan. His destiny took a sharp swerve in 1953, when his father, an immigrant Communist working for MGM in New York, ran afoul of McCarthy-era cold warriors, who invited him either to declare for America or get the hell back to Moscow. The elder Pozner must be one of the few recipients of this classic taunt who took it seriously: He got the hell back to Moscow. Eight years later, young Vladimir joined the Novosti press agency. He transferred to Radio Moscow in 1970.

Today this foremost of media Russians enjoys what may be the most secure job in television—on either side of the iron curtain. American TV journalists, Ted Koppel of *Nightline* in particular, are endlessly entertained by the novelty of hearing rigid Soviet doctrine recited in a Noo Yawk accent. "He gives us no inside information whatsoever," says a *Nightline* producer. "His value to the show is that he gives the American people the Moscow party line, pure and simple."

As for Pozner's employers (he is said to pocket $140 per U.S. appearance from the Soviet government, which apparently has never had to deal with the William Morris Agency), they love him for roughly the same reason. Pozner gives them, ah, credibility in the global telecommunications race.

For several years, American correspondents in Moscow noted an acute and growing fascination with U.S. television on the part of Soviet broadcasters and technicians. This fascination extended to both technology and programming strategy. The Russians were intrigued—who wouldn't be?—by the Americans' mastery of video iconography, by the symbology of information.

But until November 10, 1982, this interest remained academic, out of mortal necessity. Leonid Brezhnev, the original Ivan the Bear, ran Russia the old-fashioned way. Any broadcast functionary reckless enough to retool Moscow's global image along the lines of *Eyewitness News* might find himself swiftly reassigned to the gulag bureau.

After Brezhnev's death, Yuri Andropov loosened those tacit

restraints. As part of his general shakeout of the hidebound Soviet bureaucracy, Andropov permitted the telecommunications apparatchiks their furtive dream: parity of style with their Western colleagues and adversaries.

Pozner himself owes his American celebrityhood to the discerning eye of Anne Garrels, then an ABC Moscow correspondent. It was Garrels who lifted Pozner out of comradely obscurity by requesting his presence as a Soviet spokesman for *Nightline*. But the general flowering of the media Russians—the smoothly ironic news-interview guests, the "photo opportunities," the press conferences—was a force waiting to be released. By all accounts, the present premier, Konstantin Chernenko, has not attempted to reverse the trend.

There is a limit, however, to all this flowering. The limit lies at the point where image meets substance. The new media Russians may have mastered the forms of open, democratic inquiry, but there is little evidence as yet of any criticism, probing of official policies, conjecture or demand for accountability, which would give such forms meaning. (Perhaps the Soviet government's desire to keep it that way is the reason for the sudden, unexplained cancellation of a scheduled U.S. lecture tour by Pozner last spring.) Those American viewers who flip on *The Vlad and Ted Show* and fantasize an emerging Russia of McDonald's and *The Village Voice* are being seduced by images.

For a truer picture, consider what ABC News must go through in order to secure Vlad's homespun presence for an interview. First, the New York office must telex its Moscow bureau with the request—not telephone, *telex*; the Soviets want it all in writing. This must be done twenty-four to forty-eight hours before Vlad's scheduled appearance. The Moscow bureau then relays the request to the agency that regulates Soviet television, which, should it approve, submits it for final approval to Radio Moscow. In the history of modern telecommunications, only Roone Arledge himself has proved harder to track down for an interview.

It is easy to infer from all this a rather pronounced cynicism on the part of Russia's video engineers—and to envision a future straight out of the morbid dreams of conservative Midge Decter, with phalanxes of Americanized automatons marching podlike out of the Soviet laboratories and onto the U.S. airwaves, tranquilizing Jane and Joan and David and Bill and Bryant with their cunningly camouflaged, brain-twisting propaganda.

I prefer an optimistic view. In these days of Olympics pullouts and negotiation walkouts and "evil empire" rhetoric, *The Vlad and Ted Show* is about the *only* dialogue going between East and West. Wouldn't it be eerily wonderful if television talk inexorably replaced what are always called, with studied euphemism, "the talks"? We'd have global peace *and* good grooming. More you cannot ask.

Out, Out, Damned Spot

American television commercials have lately come to share certain features with American sex: Terribly Important, and highly competent as well. But . . . not all that much fun.

I began to reach that conclusion the other night as I sat through a testimonial by George C. Scott for Renault. Unless it was Wolfman Jack for Honda Rebel. Or was it Robert Duvall for MasterCard—a spot that calls forth from Duvall a fist-pumping, tightlipped burst of card-carrying sincerity perhaps unequaled in his work since Lieutenant Colonel Kilgore in *Apocalypse Now.*

Ah. There's the point. Duvall doing Kilgore for MasterCard would be *funny:* Can't you see him in his cavalry Stetson, a tracking camera keeping pace with him as he strides along a "hot" beach, ordnance blazing, choppers swooping, the strains of "Ride of the Valkyries" in the background? Duvall: *"Charlie don't surf!"* [Wheels to camera, holding up the plastic.] "But *you* can surf—or dine in any of the world's luxurious ocean-view hotels—as long as you carry this little sucker. . . ."

But *noooooo*. Such playfulness would be entirely out of keeping with the New Deadpan that has draped itself like funeral bunting over TV spots. No; instead of satire, we're getting unction—with serious hambones such as Scott and Duvall pretending to be *really worked up* over the sponsor's product. (I used to feel that John Houseman was sharing a sly joke with us in his persona for Smith Barney. Lately, I'm not so sure.)

Or else we're getting high-church tech—all those over-wrought computer wipes and overlays from the big conglomerate advertisers. Or else we're getting *Uhmuhrucuh*, from the airlines and Lee Iacocca and the pickup-truck people and practically everybody else. (I love the schizoid nationalism of the Löwenbräu beer spot: "It's brewed in *Uhmuhrucuh* . . . 600 years of Bavarian heritage in one great *Uhmuhrucuhun* beer. . . .")

It's almost—gee, I hate to inject politics into this lovely discussion, but here goes—it's almost as though the current administration were paying off an old debt: The cream of Madison Avenue, the "Tuesday Team," produced those spots that helped Ronald Reagan get re-elected in 1984—so the current round of products-and-services ads is being masterminded by those twins of zaniness, Caspar Weinberger and George Shultz.

How else to explain the curiously refunctionalized syntax of several conspicuous campaigns? "You're gonna like it there" ("there" being the inside of a Kellogg's Raisin Square); "Live it!" ("it" being a today's Chevy); "Where you're going, it's Michelob." The aim of these constructions doesn't seem to be any sort of shared delight in the nuances of language. The aim seems to be the willful obliteration of nuance, and meaning, to pave the way for a new type of modular technolanguage whose references encompass everything and nothing—the

Word made video flash. Within the sealed logic of this willfully artificial system of discourse, *whatever* is argued—or stated, or suggested, or insinuated—is ipso facto true.

(This particular strategy has been a specialty of government bureaucrats for several decades now—right, Mr. Orwell? It's nice to see that the lads are getting a shot at the really big residual bucks.)

Has it really come to this? A bankruptcy of wit so profound that Yvonne De Carlo and Martha Raye hailing denture wearers for Polident are welcomed by trade publications as "glamorous"? An air of fin de siècle about the Lite beer ads, with no campaign showing the remotest signs of replacing them as the ticklers of America's funny bone? Did Burger King really think that "Herb" was going to be a memorable honk? Are nerdy "Herb" and his many soul brothers—see the fat suburban schlemiel for Wagner paint—going to stand forever as the symbols of comic American male consumerhood? (Not necessarily: These wimps are being crowded by an equally clunky, equally artificial-seeming symbol, the Hick Who Talks Like He's Worked Hard Memorizing His Lines. See—better yet, *don't* see—the campaign for Bartles & Jaymes wine coolers.)

All in all, it's been a pretty flat showing lately for an industry that by all rights should be entering a Creative Golden Age. Never before have so many tools, and so much license, been available to advertising professionals. The advent of computer-generated images has made the video screen a canvas of infinite possibility. The era of stereo TV sound is at hand, suggesting a powerful new range of aural options.

As for freedom of expression, times have never been better.

They still nail you for outright documentable deception, of course. Sometimes. Cigarette commercials are forbidden by an act of Congress, and the networks remain squeamish about "advocacy" ads, as well as pitches for hard liquor and contraceptives.

But when it comes to designing pitches for products that *can* be sold, creative teams are battering down taboo after taboo: racial stereotyping, sexual explicitness, direct attacks on competing products, appeals to patriotism and even to God. Most of these frontiers were unreachable even in the freewheeling 1970s. The Perry Ellis "f--- you" ad has breached the barriers of print; its mutation for television is surely but a matter of time.

The Sell is rampant on a crest of tinsel.

So how come nobody's smiling? How come it's suddenly the *job* of advertising and not the *joy* of it?

Talk to different people in the business, you get different answers. To Barbara Lippert, a pungent (but refined) young content-analyst of TV ads, it's a matter of breeding, pure and simple. Look at the cultural conditioning of the current generation of copywriters: *television!* How can you expect these people to write like S. J. Perelman when they were weaned on *The Scooby-Doo/Dynomutt Hour*? "Beautiful visuals have replaced humor," Lippert declares.

Then there is the Theory of Creeping Corporatism, also known as the National Football League Analogy. To wit: As agencies grow larger through mega-mergers and more imperial in their overall psychologies, they lose the instinct for childlike playfulness that has often been the life-force of memorable campaigns. (Can you imagine a global agency, all beset with the cosmic concerns of nuclear winter and its effect on decongestant sales, tolerating the slightest risibility over the amplified crunching of a potato chip?)

Tom McElligott is a creative director who would not disagree with these interpretations. In fact, he expresses them more brutally than most. To the proposition that young copywriters lack a broad cultural resource base, McElligott hisses, "An accurate perception. They show an absence of conceptual imagination and intelligence. Advertising, at this point in time, is being written largely by people with no writing skills." As

79

for the perception that the industry is suffering from an inflated notion of its own bigness, McElligott amplifies, "We're seeing a wave of condescension from people who have no right to be condescending about anything."

That's tough talk—especially when you consider that Tom McElligott is not a member of the hard-boiled New York advertising world; his modest-size agency, Fallon McElligott, has headquarters in Minneapolis, that notorious hotbed of civility. With annual billings of $85 million (the midsize New York–based Della Femina Travisano & Partners, by way of handy contrast, bills $250 million), Fallon McElligott and its brain trust would hardly seem to have the credentials to critique the competition.

Yet this is an agency on the rise. Its accounts (half of them are regional, half national) include *The Wall Street Journal*, Bloomingdale's, Prince spaghetti sauces and—for a time—Mr. Coffee. And last May, Fallon McElligott captured more honors than anyone else—twenty-six—in the prestigious One Show Awards at the Waldorf-Astoria.

"These are demoralizing times in the industry for the creative people," McElligott insists. "What you're seeing are the results of a syndrome I call 'malicious obedience.' The clients are bullying the people at the agencies, and the creative types are striking back by giving the clients *exactly what they want*— with not an ounce of extra spark or imagination. So in an era that ought to be bursting with new ideas, you're seeing commercials that are truly horrible—they're depressing to look at. And the big reason they're depressing is that they're *derivative*. The industry is cannibalizing whatever has worked over the last twenty years."

And what brought on this dark age of client-bullying, malicious obedience and derivation? McElligott's answer is both familiar and plausible to anyone who has followed the enervation of imaginative spark in the media as a whole—in television news, in TV writing in general and in the growing cartoonishness of the daily newspaper—and, widening the scope a bit, in politics, education and several other spheres of American ideas.

McElligott's answer is that the market researchers have arrived.

"Actually, they arrived in the 1970s," McElligott maintains. "The Seventies were a terrible time for the industry. That was when market-testing took over the business. When that happened, you said good-bye to the artistic side."

The most influential of the testers is Burke Marketing Services, Inc., of Cincinnati. "A very, very, very smart company," McElligott concedes. "Their biggest client, not surprisingly, is Procter & Gamble—headquartered in the same city.

"What the Burke people do is test the brand-name retention of a product. Over the last ten years or so, the Burke score has become like some kind of mystical revelation. There are copywriters who build their careers on their ability to get a high Burke score.

"And how do you get a high Burke?" he continues. "You do commercials that go with the averages—dull, derivative but dependable commercials. At least they're dependable for products with the massive market saturation of Procter & Gamble. I wouldn't advise a small company with a small client to try it—there's not enough leverage in the market for the product to catch on that way. But everybody *is* trying it."

McElligott speaks from experience. One of the commercial campaigns that first drew attention to his company two years ago became a model for a host of derivative ads, even though it was for a regional client.

"Minnesota Federal Savings and Loan retained us to do some ads," McElligott recalls. "Our aim was to point up the way most banks promise the customer everything—toasters, golf clubs—but end up delivering nothing. So we showed this whole group of bankers in their three-piece suits dancing a guy out of the bank. The music was 'Hit the Road, Jack.'

"Well, it was funny. It won some awards. Now you see all these car commercials—Sable, Ford, Chevy, Volks—all these spots using pop music from the past. Not an ounce of imagination! Terribly derivative!"

McElligott doesn't believe the entire landscape is devoid of wit and cleverness, of course. He offers high marks to two New York agencies: Ally & Gargano, creator of the fast-talking Federal Express campaign, and Ammirati & Puris, which has done charming work on behalf of BMW, United Parcel Service and Waterford.

"On the whole, though," he insists, "with the wave of mergers and acquisitions going on, you're going to see mostly caution and spots that are strong on 'accountability.' This whole thing of everybody hopping on the word 'America' as a sort of halo is a good example."

Too bad. There was a time when aficionados of television could turn to one another and say, with satisfying world-weariness, "You know, the best thing about the medium is the commercials. *That's* where all the real creativity goes."

Now we don't even have that satisfaction.

BILL COSBY MEETS THE
MAYFLOWER MADAM

*And other imaginative new series that prove
television makes strange bedfellows*

Behavioral scientists and audience-measurement experts are
still groping for answers to the enigmatic discovery that burst
like a bombshell over the Hollywood television-production
community in December: the revelation (confirmed by several
independent studies and surveys) that the American viewing
public *didn't like all of the new shows that were introduced in the
fall.*

"It just hit us right between the eyes," admitted one stunned
network vice-president. "Nothing like this has ever happened
before in the history of prime-time television. I guess you'd
have to say it's part of the times we live in. The summit break-
downs, the whole disinformation thing. The consumer thing.
People are searching for new alternatives, new values. I think
I'll kill myself."

Another executive, who refused even to be quoted directly for fear of reprisals, confided that some networks might be forced to cancel some of the shows that premiered in the fall. Fortunately, this executive informed *GQ*, a contingency plan for just such an emergency has been on-line for several years at some of the top production studios, a plan known informally among television programmers as . . . *Mid-season Replacements!*

Life With Nancy—America's favorite petite cutup, Nancy Davis, returns to prime time to star as Nancy Cuomo, whose new hubby, Mario, is gearing up for a run at (of all things) the presidency of the United States—over Nancy's dead body! (What Mario doesn't know is that "Nancy" is really none other than Nancy Gipper, wife of the incumbent!)

In the premiere story line, "Nancy" turns up at one of Mario's big fund-raisers disguised as a Sandinista guerrilla in red A-line fatigues, and goes tumbling off the end of the speaker's platform in an effort to cause a ruckus. Featured is Barbara Bush as the next-estate neighbor, whose recurring line—"Oh, Nancy, you'll *never* fool Mario in *that* getup!"—is sure to become an instant national buzz phrase.

Guest stars: Frank Sinatra, the Beach Boys, Former Hostage Nick Daniloff.

Consonant!—Streetwise thesaurus-squad vice-cop J. T. Blfstvchyx (Kenny Rogers, in his first continuing-series dramatic role) bends the rules and sometimes takes the parts of speech into his own hands in order to root out the grammatical scum contributing to the decline of literacy in a large (unnamed) American urban center. Blfstvchyx's methods frequently put him at odds with his long-suffering superior, Captain Vern Nacular (Edwin Newman), who sympathizes with Blfstvchyx's frustration but warns him to keep a civil tongue or face conjugation.

A "twist" in this series is that Blfstvchyx, outwardly ruthless and alienated, secretly nurses a sense of inadequacy over the lack of a *k* in his last name, a lack that sets him apart from all other tough TV cops except Spenser and possibly Tubbs. In the premiere episode, Blfstvchyx talks a deranged umlaut down from a hot-wired ampersand, arrives on the scene just in time to thwart a double negative and sneers at the memory of former major leaguer Robert Ellwood Uhle.

Guest stars: secretary of Education William Bennett (as himself), the New Christy Minstrels, the letter *J*.

Make Room for Sydney—"Name me the two *primo* concepts in America right now," challenges hot senior producer Sam Langhorne del Rey (*Geriatric Sluts*), and then, before you can answer, fields his own query: "Bill Cosby and the Mayflower Madam!"

Mix the two together and you have the recipe for Del Rey's slightly offbeat but market-proven "warmedy" about a minority (Wasp) head of a typical middle-class call-girl ring (Sydney Biddle Barrows, in her comic-dramatic television debut) who presides over her charges with gentle humor, common sense and Harvard Business School managerial techniques.

In the series premiere, Sydney consoles Denver Jade (Nancy McKeon), who is convinced that credit-card Port-a-Prints have taken the romance out of prostitution; Anita Mann (Xaviera Hollander) gets a lesson in the benefits of oral hygiene; and the gang receives a surprise visit—from the cops!

The john: Augusto Pinochet.

World Court—In this syndicated weekday series, actual sitting Supreme Court Justice Sandra Day O'Connor presides over an international tribunal, and familiar stars of daytime dramas and music videos portray the various nations of the world in these based-on-fact dramatizations of actual geopolitical power disputes.

Look for Cyndi Lauper as Nicaragua going toe-to-toe with Hulk Hogan (America) in a slam-dance "cross-examination" over the mining of Managua harbor. Twist: Nations of the world *actually have to abide by* Ms. O'Connor's verdicts. Floor correspondent: Former Hostage Nick Daniloff.

K-Smarts—Being a suburban parent isn't easy—especially

when you have four children, each of whom seems to represent a different ethnic group! Just ask Kay Ann Johnson (Martina Navratilova). Her husband, Biff (Charles Nelson Reilly), is a rising young Navy test pilot. So the job of feeding straight lines to the three girls (Whoopi Goldberg) and one boy (Linda Hunt) falls mostly to long-suffering Kay.

Fortunately there is Wilford Brimley (Wilford Brimley), who wandered onto the set one day from the cast of *Our House* and never seemed to notice the difference. Wilford's familiar plaintive query—"Which one of you whippersnappers put Creamy-Yums on my poker cards?"—becomes an endearing family joke until Kay tires of it one day and beats his brains out with a graphite racquet. In between all the shopping, Kay's ongoing battle with her upper-body muscle-fat ratio and the kids' repeated (albeit high-spirited!) failures at random urine tests, there's still time for buckets of love—until an alien life-form resembling Edwin Meese crashes through the roof and demands to be taken at once to Christie Hefner.

Sample dialogue: ALF: "I demand to be taken at once to see this Hefner!" Kay: *"You?"* ALF: "No! Christie!"

Playboy's Video Magazine Presents the Girls of the United States Supreme Court—"Combining a keen sociopolitical consciousness with tasteful erotica," as the press release puts it, Playboy CEO Christie Hefner hopes that this innovative three-hour special will prove to be the de facto pilot for a weekly series of topical looks at naked women holding down interesting positions (no pun intended!) in world-leadership roles. Future formats might include *The Girls of the British Prime Ministership, The Girls of the Philippine People's Democracy* and *The Girls of the Ownership of the Los Angeles Rams.*

Mike Buckner, Medical Ethics—Got a thorny dilemma involving a comatose patient, a life-support system and a will naming a blonde divorcée in a diaphanous gown as sole heiress? Don't pull the plug—pull the phone off the wall and dial B-U-C-K-N-E-R. (You can find his "Med-Eth" listing in the classified ads, right below "Lonely Hearts.")

That'll put you next to a guy who's knocked heads with a categorical imperative or three, a neo-Hegelian breed of urban theorizer who handles only those cases that elude the sentimental pieties of the bourgeois moralists. Buckner (Elliott Gould) is one tough Manichaean—he packs a *k* in both his first and last names—who has been known to stop rogue hospital administrators in their tracks with a tersely barked "Act only on that maxim through which you can at the same time will that it should become a universal law!" But he's sensitive enough to seduce a beautiful woman Gnostic (Shelley Hack) with the observation "Life has a value only when it has something valuable as its object."

In the premiere, Buckner is summoned from his dwelling place, the hold of an eighteenth-century umiak, to help a distraught plastic surgeon inform her patient that she has accidentally given him the hocked lips of a destitute Andrew Marc model.

MTV Vice Versa—Finally, a series that probes beneath the surface of the music-video genre to extract a gritty postmodernist idiom: hot, *noir*, seething with urban menace and completely lacking in earth tones.

Mikey and Petey (the child actors Peter Michaels and Mike Peterson) are a brace of angst-ridden VJs continually going "undercover" in order to nail operatives of the vidrock underworld who try to smuggle drug-related lyrics onto the playlist. Accompanied by a thumping sound track consisting of current gunfire from TV detective shows, and wearing the latest designer fashions from OshKosh, Mikey and Petey do battle in a Brechtian vision of Burbank with an assorted array of celebrity guest supervillains.

In the premiere, the duo is forced to turn its video-editing console upon a porn-rock queen (Tipper Gore) who is intent on coercing the United States Congress into replacing the present national anthem with a new side by Twisted Sister (Van Halen).

America Did It—The Public Broadcasting System has already

begun to feel the stings of its critics, even though this thirteen-part series documenting the retroactive culpability of the United States in most of history's great calamities will not begin its run until Washington's Birthday.

Distinguished Marxist scholar and critic Iva Grudge recounts, with impressively annotated evidence, the process by which American imperialism, fueled by the engines of capitalism and Einstein's theory of relativity, actually *reached back in time* to influence such pivotal epochs as the Sacking of Troy, the Fall of the Ottoman Empire, the Defeat of the Spanish Armada and the premature death of Wolfgang Amadeus Mozart.

As a concession to "the full spectrum of ideas," however, PBS executive producer Phel O. Traveler has agreed to broadcast a panel discussion after each of the thirteen episodes, the panel consisting of Former Hostage Nick Daniloff, Christie Hefner, Supreme Court Justice Sandra Day O'Connor and the entire cast of *Time and Again*.

"With this dynamic new lineup of bold concepts and a creative mix of solidly established formats and ground-breaking new—uh—concepts," said the studio executive, finally finding his voice, "we can position ourselves dynamically for the—ah—the coming. . . ." His voice trailed off and for a moment he looked deeply confused.

II

Players

If Charles Dickens or Mark Twain were alive today (I console myself constantly), they would probably be writing about television. (A sudden dark thought intrudes: If Dickens or Twain were alive today, God knows they would probably be *on* television—Twain as the last act on an HBO Comedy Showcase; Dickens selling the *Encyclopaedia Britannica* or hosting some endless PBS series. . . . I'm really sorry I even brought this up.)

The point is, the universe of television is, if nothing else, rich with characters. Not necessarily the sorts of characters you would want to seat at Thanksgiving dinner at your Episcopalian uncle's country house outside Charleston, South Carolina, but . . . characters. *Players,* as we learned to say in the

Wall Street–soaked lexicon of the Eighties. In this section, you will meet some of them.

If Robert Pittman was the definitive Eighties "Industry" figure, Morton Downey Jr.—Pittman's most sulfurous humanoid creation—was the definitive TV personality. Downey's brief syndicated reign as a crass and vicious talk-show host originating at station WWOR in Secaucus, New Jersey, marked a sordid new epoch in public-affairs programming: the cynical and irresponsible stimulation of adolescent aggression (through Downey's studio audience, "The Beast," as I called it) as a competitive ratings device. MTV had invaded the Town Meeting.

The concluding thought of my profile of Downey ("It Came From New Jersey") suggested that Downey's scabrousness amounted to a glimpse of television in the twenty-first century. Several months after that, Downey himself appeared to negate that prediction by self-destructing: His show was canceled in a miasma of bad ratings and the host's own increasingly eccentric public behavior—his dubious claim, for instance, that he had been assaulted in a San Francisco airport.

But Downeyism survived Downey. The street-gang hooting of his studio audience, The Beast, embedded itself in American pop-cultural style. (Runners at the back of the pack in the New York City Marathon took up The Beast's "Hoo! Hoo! Hoo! Hoo!" chant as they passed through echoing tunnels along the route.) Downey's middle-aged-punk persona began to replicate itself in any number of similar formats around the spectrum—most ludicrously in the jacked-up hostility of the elephantine John McLaughlin, on McLaughlin's new attack-interview show on the Consumer News and Business Channel (CNBC). This was ironic, given many people's suspicion that Downey had tailored his own persona after McLaughlin's legendary tirades on PBS's *McLaughlin & Co.* It was doubly ironic when, in December 1989, Downey himself fetched up on CNBC as cohost of a program called *Showdown.* The format included a studio audience.

Among the other characters visited in this section:

In "Real (Sick) People," Van Gordon Sauter, the executive who presided over the horrific mid-1980s plunge of CBS News from its historic pre-eminence into bathetic dissolution, is observed as he begins a new career: as West Coast impresario of a syndicated program in which real people receive real diagnoses for real illnesses, in front of a real TV camera. The show later died of a not-so-rare disease—mediocrity—and Sauter was last glimpsed as the panelist on some syndicated show or other about the movies, or something.

"The Voyeur" is an encounter with that shameless apostle of Reagan-era lubriciousness, Robin Leach, the host of *Lifestyles of the Rich and Famous*. Leach has since gone on to parody his persona, if that is possible, as a ubiquitous commercial pitchman. "The Most Dangerous Man in Television Is . . ." (an arguable title, in retrospect) brings us into the office suite of Al Masini, the man who did for Leach what Bob Pittman did for Downey: created him, through creating his venue. Masini is the mastermind of *Lifestyles*, not to mention *Entertainment Tonight*, *Solid Gold* and other expressions of the Yuppie gestalt. His newest project, scheduled for satellite-delivered syndication in the fall of 1990, will push trendiness to the ultimate: It will cover news that hasn't happened yet. *Preview, the Best of the New* will be a daily half-hour look at forthcoming events in movies, television, music, scientific and technological breakthroughs and something called "living," to be reported by the inescapable Mr. Leach. If the millennium is to bring about the end of the world, and if God has a P-R department, chances are you'll hear about it first on Al Masini's *Preview*.

Moving from the future to the past, "Joe 'The Living Legend' Franklin" is a favorite of mine—a profile of the often-caricatured late-night host and patron saint of the sort of people William Saroyan called "magnificent nobodies." Like the Lady in the Pillbox Hat, Franklin is happily suspended in

93

a prior era. How interesting—and how characteristic of this medium's indifferent glare—that the station that tolerates his late-night innocence (WWOR in Secaucus) was also the perpetrator of Downey's befouling design.

George Will is no longer doing regular commentary for ABC's *World News Tonight*. (He can be seen and, more to the point, heard, every Sunday on *This Week With David Brinkley*.) Bill Moyers is no longer even *with* CBS News; he has long since returned to PBS, where his interviews, essays and series continue to be the glory of nonfiction television. ("A ship deserting the sinking rats," was the way some wag put it.) Nevertheless, I've decided to retain "Where There's a Will, There's a Moyers"—if for no other reason than to acknowledge two thoughtful men who have lent television in the Eighties the dignity of their authentic visions.

"The Apprenticeship of Shelley Long and Kitty Felde" and "Norman Mark Gets the Last Nyah-Hah-Hah-Hah-Hah" are visits with people who in certain ways help form the spine of American broadcasting. Kitty Felde and Norman Mark are talented, dedicated journeymen—good enough, in a just universe, to make it to the top, but denied ultimate stardom through any number of wrong turns and idiot circumstances. The fact that they hang in, struggling and perfecting their craft, invests the medium with what little radiance it can claim.

It Came From New Jersey

The beast is loose, and it's helping make Morton Downey Jr. *the most horrifying show of the Eighties*

The elevator doors slide open on the studio floor of the television center. Morton Downey Jr.'s piscine eyes bulge left, then right.

"Oh, shit," Downey mutters. "The audience is here." He says it with the unconvincing moue of a Washington hostess murmuring, "Oh, shit. The secretary of defense has just arrived."

Downey bounds from the elevator, skipping on the balls of his feet, which are snuggled in Italian tasseled loafers. It is more than an hour before tonight's taping of *The Morton Downey Jr. Show* on Superstation WWOR-TV in Secaucus, New Jersey. But already the audience has come in from the boroughs and the industrial darkness. Already it has coalesced into the shape and the mood of a sentient animal, an elongated beast lying patiently outside the studio door.

Downey sprints alongside the flank of the beast, high-fiving its several hundred hands. Lots of black leather. Football jerseys. Chains. And the guys look tough, too. The beast stirs: It recognizes its master. Its many eyes are already filmed over with a kind of erotic lust for the theater of abuse to follow. It commences a tremendous guttural bark: *"Mort! Mort! Mort! Mort!"*

Many Americans are not yet aware, my friends—as Downey would doubtless put it—*not yet aware* that there is any such thing as a *Morton Downey Jr. Show.* LIKE HELL THERE ISN'T! And I'll tellya—wait, lemme finish, you'll get your turn, little guy—I'll tellya something else! A lot of those *bubbleheads* and *squeaky-faced wimps* who have seen it since it went on the air last October—they're saying, "HEY! DOWNEY'S NOTHING MORE THAN A *THROWBACK!* Like Joe Pyne in the Sixties! Fist-in-the-mouth television. Right?" WELL LEMME TELLYA! *THEY CAN KISS MY BUTT!* BECAUSE THAT'S *BULLCRAP!*

No. Downey is exactly what his publicity claims him to be: the talk-show host who will take the genre into the twenty-first century. A frighteningly accurate assertion.

The secret ingredient is Downey's audience. Not the pasty-faced matrons of Donahue and Oprah but . . . kids. Working class, Trans-Am owners, pro-football fans. They come to *rock and roll.* They've seen the show. They know what's expected of them: to cheer when Downey screams "SHUT UP, FLESH-FACE!" at a guest who starts to disrupt his tirade with a coherent debating point. To whoop and dance when Downey literally wraps himself in an American flag and offers a Tehran-born student the opportunity to kiss his ass. To bellow frothing invective as Downey lavishes such hateful ad hominem sarcasm on a panel of porno actresses or robed Ku Klux

Klanspeople that he inadvertently confers a kind of dignity on their helplessness.

It is the audience-as-attack-dog that transforms Downey's cretinous vulgarities into a sort of performance art—a sulfurous music video without the music. *Exactly.* How could it be otherwise? The producer of the *Downey Show* (along with MCA, the new corporate owner of WWOR) is Quantum Media, Inc. The president of Quantum is Robert Pittman, the man who invented MTV.

Downey dashes into the makeup room, where he peels down to his boxer shorts and socks, indifferent to the presence of the WWOR anchorwoman in the hairstylist's chair. "*Very* strong, *very* strong demos [demographics] with the kids," he is saying to his own reflection in the mirror. He slides on a pair of brown slacks, notches the Gucci belt. He wears lots of gold. "This is the first young people's talk show. These kids keep getting told in school, in their jobs: Keep your lips buttoned; don't get out of line; don't talk back. Well, my friend— they come to *this* show, and here's someone who's *doing* it . . . and *getting away with it* . . . and *letting them do it*!

His face, at 55, looks like two profiles stitched together, but badly—the watery blue eyes aligned too far to the outside, the chins overlapping to form a point like the bottom of a valentine heart. The hair, brushed up and back Bobby Darin-style, is jet-black. But what really dominates Morton Downey's features is the teeth. Rows and rows of them, pure and blinding porcelain, welded into his mouth like piano keys. It is these teeth, which flash horribly when he speaks (*the canines!*), that signal an affinity between Downey and the audience-beast.

He was a radio man for five years. This is his first television show. The dossier on his peculiar career is by now fairly well known to his cult fans: son of the late beloved Irish tenor Morton Downey Sr. and the actress Barbara Bennett. Former rock-and-roll singer and songwriter (he coproduced the Sixties classic

"Wipeout"). Adventurer and hero (he claims to have smuggled starving Ibo tribesmen out of Nigeria during the Biafran war). Former vice-president of the Canteen Corp. A cofounder of the American Basketball Association. Presidential candidate in 1980 for the American Independent Party.

As of this night in early November, *Downey* is available five nights a week to about ten million American households, 11 percent of the viewing public. That could change soon; syndication plans are a possibility. Meanwhile, the low profile might be working to the program's advantage. Its producers are still booking guests who are innocent of what they're getting into.

Tonight's guests, for example: Two distinguished academics will debate each other (*or so they think*!) on whether a national policy should be established for withdrawing health care for old and hopelessly sick people. Or, as Downey will frame it at the top of the show, "I wonder whether we're still CIVILIZED tonight, my friends! I wonder whether the GOVERNMENT . . . has the RIGHT . . . to END A PERSON'S LIFE!"

Half an hour before showtime, the beast is released into the studio.

It is impossible to sense the full adrenaline frenzy of a *Downey* audience by watching it on TV. Only inside the studio can one feel the hunger for action—the hysteria—like a kind of barometric pressure on one's skin.

They file in, looking around, cracking gum, fiddling with their neck chains, and fill up the bleachers, where they sit gaping down at the lighted but empty set. And what a deceptively bland-looking little instrument of terror that set is: a dais of chrome and fiberboard. A chair for Downey, chairs for the guests. But Mort's chair is adjusted several inches higher than the others. The guests' chairs whip back and forth, but—subtle designer touch—Downey's chair swivels, the guests' chairs don't. (The production staff has bolted them solid.) Meanwhile, the main camera on Downey is positioned low, near ground level, to emphasize his domineering presence over his guests. It's amazing how docile people become on that set.

Downey is killing time by pacing around the runway behind the bleachers, beneath a bevy of butts. I decide this is as good a time as any to ask him where the rage comes from.

The answer seems surprisingly disarming. "I was disciplined hard as a kid," he says. "Military school at 11. Jesuits."

But—but wasn't he the son of the beloved Irish tenor Morton Downey Sr., the darling of radio's Golden Age?

"My father," says Downey, and shows a few dozen teeth. "I only saw him every three weeks, when he came in off the road. We lived on Park Avenue and in Connecticut. My parents were divorced. I never saw my mom from age 7 till age 21. My grandmother would watch us while Dad was gone. She'd make a list of all the things we'd done, all the misbehaving. Dad would read that list. Then he'd take us up to his room, where he kept this elephant tusk carved into a long shoehorn sort of thing—Paul Whiteman had given it to him. He'd take that shoehorn and he'd beat us with it."

Showtime.

The theme music—a kick-ass hard-rock riff—lashes out at top decibel. A floor director whips the beast into an orgiastic tumult of whistles and applause.

"MORT! MORT! MORT! MORT!"

Downey makes his patented entrance. Tracked by a long-range camera, he comes hustling down the same runway where he'd been killing time. Now he's flanked by two assistants. He seems to be studying some blue note cards. Just as he reaches the rim of the set, he flips a card to each assistant, then breaks into a full sprint for the dais. This is a bit of performance kitsch that Downey cooked up—"It makes me look like I'm getting information right up to the last second," he told me. In the context of what usually follows, it makes him look more like a gang leader getting an escort by his body-guards to the killing field.

The show's first segment is deceptively calm. The guest is a man named Sydney Rosoff, chairman of the Society for the Right to Die. Rosoff says that everyone should have the right to terminate his or her life-support system if recovery seems hopeless.

The beast isn't sure how to feel about this. It gives off some ruffs and woofs, waiting for the attack cue from its master. Downey, a lighted cigarette between his fingers, has slid off his chair and now towers over Rosoff. The beast growls in its throat. Rosoff shrinks in a bit, a suddenly naked and alone man.

"How about *this*," Downey snarls. "I see this as a *progression*, to the *government* having this right."

WOOF! WOOF! grumps the beast.

But the segment ends with no ripped flesh. Rosoff climbs out of his chair, a dopey grin on his face. He's a man who has looked into the *jaws*—and survived! Back after this.

Now Dr. Daniel Callahan is in the chair. He is chairman of the Institute of Social Ethics and Life Sciences and wrote *Setting the Limits: Medical Goals in an Aging Society*. The book argues for an age limit on technological life-support systems. Grrrrrr, WOOF! But Downey is the picture of suave solicitation.

"If we set the age limit up here [hand at eye level] today," he asks reasonably, "who's to say tomorrow it isn't set here . . . and lower . . . and lower?"

Downey offers Callahan two minutes to state his case without interruption. "I don't want to be a bully"—the porcelain teeth flash like knives; the beast stirs—"*do I look like a bully to you, Doctor?*" Downey turns, teeth still bared in a grin, to the audience. "*My gang is not a gang of bullies, either.*"

Knowing chuckles from the awakening crowd.

Callahan, an earnest, curly-haired man in glasses, launches

into his case: Americans enjoy a wealth of high-technology life-extension care . . . it costs a lot of money . . . thirty years from now, 50 percent of the federal budget will go toward health care for the elderly . . . we have to rethink . . . there will have to be an age cutoff eventually . . . the late seventies or early eighties. . . .

And then Callahan carelessly bares a slice of throat. "I'm really very impressed by the British system," he says. "They provide no access to dialysis or expensive heart surgery, but their overall health care is terrific."

Downey is upon him before his last syllable dies away. "Their system says if you're 55 and need dialysis, you can't get it." "Right," says Callahan, "but I wouldn't—" "Well, the British did, and you just said you *ad-miiiiiiiirrrred* their system!"

Olé! The bedlam from the bleacher seats is deafening. The beast senses attack; its forest of arms shoots into the air. Over the din Morton Downey suddenly screams into Callahan's face, "FIFTY-FIVE YEARS OLD . . . LEMME TELLYA, PAL, I'LL BE 55 in THREE WEEKS AND *NOBODY'S GONNA CROAK ME!*" Whoops, howls fill the air.

"I said the late seventies—" begins Callahan.

"THIS IS THE SAME CRAPPOLA—ALL THE POPULATION EXPERTS STATE 80 YEARS, SO YOU START THERE! THEN THE NEXT JERK WHO INTERPRETS THE LAW SAYS 70! THEN YOU GET SOME *OTHER BUBBLEHEAD* IN THERE, AND *HE* SAYS 60! AWRIGHT, HOW CAN YOU BE SURE IT'LL STAY AT 80? *HOW DO YOU KNOW?*"

"We don't—"

Downey thrusts his lighted cigarette toward the camera. "UNCLE GEORGE, YOU WATCHING TONIGHT? YOU WERE 93 YEARS OLD LAST WEEK; WHADDAYA SAY TO THIS GUY, HE WANTS YOU CROAKED RIGHT NOW BECAUSE IT'S *COSTING TOO MUCH MONEY TO KEEP YOU ALIVE!*"

Screams! Taunts! A waterfall of mockery from the seats!

"Excuse me, I *didn't* say I want him croaked—"

From the beast: "YOU'RE A ROACH! GO TO RUSSIA!"
Station break. Don't go 'way. We'll be right back.

Now Dr. Richard L. Rubenstein has joined Callahan on the set. Rubenstein is president of the Washington Institute for Values in Public Policy. Under normal circumstances, he would be an opponent of Callahan's; he disagrees that age should be a criterion for terminating health care. But in this arena, this pit, such nuances seem laughable, the fine distinctions of life on another planet. The two men draw together, wary and grim.

Rubenstein has a go at the pretense of debate: Yes, limits must be set. But targeting age groups runs the risk of the "bureaucratic possibility" that such groups would be considered "surplus." In a time of national crisis, such groups might be eliminated.

Downey isn't listening. Rubenstein doesn't exist. Downey has targeted his own victim for the evening. Turning back to Callahan, he asks him offhandedly, "Your mom and dad alive, or are they dead now?"

There is a long, tense moment before Callahan replies evenly, "They're both dead."

"Would you have cut off medical care to let them die?"

WOOF! CHUFF! CHORTLE!

Callahan draws a breath. Then he says, "I should make one thing clear: We need decades of discussion and dialogue on this—"

"You're safe, Uncle George, you're safe. . . . He's not gonna killya tonight. . . . Nazi Germany started the same way. They wanted to take some time to build it up, didn't they?"

"I reject the analogy!" Callahan, twisting in his fixed seat, has finally risen to the bait. *"I won't call you the Dr. Goebbels of the media, and you don't accuse me of Nazism!"*

The beast is quivering with violent glee—"GO! GO! GO! GO!"—but Downey prowls calmly. "You can call me the Dr. Goebbels of the media; that's quite all right . . . *and I will, whether you do or not, refer to you as the Nazi in medicine."*

Amid the thunderous riot of joyful bays and war whoops comes a sound so singular, so anguished and pure, that it remains in the consciousness long after all the other sounds of this grotesque hour have congealed. It is the cry of a surprised and wounded man: "OH, NO-O!" The beast hears it and bellows louder.

But now Rubenstein is on his feet. *A guest has left the low, unswiveling chair!* The beast loves it: "GO! GO! GO! GO!"

Rubenstein stands there, this white-haired man in a gray suit, stands there until even the beast seems a little abashed. And then, pointing at Callahan, he says, "I have spent thirty years studying Nazism! I wrote three books! I know this man! I disagree with this man! But you *cannot call him anything like that*! *It is absolutely unfair!*"

Downey has backed up to the rim of his audience. He shrugs. "The doctor is entitled to his opinion, I'm entitled to mine—"

"When it comes to a man who has worked as hard as he has—"

Now the camera is on Morton Downey's face, and it is suddenly transformed into a convulsion of tics and winks. The eyes bulge, the porcelain teeth are bared.

"*ADOLF HITLER WORKED HARD TOO! ARE YOU SO DUMB? YOU WROTE A BOOK ABOUT AUSCHWITZ!*" Bedlam. Theme music. Break.

Back near the runway, one of the young rock-and-roll boys of Morton Downey's production staff is gazing at Rubenstein's image on a monitor screen. There is something like lovelight in the kid's eyes; his face is a mask of beatific awe.

"It's great television," he croons, to himself as much as anyone. "You can see the sweat on the top of his head. . . ."

On the morning of the day I drove over to Secaucus to watch the taping of *The Morton Downey Jr. Show*, a magazine had come in the mail. It was a commemorative issue of *The Quill*, a professional journalist's monthly, and in it were reprinted some articles written decades ago.

One of them in particular had caught my attention. It was from the late 1940s, the very dawn of television—about the time of Morton Downey Sr.'s great national fame.

The article was full of the stentorian phrases of the time— "the vast and unlimited potential of this new medium," and so forth. But what really fascinated me was the accompanying photograph. It showed a pioneer television cameraman— shooting 16-mm film—perched on top of a station wagon in the Chicago Loop. Below him on the bright sidewalk, a group of passersby had paused to glance upward—men with wide ties, women in pillbox hats. Their faces told it all: those smiles of arrested curiosity, the delight and inclusive pride just starting to spread, that are the special and irretrievable qualities of faces from that era.

I did not see any such faces leaving the WWOR studios that night in Secaucus. I saw satiation; I saw the afterglow of adrenaline rush. I saw faces that were already forgetting what the excitement had been about.

I saw the face of television in the twenty-first century.

REAL (SICK) PEOPLE

*In his quest to go Hollywood, former news whiz Van
Gordon Sauter discovers that patients are a virtue*

Van Gordon Sauter remembers the exact moment it hit him:
There were dollars to be made in diseases! A fortune in phle-
bitis, riches in rickets, megabucks in mastoiditis—Gold in Them
Thar Ills.

"It was June 1987," says Sauter, speaking of a time not yet
a year after he himself had been surgically removed, like a
rejected organ, from the presidency of CBS News. "I was giving a speech to the American Medical Association's annual
broadcast meeting at Rancho Mirage, California. You know
how it gets after you give so many of those things. I was just
standing up there, flapping my arms like some robot at Dis-
neyland—when suddenly I realized that *I was looking at a whole
roomful of Judge Wapners!*"

Leaping lymph nodes! Judge Wapner . . . *People's Court* . . .

AMA doctors . . . *People's Pancreatectomy*, right? Before you could hum two verses of "(It Ain't Hard to Get Along With) Somebody Else's Troubles," Sauter had mentally memo'd himself a high-concept premise: a strip-syndicated early-fringe vehicle in which viewers would be allowed to gape and listen, *for the first time on TV*, inside the examination rooms, the labs and the offices of actual, working, *good-looking* physicians as they dished out heaps of bad news to their patients.

Give it to me straight, Doc—how long is your option?

And thus was conceived *Group One Medical*, a Sauter-Piller-Percelay production in association with MGM/UA Telecommunications, Inc., offered five days a week in upwards of eighty-five American cities.

It's an inspirational story in itself, really—worthy of a treatment for a TV movie: Sauter, flamboyant and controversial network news mogul, former wunderkind; career in ashes following series of disastrous management decisions at CBS News; suddenly reborn at the relatively advanced age of 53 as a Hollywood-entertainment impresario.

Van Gordon Sauter, the Grand Mal Moses of reality programming.

Ah, yes. Reality programming. That heaven-sent antidote to the writers' strike and its aftermath, not to mention the long-delayed answered prayer of the unknown network president, who shrieked in the sweet long ago, *"There's not even enough mediocrity to go around!"*

He was talking about *scripted* mediocrity, of course, and he was right. And that was even before cable, before superstations, before Siskel and Ebert. But those days are over. With the recent advent of reality programming—controlled real-life situations in which the misfortunes of actual people are presented as edifying entertainment—there is now plenty of mediocrity to go around. More than plenty, if you count reality programming's inevitable and almost instantaneous offshoot: scripted-, or simulated-, reality programming.

Give it to me straight, Doc—are you a doc?

Did I say "recent"? Can *People's Court* be eight years old already? Can it have been 1980—the outset of that Rancho Mirage of a decade—that a retired judge named Joseph Wapner began hearing small-claims-settlement cases in a studio-courtroom toward the greater glory of American jurisprudence and Ralph Edwards/Stu Billett Productions?

Yes, it can. And the purveyors of reality programming have learned quite a lot since that big bang, that spontaneous combustion of a genre. They have learned, for instance, how to cover their asses.

Back in 1980 the concept of "entertainment" hadn't quite attained the all-embracing holiness that it enjoys today. Close, mind you, but not quite all-embracing. The *People's Court* people, for instance, never thought to promote their new concept as a kind of pop-cult-equivalent experience for Harvard Law School; they offered it up as standard honest voyeurism. And took a terrific drubbing from certain critics, who were shocked at this arrant mongrelizing of entertainment and the august sanctity of the courts.

But, boy, Your Honor, did the show mop up on the bottom line. *Big* ratings in the late afternoon, but, just as important, *People's Court* ran on an almost-invisible budget. Reality proved not only popular but cheap. Real plaintiffs didn't drag down soap-opera salaries. Not even Judge Wapner himself required the care and feeding of, say, a Redd Foxx.

Give it to me straight, Judge—how much do you make?

And so within a very few years, the early-evening pre–local news hours were filled with this sort of stuff. Ordinary people, caught on the barbed wire of life's little torments, thrashing to get loose for the titillation of the folks at home. And always under the legitimizing gaze of a robed authority figure.

Superior Court. Divorce Court. The Judge. Americans couldn't get enough of watching old men whack their gavels. And every one of these offshoots shared an interesting quality: They were scripted. Even as Edwards/Billett was selling reality as entertainment, its imitators had turned it around; they were selling entertainment as reality.

Or quasi-reality, anyway. Although the simulation disclaimer was pretty fine-print stuff in the credits, the make-believe-judge shows were not falsely presented. Still, they needed a rationale, some high-sounding claim of Redeeming Social Value, to justify the fake-documentary look.

And so the marketing concept took hold that these entertainments were *good for you*! And what's more, it didn't even hurt: That even as you salivated over the slit-skirted slut on the witness stand and wondered whether she'd get nailed for sleeping with her husband's sister's tax accountant, you were learning some valuable case law, real insider stuff that would come in handy if your own slut—oh, never mind.

That was the evolving strategy of reality programming out of Hollywood in the early Eighties—the high-water-mark era of the docudrama, the predawn of Morning Again in America, you may recall. That was the genesis of the form that has lately decayed into such morbid freak shows as *America's Most Wanted*, the noxious Fox Television series that dramatically re-creates violent crimes—actorish bodies twitching and jumping as bullet after simulated bullet sinks wetly into them—and then flashes the likeness of the real-life at-large perpetrator. *America's Most Wanted* has led to a couple of dozen capital-case arrests and has contributed to the cultural acceptance of gunplay as spectator sport. It's a measure of this country, and these anesthetized times, that the series has been praised as a public service.

But meanwhile, back in the early Eighties, by one of those fascinating coincidences, a similar "reality" strategy was starting to manifest itself on the other side of the country—in the network news citadels of New York City. Its mastermind was one Van Gordon Sauter, the president of CBS News, who had come to believe that, hell, *reality* needed some reality programming.

Sauter began to tear apart the philosophical foundations of CBS News—information selected on the basis of public interest and presented concisely, without dramatization. In the ruins of these foundations, Sauter erected his philosophy of "moments"—trends and political currents as refracted in the glimpsed lives of ordinary people (farmers, laid-off factory workers) who were "experiencing" these currents.

It was in those moments, and not at the moment of Sauter's speech to the AMA, that *Group One Medical* began to be born.

"It was easy for me, when Van talked about *People's Court* as a prototype entity, easy for me to get a sense of his interest in creating a reality medical show. I said I'd be quite pleased in working with him. I was invited to be part of the creative process."

That's Ron Pion talking. *Doctor* Ron, ob-gyn, a 57-year-old state-of-the-art California medico-media smoothy who attended that Rancho Mirage confab, did lunch with Van and Van's people at Scandia afterward and, après Scandia, rang up some pertinent MGM/UA people on his car phone to say he was coming in with a concept.

Dr. Ron, a former NBC News medical correspondent, became *Group One Medical*'s technical consultant. ("Initially, there was some thought of my being on-camera.") Dr. Ron was put in charge of coming up with talent—doctor talent and patient talent. Since nearly everyone in Southern California is an actual or an aspiring talent anyway, this did not prove to be the problem it might seem.

"I started by looking through a California AMA picture book of active members," Dr. Ron says. "Then the MGM people and I started to highlight those people who *had a look*. Then—"

What *kind* of look? I rudely interrupt, fascinated. Reality always fascinates me.

"The look kept changing," says Dr. Ron. "Some people on the creative team wanted a man, some wanted a woman; some voted young, some old; some voted a look of confidence, some a look of caring. . . ."

The creative team finally voted on three doctors: one with a look of Tom Selleck, one with a look of Jessica Walter and one with a look of Lou Gossett Jr. The three would more or less play themselves on-camera, listening to patients describe their complaints, providing diagnoses and just plain *relating* with them in a caring but confident sort of way. At the end of each program the three doctors would huddle for a few "moments" and do a little cross talk about the day's horror sto—excuse me, the day's cases, just like those "real correspondents" on CBS News' *West 57th*.

And the patient talent? A slightly larger order, but no problem, really, for Dr. Ron.

"I wrote a 'Dear Editor' letter to *Los Angeles County Medical Association Physician* magazine," says Pion, "asking colleagues to loan us their patients. I wanted our doctors to be able to borrow these patients in a continuing-care arrangement. It's similar to what we doctors call teaching rounds, or case presentations, in which permission is obtained for the patient to be presented to a body of professionals for the purpose of teaching."

Ah! Teaching! Glad Dr. Ron brought that up! *Teaching*, of course, is the hortatory cornerstone of *Group One Medical*—its mission, its raison d'être type of thing. What! You thought this was some kind of *entertainment show*? Just listen to Dr. Ron.

"Look up the word 'entertain' in your dictionary," he prescribes. "You'll find it says 'to hold in the mind.' [I did. The doc had given it to me straight.] The ultimate purpose of this show is that, truly, someone may be assisted. I believe the American public is desirous of having more health information. My own bias has been that it would be nice if patients with similar conditions tuned in."

Now, *that* would take one hell of a lot of "Dear *TV Guide*" letters from Dr. Ron, but who's to say? Meanwhile, let's get down to cases—the sorts of cases *Group One Medical* will be depicting for the theoretical edification of its viewers.

"First of all, it's all real-time conversation," Dr. Ron assures me. "Edited down, of course. But no rehearsals, no retakes except for technical problems."

But the patients' reactions to bad news, I press. Isn't it a little exploitive for a camera to be on someone—even if he's volunteered and is getting a token fee—at the moment of a life-shattering discovery?

"No. On our program, *nobody ever learns anything before the camera*," the doctor says. "That's too exploitive. No way in the world will the patient-physician confidentiality be broken. It will always be *last week* that they've learned that they have cancer, learned they have AIDS. What you will see is the patients as they *continue to experience* the diagnosis."

I have no reason to doubt Dr. Ron's word, and yet his choices of examples are interesting. On the promotional "vignette" tape that MGM/UA has released to stations and potential sponsors, there is one exceedingly memorable tight-focus vignette—a "moment," if you will—of a middle-aged man raising his expressive dark eyebrows and mouthing with incredulity, "*Cancer?*"

Another "moment" on the tape shows the Selleck-type doctor saying to a patient, "First of all, let me ask you your sexual preference." The patient responds that he is gay. It's not clear to me how either of these moments can be fit retroactively into the "continuing to experience" rubric. (The gay patient learns to his evident surprise just moments later that his previous visits to other doctors may not have resulted in adequate tests for the HIV virus.) But I'm willing to believe that some explanation exists.

What I am considerably less willing to believe is that *Group One Medical*, or its soon-to-be-burgeoning imitators (something called *Family Medical Center*, a scripted medical show taped by documentary-style hand-held cameras, was set for fall syndication by Lorimar Television), will deepen any lay viewer's comprehension of medical theory beyond a few useful palliatives.

In fact, I am deeply convinced that *Group One Medical*, like most other self-justifying programs of its genre, is running counter to the old Hippocratic admonition to "first do no harm."

The harm done by reality programming is doubtless unintentional, but it is harm just the same: the harm of falsely suggesting to the culture that there are no distinctions between entertainment and education—or entertainment and specialized knowledge, or entertainment and heightened citizenship (or, in the case of the fading televangelists, between entertainment and sacredness). The magnitude of this passive lie can be grasped if one imagines prelaw or premedical students actually studying for their professions by hunkering down, notepads in hand, before fringe-time broadcasts of *People's Court* or *Group One Medical*.

It is monstrous—and pitiful—to imagine what calamities await an individual, or a culture, who believes himself to be "experiencing" the process of education through entertainment television. As social critic Neil Postman, among others, has argued, nearly everything that defines entertainment is inimical to education, and vice versa.

This video-generated myth of learning by entertainment, or learning stripped of rigor and discipline and incentive, is worse than banal. It is insidious and is helping to make respectable a growing national contempt for literacy and learning. The result? A widening gulf between unspecialized consumeroid Americans and a new, paternalistic managerial and technocratic elite. As suggested, the consequences of this rift—a passive, depoliticized, credulous body politic—are unlovely to imagine.

Give it to us, straight, Doc—how long have we got?

THE VOYEUR

On his Lifestyles of the Rich and Famous, *that Brit, Robin Leach, has plucked open America's soul and read the price tags*

"*Naow we'll jungle-hawp to a Brazilian island and tolk to a plawstic suhgeon whom the rich have moide foymous. . . .*" If Robin Leach should ever come by your house (hey, it could happen; Robin Leach gets around, and you've made a bit of a name for yourself, haven't you?), don't let him inside your bathroom.

"*Hit's nao awccident that his clinic is in raomawntic Rio day Janeiro. . . .*"

He will pluck open your medicine cabinet—he does this routinely, reflexively, he admits without guilt—and eyeball the price on your innermost plastic bottle of Johnson's No More Tears baby shampoo. . . .

"*Dr. Ivan Pitanguy aowns this mawnsion that's just a samba-beat away from his clinic—and hit's a mawnsion that is filled with his wuld-renowned awt collayction. . . ."*

And Robin Leach may come to a terrible judgment. He may conclude that your house (while perhaps perfectly acceptable, mate, don't get a bloke wrong) is not of sufficiently—what?—pharaonic scale to merit a full-fledged, helicopter-and-zoom-lens visit from the crew of his syndicated TV show, *Lifestyles of the Rich and Famous* (a title so sumptuously vulgar, by the way, that to experience its maximum resonance with the libido, one should tongue its syllables only in Leach's own oleaginous cockney rolls: *"Loif-stoyles of the Reech and Foymous"*).

You may protest. Okay, so you're not rich. But you're famous. Or soon will be, a little. That one-act of yours had small but tony notices. Your cameo spot in *The Natural* is attracting some interest at Fox. You can *explain* about the goddamn Johnson's. . . .

Forget it. Here's what you're up against: *"The success Clint Aistwood has won from his blokebustah films allows him to lead the loifstoyle he pleases. . . . When money is no object, celebrities can hoide from the maddening* [sic] *crowds in rawmbling mawnsions behind groves of soipress trees. . . ."* You got a cypress tree, Mac?

Well. It is easy—tempting, in fact—to continue in this vein, having a bit of *Saturday Night Live*-ish sport with Robin Leach and his accent and his unctuous keyhole-peeper's fascination with swells and loot and conspicuous consumption, and with that rat-a-tat-tat patois in which he expresses it on the air each week, for one full hour, in nearly two hundred American television markets.

Tempting but idle. Worse than idle. Robin Leach is dangerous to ignore. Like an alert European visitor of another time, name of de Tocqueville, Leach has plucked open America's soul and read the price tags. He has isolated an appetite beneath the appetite. He is rat-a-tatting a message that the faltering genre of U.S. television known as "infotainment" might do well to decode. (As indeed a part of it has: Both Para-

114

mount, Leach's old employer at *Entertainment Tonight*, and Columbia hustled out pilot imitations of *Lifestyles*. At least three other competitors are on the drawing boards. Local TV newscasts pay their imitative homage. And Leach claims, with a characteristic shrug of amiable indifference, that Barbara Walters has revised her act on ABC since *Lifestyles* became a weekly series last March.)

Leach's message to his competitors in video-voyeur journalism is this: You're gunking it all up, mates. Losing your own focus. A certain yeasty preciousness is creeping into a programming form that should thrust forward on the ballast of its own perfect insignificance.

"They're losing focus," Leach says. "I mean, *Entertainment Tonight* doing a piece on the anniversary of the Tylenol murders. Well, that's journalism, isn't it? That isn't what *ET*'s about. I don't even think most of these shows handle celebrity interviews right. I have a sign above my desk at work that says, NO MORE 'I WANT TO STRETCH.' That's the phrase every starlet on *Three's Company* uses when she means she wants to expand her career, do Shakespeare. 'I want to stretch.' Look, the guys that make beer or put doors on cars every four seconds—they don't relate to 'I want to stretch.' What are they gonna do—put *bumpers* on tomorrow?"

Leach does not consider *Lifestyles* to be a competitor (or a comeuppance) to *ET*, although he walked away from the latter show, in an uncharacteristic burst of bitterness, after a series of confrontations with its executive producer, George Merlis—who left some months later, after a series of disagreements with Paramount executives.

Leach's departure from *ET* gave him the opportunity to devote his full attention to *Lifestyles*, which he created in collaboration with Al Masini, the president of TeleRep Inc. and a founding genius of *Entertainment Tonight*. *Lifestyles* was conceived as an occasional syndicated special. The first such special (spotlighting the lifestyles of Kenny Rogers, Liberace, Loretta Lynn, Christopher Reeve, Donald Sutherland, Roger

Moore, Linda Evans, and Michael Caine) aired in August 1983 in 175 markets; it averaged an 11.9 rating—an impressive number in late summer with relatively little promotion. (Then again, its title is its own promotion.) A second special, in January, averaged—says Leach—six ratings points ahead of all projections, even though most local stations used the show as cannon fodder against its heaviest competition of the week. After that showing, *Lifestyles* made its debut as a syndicated, satellite-delivered series in March.

Leach absorbed a good deal of programming strategy from his time at *ET* and earlier at Cable News Network's *People Tonight*—his video apprenticeship after almost twenty years in America as a freelance tabloid gossip columnist. Despite its illusion of opulence, *Lifestyles* is a relatively cheap show to produce—about $300,000 per hour. Leach maintains a permanent staff of only forty-three people, including five producers. He collects much of his raw material during a couple of manic European tours a year, during which he might conduct twenty-two separate interviews in eleven days. Back home, his production staff stitches together as many as four separate programs in one editing session. Clearly, this is a no-nonsense, cost-effective process. (Leach must have time for only a *peek* into those medicine cabinets.)

But this practicality reveals a good deal more of the essential Robin Leach than his insouciant video image. Leach, you must understand, is a *bloke*—a fellow who gets along by identifying with auto workers, not autocrats. His father back in Harrow (a district right outside London) was a sales manager for the Hoover vacuum cleaner people. The son was writing for village newspapers at age 11 and for the Fleet Street newspapers at 17. At age 21, in 1963, he put aside his job as show biz reporter at the *Daily Mail* and shipped over to America to have a look 'round. He caught on to American newspaper ways, developed a knack for getting celebrities to talk to him and built a comfortable career as a freelance gossip for several British, Australian and American papers, most notably Rupert Murdoch's *Star*.

Leach is a good deal shrewder and less ingratiating than he sometimes appears onscreen. He views the frequently vilified Murdoch with a detached professional admiration: what matters is that Murdoch *made it*. This value-free appreciation of success is a key to Leach's instinctive rapport with American TV watchers. In its heart of hearts, *Lifestyles of the Rich and Famous* is as distinct from *ET* or *PM Magazine* as those programs are distinct from *60 Minutes*.

The most striking effect of *Lifestyles*, at least upon first viewing, is its intense compression. Within the standard hour format—a *lot* of airtime for this sort of thing—not a word, not a second of visual imagery, is extraneous to the formula. The writing, for its genre, is brilliant, the best on television—an unrelenting, pared-down staccato of wised-up sentences burnished hard with the vernacular of vicarious greed.

"A winding staircase holds 3000 bottles of vintage wine—stocked for his customers, 14,000 of the wuld's wealthiest!" (Leach's associate writers are fellow Brits Jeff Samuels and Malcolm Boynes, both tabloid veterans who can dish it out with the best.)

Leach insists on a similar tightness for the videotape images that illustrate the ten—*ten*—separate *Lifestyle* profiles shoehorned into each hour. It is in the editing of the video that Leach's subtle but ironclad formulas reveal themselves.

Leach himself almost never appears on camera. Who cares about seeing Leach? (This, he believes, is his legacy to Barbara Walters; her recent specials feature much less Barbara and much more subject.) And there are very few "talking head" shots of anyone on *Lifestyles*. The star's (or starlet's) voice may be heard answering interview questions—"I think [*pause*] you have to play hard to release the pressure," Heather Thomas may confide—but you won't see Heather's lips forming that immortal thought. What you'll see is a shot of Heather playing hard; in this instance in a hot-air balloon. ("This is a very spiritual sport,

I think. We're floating. We're not forcing ourselves through the winds, we're *floating*.")

Which somehow brings to mind an even subtler and more subversive dictum of Leach's: *minimal celebrities*. Robin Leach—it can now be revealed—is as weary of "starbabble" as the rest of us. His principal departure from other infotainment programs involves his determination to do something about it. This may sound like a direct contradiction of his show's self-proclaimed subject matter. Only partly true. It is no accident that *rich* precedes *famous* in the show's title.

"I don't find stars fascinating at all," Leach says. "I have to do a few on each show so I can put their names in the listings; otherwise nobody would find us. But I don't think the public identifies with stars as much as everybody in this business thinks—at least not the stars' work, their roles, their careers. Ordinary people can't relate to that.

"I like the captains of industry. The big achievers. I loved the plastic surgeon piece, it was the best profile on that show. My theory is this: People relate to the big winners of life. Power. That's what they fantasize about. Power and what it can bring you. People want to open those famous doors and get inside and see what's in the drawers, what kind of sheets are on the bed. It's not fan journalism I do, it's silk-pajama journalism."

Just how deep does Robin Leach's regard for "the big achievers" extend? (One recalls a segment in which the *Lifestyles* camera dwelt lovingly on a $10,000 .38-caliber "extra-special handgun.") Are there any "captains" whom he would *not* profile? What about a captain of the underworld, a cocaine baron?

Robin Leach did not even have to think about it. "The audience would love it," he replied. "Of course I would do it." He paused, staring off—no doubt into some ineffable, ultimate medicine cabinet.

"Theah's *naobody* I wouldn't do," Robin Leach says.

". . . *So he makes the maost of his toime hawping to his island, where he's met by a chauffeur-driven jeep*. . . ."

The Most Dangerous Man
in Television Is . . .

. . . Al Masini, who finally landed a job after 250 job interviews. Since then he's done nothing less than change the very way we watch the tube

On January 16, 1985, a 50-ish man in a tab-waisted suit, a balding man with an alarming set of teeth, a man named Al Masini, stood up and gave a speech before a group of television producers, directors and writers in Los Angeles. Masini's first words were "Thank you for inviting me today. I'm really honored to be here." That sufficed for the loosening-up portion of Masini's speech, the way-with-words demonstration, the part where the speaker shows what a droll sort of fellow the audience is about to enjoy.

What followed during the next forty minutes or so was an astonishing performance, a rare, virtuoso excursion along the Cartesian coordinates that define the innermost secrets of television strategy.

Masini gave them the fundamentals. He talked building

119

blocks; he talked revenue pie and station reps and straight barter and scarcity of available time. He laid a little M–F 3–6 P.M. kid strip on them; he divided the OPT pie; he talked the new 12/12/12 rule; and he laid down a general rule for success (syndicated specials distributed on a cash basis must be sold in at least one hundred markets, if you have to know). Masini gave them some overestimated delivery and make-goods; he went double-exposure and common-window on them and showed them the NATPE blitz. Hell, he even gave them his formula to get a program on the air. (Select some type of program missing from the TV spectrum. There. Now *you* do it.)

When Masini was finished, there probably wasn't a dry résumé in the house. (I wasn't present. I saw the transcript. I won't say I wept, but there was a lump.) Those producers and directors and writers must have thought they'd seen the second coming of Faye Dunaway in *Network*. Masini had taken them methodically as a metronome into the double helix, the headwaters of the Nile, all the first-cause principles of television's blind, dumb, deus-ex-machina logic.

And make no mistake: It is *logic*, not dreamlike "creative process," that sets the terms for television's programming choices. Why, then, do most shows and most new concepts fail? Because the logic is so difficult. Labyrinthine. It yields only to an infinitely patient, methodical, almost hyperdialectical mind. A mind like Al Masini's.

Just who *is* this Al Masini? In order to conjure him in his full backlighted glory, it is necessary to first conjure Mary Hart and the formidable leviathan that is *Entertainment Tonight*; Robin Leach and *Lifestyles of the Rich and Famous*; the top-pop recording series *Solid Gold*; Ed McMahon and the talent-scouting *Star Search*; and Operation Prime Time, the landmark series of prime-time specials offered by an ad-hoc collective of independent and affiliate stations.

Solid Gold, in its sixth season, has been the number-one-rated first-run syndicated series in reaching women in the 18–49 age-group, the prime target of commercial programming. *Entertainment Tonight*, in its fifth season, is a close runner-up. *Lifestyles* increased its stations' ratings in that time period by an average of 40 percent in its first year. *Star Search* added 40 percent more viewers after its first season. OPT is one of the great conceptual breakthroughs for independent (non-network) stations in television history.

Al Masini invented them all. Which is to say that not only did he conceive the thematic premises for these wildly, improbably successful new formats (*"Select some type of program missing from the TV spectrum"*), but, more eerily still, in nearly every case he brought them to the airwaves by pouncing upon some buried marketing strategy, some device left unused or unexploited or even unsuspected by all the other blood-scenting dorsal-fin types who swim in Masini's sea.

In April, Masini masterminded yet another syndicated series, *The Start of Something Big*. It bore the earmarks of previous Masini successes (we will exempt certain offerings of OPT from the following rap sheet): an unabashed, almost voyeuristic obsession with celebrities in the uppermost reaches of the "Q" rankings (BOB HOPE! JOAN COLLINS! RAQUEL WELCH! JULIO IGLESIAS! LUCILLE BALL!); an editing and pacing style reminiscent of a frenzied refugee from the Universal back-lot tour; and a "concept" that is high-definition to the point of imbecility ("It reveals the secrets of how famous celebrities and some important things around us started," gushes the promotional copy). And finally, in Masini's own modest appraisal, his latest creation is ultrapromotable and exploitably newsworthy—just like its predecessors.

The above descriptions are not intended as unkind. They merely seek to describe what manifestly *is*. I can hardly be churlish; I spent several gratifying, Walter Mittyish months as *Entertainment Tonight*'s media critic, and damn it, I enjoyed the fast track, thank you, Al. Hey. Barbara Howar dragged me to dinner at Elaine's once. (Of course, she dragged the entire New York bureau of *ET* as well, and I seem to have disgraced the entire table by loudly insisting, in a late, moist epiphany, that we all pledge on the spot to use our talents always for good, never for evil—but that's another yarn.)

The point of all this, I guess, is that Al Masini is a living corrective to one of the television industry's most inane myths: the myth of the videobabies as TV's essential visionaries. Those shiny-eyed, hermetic, beatific kids who *grew up with the medium*, see, and know how to program 'cause they've, like, internalized the tube's whole nonlinear semiotics. Silverman in his mid-Seventies glory. Brandon Tartikoff, Silverman's protégé and now the head of programming at NBC. Bob Pittman, the ascetic guru of MTV.

Smart cookies, every one. But insiders. Kids with resources, clout, an established apparatus. Middle-aged Masini has none of this. He's a rep, an agency man. Whatever schemes he devises must be methodically constructed step by step, using other (cautious) people's cameras and transmitters. Al Masini is a businessman. Al Masini sits down and reads the organization charts, the rate cards, the executive biographies—even the damned engineering manuals. He may be the most dangerous man in television today. And he isn't even precisely *in* television.

"I'm very analytical—I'm thorough, I'm plodding, and I try harder," Masini allows from behind his desk in the Manhattan office of TeleRep, the company that serves as a base for his eclectic operations. The modesty of that self-appraisal was undercut slightly by the *fact* of his desk—a thrusting, phallic wedge of mahogany with a wingspan of fifteen feet, a power desk if ever there was one. Telephone messages coat the surface like pink litter. Masini smiles, showing those perfect, alarming teeth, pleased at the chance to consider his gift for consideration.

"I actually *memorized* that engineering book," he says. "That was back in 1953, when I was a kid working at Station KFBB in Great Falls. I was so naive I thought they'd ask me questions from it. I was working nights for free."

He eventually wound up in the film-editing department at CBS—after writing 800 letters of application and enduring 250 job interviews. (Not that Masini knew anything about editing film; he read every book on the subject that he could find the night after securing the job.) He used this humble vantage point to study the organization structure at CBS. "I wanted to find the job with the most visibility," he says. He found it in a sector that only a Masini could love: the drab, unglamorous clearance department, where functionaries acted as liaisons between the advertising agencies and such shows as *Ed Sullivan* and *Playhouse 90*. "It was where you got to meet everybody." Masini shrugs, impatient at having to explain the obvious.

The actual call for the job interview caught him by surprise. "I telephoned my mother and said, 'You must bring down a new suit for me,' " he recalls. "We set up a relay team of my friends between our house and CBS. I actually changed suits in the corridor." Thorough. He got the job, learned sales—"It was apparent to me that *everyone* who got to the top got there through sales"—and soon afterward left the network to join a station-representative firm, where for the next twelve years he acted as an agent, selling the stations' local commercial time to national advertisers.

Again, Masini was shrewdly trading visible status and prestige for real power. He learned how local television stations operated. He became the unofficial sales manager for each of his client stations. That expertise led him logically into programming; he became an ex-officio programmer for those same stations. By 1968 he was ready to organize his own agency, which he called TeleRep. He started with billings of $9 million from three stations. Today, TeleRep bills $685 million from forty-five stations, making it the third largest agency of its kind, with seventeen offices around the country. Along the way, Masini invented strip programming (the practice of running syndicated series five nights a week) and spot pricing (allowing sponsors relief from being billed according to the ratings, in certain instances). Masini's education was coming along nicely.

His next step was to invent a mechanism that united independent stations and network affiliates in a collective programming thrust. At that time, the independents were clearly second-class citizens, and their prime-time menu of *Gilligan's Island* and *F Troop* reruns was not making a dent in the network ratings. Masini spotted an opportunity and outlined it in a 1976 speech to the Independent Television Convention in Los Angeles.

"I told them, 'Even if you have to share your product, you have a joint need to pool your resources.' Nobody picked up on it at first. Obviously, they couldn't mount a regular series; there was no money to experiment with. What they needed was an *event*—highly exploitable. It had to have *stars*. Preferably, it should be based on a book."

What resulted was Operation Prime Time, a station cooperative venture that by now has yielded nearly one hundred hours of national programming, including the Emmy Award–winning *A Woman Called Golda*, as well as *Sadat* and *Smiley's People*. From the first, OPT offerings equaled and frequently surpassed their network competition in the ratings. Suddenly Al Masini was more than a success model for independent-station people. Suddenly, he was a god.

But Masini's greatest triumphs lay ahead. With *Solid Gold*, in 1980, he realized a delicious satisfaction: the establishment of a successful weekly prime-time series independent of the networks' hegemony.

"I try to fill a void," he explains with his usual oblique simplicity. "I felt the timing was right for a hit-parade type of show. And the best way to get a rating is to appeal to the family."

A *nightly* series—*Entertainment Tonight*—was next.

"You must have an idea," says Masini, "of the void you are filling not only for the audience but also for the station. I noted that there was virtually nothing except game shows for local stations in the prime-time access period of seven-thirty [Eastern time]. I conceived of *ET* by deduction. I knew we couldn't create whole scripts for a show five nights a week. It had to be a sort of news show. I knew that movie and *People*-type magazines were big business. Fine; I factored this in.

"My biggest problem then was timeliness. How to distribute a news show off-network so that it's fresh each night? Well, earth stations. Satellites. Then I had to build in a plan for *financing* the earth stations. I formed joint ventures. I gave pieces of the show away—but what I got in return was *clearance*. And finally, I proposed that the local stations could have an hour-long recap of the week's *ET* segments. This served two purposes: It amortized our production costs, and it gave the stations some extra minutes of local commercial time."

Out of this compilation of abstract, deductive and purely *business* decisions came the show (produced by Paramount) that, along with MTV, was the definitive TV breakthrough of the 1980s.

Entertainment Tonight may never win a Peabody Award, but like so many of Masini's brainstorms, it works with the audience—and not *quite* for the reasons that seem most blatant. In this case, it is not just the parade of celebrities that has kept *ET* hot for so many seasons.

"*Pace*," says Masini. "*ET* works because of its pace."

And how does Masini ensure that the pace retains its unwavering pitch of intensity week after week, even though he remains across the continent from Paramount's production studios?

"I build in formulas," says Masini, "so that the pace is controlled not by the director but by me. There are eight distinct elements I insist on. . . ." He pauses. We are getting into classified territory.

"I am very cognizant of all the angles," says Al Masini, smiling and showing those alarming incisors.

Joe "the Living Legend" Franklin Is a Very Lovely Guy. We've Got Proof!

The venerable talk-show host loved the Forties so much he decided he'd stay there

"I am going to answer the telephone," Joe Franklin's voice is saying on the other end of the telephone line—to someone else in his office; Joe Franklin hasn't yet quite got his mouth to the receiver. Joe Franklin takes all his own calls.

And then, upon hearing my request:

"You are hitting me at a *crest*, my friend. I am on a *roll*. This is the *right time* for me to do a slick interview. I will give you stuff that will get on page *one*, that will get on page *four*, all over the world. I got my *doctor* here, spraying my throat. I will see you at eleven-thirty Friday. I love your vitality."

My *vitality*? It has been a long time since anyone has complimented me on my vitality. And Joe Franklin has never even met me. Already I am liking Joe Franklin's vitality. So at several minutes before 11:30 A.M. on Friday, I am killing time in the rain below his office—perhaps his suite of offices—at 42nd Street and Broadway, in Manhattan's famed Times Square district.

Joe Franklin. Mister Memory Lane. The longest-running television-talk-show host in history—thirty-six years—he entered the *Guinness Book of World Records* with broadcast No. 21,050 on WOR in New York on June 1, 1985. Joe Franklin. A man whose guests over the years have included the likes of Woody Allen, Barbra Streisand and (in his *Death Valley Days*) Ronald Reagan. The likes of "Weird Al" Yankovic, they have included. And Jerry Vale and Margaret Whiting and Lou Jacobi. A man who has earned the plaudits of the critics ("A kind of weird reverse charisma," enthuses Wayne Robins of *Newsday*) and even his own publicity ("Joe Franklin, I salute you, your fans salute you, and the world of TV and radio salutes you," wound up an emotional Joe Franklin press release of a few years ago). A man who has had the distinction of being parodied by Mister Billy Crystal, ladies and gentlemen! A Living Legend!

No chrome-and-glass aerie for this legend. No Scandinavian, no Donald Trump. Brick. Honest brick, and cornices. The address scribbled on my scrap of paper corresponds to the number above a small lobby entrance cheek by jowl with S&L Tuxedos (second floor) and Times Square AC (boxing). Across 42nd Street is the famed Les Gals 25¢ Live Revue XXX Movies, plus a second-story window bearing the identification "NEW YORK SCHOOL OF LOCKSMITHING."

I take the automatic push-button elevator to the fourth floor and step into a lost era. Bare tile floors. Hardwood molding. Office doors with frosted-glass windows. *Good evening, ladies and gentlemen of the radio audience. Coast to coast, border to border.* A cardboard arrow taped to one wall announces: "CHINESE ACUPUNCTURE RM 408." Wrong era. My man is in 417.

I stride past the open doorway, glimpsing what I think must

be the maintenance man's cubbyhole, before I realize that this . . . *is* . . . *it*. A hand-lettered sign directs the eye: "MEMORY LANE."

"Eugene McCarthy's doing my show; yeah, he's a great friend of mine, and Roger Williams, the great pianist. You work at CBS? Larry Tisch is a fan, a fan-*natical* fan, my God. Oh, he calls me. We have dinner together. I never follow through; I got too much on my mind. I've written twenty-three books, this one you're gonna love." Joe Franklin presses a soft-cover edition, still in the original cellophane, into my hand. I have not yet introduced myself. A telephone rings; Franklin bends down to scrabble for it amid some stacks of papers on the floor. My trench coat is not fully off. I examine the book's title: *Joe Franklin's Show Biz Memorabilia*. The author is listed as Sandra Andacht. I do a pretty good double take. And then I begin to gain awareness of where I am.

In the center of what might once have been a root-canal specialist's waiting room, I face a small and somewhat waxen man who is perched on the edge of a frayed sofa talking into a black dial telephone. "Hello? Speaking," says Joe Franklin. Another telephone, muffled and invisible, is ringing. The small man is dwarfed—nearly engulfed—by the vertical silage of his belongings; this office is a fallout shelter of show-biz detritus, a time capsule of glitz.

There are stacked cardboard boxes bursting at the seams with press releases, glossies, photocopies of notices. There are industrial gray metal shelves bent under cubic yards of old LPs— 78s. "I gotta lotta good news for ya, Ben," says Joe Franklin into one of two phones he's holding. "Today's gonna be the best day of your life, okay? I got my doctor here, spraying my throat. I'll talk to ya." Other shelves groan under canisters of film reels. There are old Sunday newspapers, complete with comics. A fragment of wooden cabinet tilts against the venetian blinds. I turn to look behind me. On the wall, half-hidden by another cabinet, is a gigantic tinted photograph of a platinum blonde, a satin doll. A page of sheet music is pasted to the open cabinet door. Its title reads: "Joe Franklin's Televising in Secaucus."

Secaucus, New Jersey, is the home of WOR's television studios. I would never have dreamt that people would gather around to sing about it. But in this room anything seems possible.

"I dunno how to say it without bragging," I hear Joe Franklin say, and I realize he is talking to me, "but I'm really hot with the campus crowd. Letters? Can't count 'em. Can't count 'em. Can't count 'em. Can't count 'em."

Both telephones ring again, and he dives for them. It is then that I notice the suits.

The suits are wadded into a mound of worsted and gabardine on the other half of the sofa where Joe Franklin is sitting. Houndstooth arms splay; natural shoulders lie crushed. It is as though a tour bus of empty suits has crashed and rolled on his couch. These must be the clothes he wears on *The Joe Franklin Show*. But what—? Why—?

I begin to form a question—but now Franklin is passing me one of the phones. "It's Irving Fields, the greatest pianist in the world," he tells me. "Talk to him. See what he says about the experience of being on my show."

I put the receiver to my ear. Irving Fields tells me he's at the Plaza and I should come over for a drink sometime. "Ah," I say. "Ah . . . I guess you've been on *The Joe Franklin Show*— a lot." Fields tells me he's been on about 400 times "in the last 400 years." He seems to feel that a quote is called for, as do I. "Stamina," Irving Fields says at last. "I guess that's what keeps him going."

I thank him and hand the receiver back to Franklin. He passes me the other one. This time it's another frequent guest, Judi Jourdan. Judi Jourdan of the Shower Singers.

"We get people from all walks of life," she explains to me. "We do cabaret; we also teach a course." There is a silence.

"All walks of life," says Judi Jourdan. "The best get on Shower Singers. Wonderful things happen to them. One of our girls was up for the lead in a Broadway show."

"Talk to him for thirty seconds," Joe Franklin is saying into the other receiver. "Tell him why I pulled for that beauty cream." I find myself talking now to a sponsor, a pharmaceutical man named Henry. Henry is speaking for the record. "To some people, he's like avuncular," he says. "Like an uncle, you know. He's a tower of strength, on a macho basis. He, uh—" Henry is groping. "He covers all bases and crosses all boundaries."

Joe Franklin is wearing suit pants—windowpane pattern on navy blue—a red-and-gray-striped shirt and a pink-and-brown necktie with crossed tennis racquets. We are talking now about the secrets of his success. "I got one great thing going for me," Joe Franklin is saying. He gives it a beat. "I'm not tall. If I was tall, like you, I couldn't walk in the street. People wouldn't leave me alone."

From the hallway have been coming the notes of somebody running the scales on a trumpet. Now Franklin's thought is totally interrupted by an intruder in the tiny and bulging office. "It's the fire marshal," explains a small elderly Hispanic man named Hector, who may be Franklin's assistant. I turn. Sure enough, there is a man in a white uniform shirt, holding a clipboard. Franklin stares, suddenly at a loss.

"He wants your autograph," says Hector. The fire marshal, a young man, grins and nods, pushing forward his clipboard. "My name's Lieutenant Joe Amadeo," he says.

Franklin has recovered his wits. " 'Joe,' same as me," he points out graciously. "Joe, you are a great man."

"Oh, thank you," says Joe. After he has left, Franklin says, "That's a funny bit. I thought he was comin' here to give me a summons. Hector, you're a lovely guy."

He picks up the thread. "I'm the last of the organics," he explains. "The last of the organics in a world where it's gotten

130

very, very plastic. Joe Franklin doesn't change. He symbolizes something solid. With the jacket and tie. I say, 'Good morning, ladies and gentlemen. . . .' " Something clicks in his mind. "You read that certain stars, the great ones, wouldn't do television talk shows. I've got proof." He glances upward significantly, at the canisters. "Ronald Reagan, *five times*. Charlie Chaplin—the great ones. You read that Cary Grant, Elvis, Gary Cooper never did a talk show. *I've got proof.*"

His age shocks. He is 58, three years younger than Johnny Carson. He seems older—not so much in appearance as in the context of his career span (he's been in broadcasting for forty years) and his inner calendar: He communes with an era defined by the Second World War. (The platinum blonde on his wall is Dolores Moran, he says, a third lead for Warner Bros. of that time. Asked whether he knew her, Franklin shakes his head, shrugs. "She typifies the Forties," he explains.)

He drives over to Secaucus Tuesdays and Thursdays to tape his five daily *Joe Franklin Shows*. The shows are aired at 1 A.M. on WOR in New York, and they get out around the country on cable. A recent ratings survey estimated his New York viewership at over 50,000 households a night. Yet his sense of being hot with the campus crowd may be accurate, in a weird sort of way: A fairly heavy collegiate sampling shows up in his demographics. It has been suggested, not entirely kindly, that viewers wised up on David Letterman's show-biz ironies regard Joe Franklin as a kind of field assignment in camp. And there was that Billy Crystal thing. Of which more later.

In addition to the television show, Joe Franklin does a weekly stint, *Joe Franklin's Memory Lane*, on WOR's sister radio station. This marathon of swing and big-band nostalgia is accomplished in two heroic shifts: Franklin is on the air from 7 until 10 P.M., and again from midnight until 5 A.M. "They want me to do it every night," he says with typical modesty, "but I'm going to start phasing out. In a couple of years, I wanna go behind the scenes, produce." (Later, going through his press clippings, I notice he has said exactly the same thing to an interviewer a couple of years ago.)

Radio is his true medium, just as fin de siècle is his true moment in time. Perhaps they are interwoven. Although his television career has spanned more than three decades, it was radio that first enchanted the young man who worshiped Eddie Cantor, and followed him through the streets of New York, and sat in NBC Studio 8H for every one of Cantor's nine-o'clock Wednesday broadcasts of *Time to Smile*. "I was very, very close with him," Franklin says. "I worked with him. After the Golden Age of Radio was over, in the Fifties, he had another show, *Ask Eddie Cantor*. Eddie would respond to letters from listeners." Joe Franklin pauses a beat, leans forward, his voice swelling a little. *"I wrote the letters!"*

I am again conscious of a presence behind me; another visitor. "I am nerviss," says a voice. "Believe me, I am nerviss." I turn. A young black man is standing there, staring at Joe Franklin. His name is George; he is an "impressionist." "I watched you since I was a kid," George tells Franklin. "I watched you with Woody and with Cosby." "Boy, this guy's got a memory, God bless him," Franklin tells me. I am sitting in the middle of a force field; I'm an impediment between George and his Lourdes.

"I gotta get things working," George says, almost under his breath. "I need some exposure. I got chills," he says, staring again at Franklin. He looks at me. "This man is an institution," he says. *"Forget* about it. *Forget* about it. *Forget* it."

George launches into some voices. "Hul-*lo* a-gain ev-ree-*body*, this is *How*-wud Coss-*ssell*." The voice goes all soft and raspy: "Ah'm *fazz't*. Ah'm *preddy*. Ah'm *the Greatisss'*." For some reason I glance down at the man's shoes. The yellowish soft-leather tips are wet from rainwater.

Joe Franklin is rummaging around him. "Do you see a blue datebook?" he asks me. I rummage, too, and find it on a chair under a stack of photocopied news stories, which slide to the floor as I extract the book.

"Leave it, don't worry about it," says Franklin, reaching for the datebook. "Lis-sen," he says, riffling the pages. "I'm gonna make up a cabaret show. George, give me your number; I'll call you tonight between five and seven. My word of honor." George is fairly jiggling with happiness. "Very good, very good," he says.

After George has left, I ask Joe Franklin about The Parody: Billy Crystal's on *Saturday Night Live*. It is a topic I have not been eager to raise. Crystal's evocation of Franklin had been brilliant and wicked; a merciless send-up of a doddering, past-addled talk-show host nattering on self-importantly with his menagerie of show business's misbegotten.

I expect Franklin's response to be grandly dismissive, perhaps even wounded—anger seems truly foreign to his soul. I am surprised at the directness of his answer.

"Billy Crystal made me a superstar," he says flatly. He considers. "I'm great now, but I was very, very, *very* hot when he was doing me. I'd give anything to get him back on that show."

I look at Franklin; he looks at me. A moment passes. "But you know," says Franklin, leaning forward on the sofa as the phone rings, "he was doing a *satire of a satire*. 'Cause I'm putting the world on. That's something only a select few can see."

The phone keeps ringing. "I'm very, very close with my audience out there," Joe Franklin says. "They can read between the lines. They know my moods. The critics say he's bland, he's neutral—my audience can read between the lines. They *know* I'm not bland or neutral.

"They meet me; they say, 'Joe, you gave that guy a zinger last night; I'm proud of you, Joe.'" He reaches down, feels for the phone, picks it up. "Hello? Speaking. Yes, my dear . . . I promise . . . if it means anything, I'm a personal friend of the governor."

133

The Apprenticeship of Shelley Long and Kitty Felde. Kitty *Who?*

Sometimes our stars shine brightest when they're out of view

When Shelley Long was 19 years old and just plain old Shelley Long, not the star of *Cheers*—there wasn't any *Cheers* back then; there was barely a Brooke Shields—she did industrial theater. She traveled around with an industrial theater group out of Chicago. The group did industro-theatrical things for, among other clients, Kentucky Fried Chicken. Shelley was in the chorus. She was a Las Vegas–type lounge singer in this industrial theater chorus performing for Kentucky Fried Chicken. The first show she ever did was in Hawaii, at a Kentucky Fried Chicken convention. Shelley and the group performed skits and songs built around issues of importance to Kentucky Fried Chicken franchisees.

I love knowing that. And not because it gives me, the professional TV critic, an excuse to feel superior toward the tin-plated world of TV actresses. The thing that kills me is that I didn't know it back then, at the time, back when I was writing a TV column in Chicago and Shelley Long's name kept cropping up on the fringes—on local TV commercials, in the Second City improv cast, in *dinner theater* for gawdsake. Shelley Long, this wiry little Junior Miss scrapper from Fort Wayne, was someone you knew would make it out of town someday; her conspicuous will of iron would get her past this dreary apprenticeship.

I knew vaguely about some of the stuff Shelley Long was doing. You couldn't avoid knowing; Chicago was not exactly the Napa Valley of actresses. But—pardon me—who cared? I was busy keeping up with the major established national talents—your Arte Johnsons, your Judy Carnes. Your Golddiggers, I was busy keeping up with. Destiny's darlings, all. A man's attention span is only so wide.

I certainly didn't know or care about Shelley's industrial theater group. And I didn't know that she had played a drug addict in an Allstate educational film. Nor that she wrote film scripts for the *Encyclopaedia Britannica*. And a comedy film for Quaker Oats, and another one about—we may as well get this all out on the table—changing a tire.

What would I have done with all this information had I possessed it? Probably nothing. But there is a chance that a lot of the TV columns I turned out in the ensuing years, and perhaps even a novel or two, might have been subtly changed, deepened, by that knowledge.

Shelley Long's secret precelebrity life, or rather, her unremarked attitude toward a chosen way of life, is part of a larger and invisible pop-cultural enclave. Invisible, at least, to most of us who professionally interpret the established pop culture. Nevertheless, this enclave is the primary feeder system into the performance tier of the pop culture, particularly in network television. Moreover, the conventional wisdom about TV performers is that they are, essentially, as transient and interchangeable as Rolaids. The occasional wisp of contrary evidence—Shelley Long, say—suggests that the inhabitants of this feeder enclave are worth getting to know. But this kind of linkage almost never happens.

You must understand this about television critics. As a group, they (we) can't muster much of a damn about feeder enclaves. What obsesses us is television *management.*

Silverman. Tinker. Arledge. Tartikoff. Sauter. These and others are our Cagneys, our Pecks, our Norse gods (and, in some cases, our souse gods—but that's another story). Power is the source of our thrall. They control entire economies, they set the nation's cognitive agenda, they are at home with such thrilling inside jargon as "bottom line."

You can see why we make fools of ourselves over them.

Network management types are the real stars in the eyes of today's engagé TV critic, schooled in the public-interest implications of television over and above its traditional show-business themes. Which is all fine and useful.

But there is an implied, and reductive, corollary: that the people at the broad, energetic base of television's pyramid, the thousands of mostly young, mostly imaginative, performance-oriented foot soldiers, are interesting only as a *class*— and then only because of the predictable and limited nature of their behavior.

This attitude is one good reason why so much daily TV criticism is so dutifully, sensibly, and nobly sterile these days.

Not that young performers go utterly unnoticed, God knows. As soon as one gets sucked from anonymity into the funnel and spat out the narrow end into the blinding glare of regular-series immortality, all the hellhounds of publicity commence their terrible bowwow. Then it's how-I-work-out time on *Entertainment Tonight*; it's all tofu and rumored love affairs and whether one got along with Victoria on the set of *Giving Attitude.* After watching a newly arrived young star reel through this long march for a few weeks, you begin to detect an almost Russian note of threnody beneath that most banal of show-biz surface lines: "I'm really a *very private person.*"

What makes it all so maddeningly dismal is that none of this publicity strip-mining, this reflexive mass-market lobotomizing of TV personalities, has ever (to my voracious knowledge) yielded up the slightest morsel of truly humanizing information. About anyone. Look. Let's imagine that Jane Gallagher really lives. Remember Jane Gallagher? Holden Caulfield's checkers partner in *Catcher in the Rye*? The girl who wouldn't move any of her kings off the back row because she liked the way they looked? Because of that single, sublime detail, a good part of the literate male baby boom grew up in love with Jane Gallagher. So let's say she comes out of her thirty-three-year seclusion and throws a press conference.

Do you know what Barbara Walters would ask her, first crack out of the box? *What kind of tree she'd like to be!* And by 6 P.M. the following day, everyone would have forgotten the hell about Jane Gallagher. Which would qualify her for the cover of *People*.

That is what I mean by the lack of truly humanizing information. Shelley Long, doing her Las Vegas lounge act limning the issues of importance to Kentucky Fried Chicken franchise-holders, is an updated version of Jane Gallagher shepherding her kings on the back row.

The point, I guess, is that—well, there are several points.

One: There exist all these kind of shaggy, quixotic, affecting people who are beating their brains out trying to crack the big time in network television. Two: A lot of these people are managing to be grass-roots custodians of the system, performing all of these localized acts of imagination even as they struggle. Three: It's important to know about these people and their work, for reasons that have to do with the soul—the soul of television as well as the soul of the critic. And four: It's no good pouncing upon them after they have emerged as brand names, for by then their wonderful serendipity has been compressed to the length and width of a press release.

Accordingly, I rise to nominate for the next Shelley Long, a woman who needs a *lot* of introduction—Kitty Felde!

Don't ask. You have never heard of Kitty Felde. *Entertainment Tonight* has never heard of Kitty Felde. *I* would never have heard of Kitty Felde had she not written me a smarty-pants letter about three years ago listing some structural objections she had to a novel I had just published. The novel was at that moment headed for remainder bins everywhere. Ms. Felde chose to type her criticisms on the back of a publicity still featuring the tooth-strewn likeness of one Kitty Felde, Actress, Los Angeles.

Here I was, having my nose rubbed in my literary shortcomings by Suzi Success. This was not what you would call a textbook beginning for a beautiful friendship. My return letter flattened palm trees as far south as Costa Mesa.

But eventually the correspondence settled into a kind of desultory exercise in mutual truculence, a transcontinental *mot juste* marathon. I had acquired, in early middle age, a pen pal.

But there was more to it than that, I soon realized. Here I was—a licensed television critic—suddenly blundering into etymological contact with an actual television *performer*. Better, a performer who hadn't made it yet. The letters soon made clear that this woman was struggling. Ford truck commercials, unemployment checks, melodrama theater, sheet-selling at Penney's. All the stuff you never hear about from Madeline Kahn.

I began to take an anthropological interest in Kitty Felde's mail. I began feeling almost *Samoan* about her. Her travails (many) and her triumphs (few) triggered a certain academic fascination.

When Kitty got hooted from The Comedy Store stage (she had tried to build a stand-up comedy routine around her typical Catholic high-school education), I raised a speculative eyebrow. I tapped a pencil to my teeth when she was rejected for the job of sportscaster on KABC radio's *Sportstalk*—she is a passionate Dodgers fan—and allowed myself the barest nod when she disclosed that she had enrolled in a sportscasting class at Santa Monica City College.

It wasn't all blind alleys, of course. She had her glory moments, her brushes with the big time. One of her partners in a repertory comedy group turned out to be Larry Hagman's daughter. The director of the blues-oriented cabaret version of *Hamlet*, in which Kitty played Ophelia on two hours' notice, was the guy who plays the bartender on *Love Boat*.

Hazily, a composite view of 29-year-old Kitty Felde began to take focus: Kitty in perpetual transit about the wide end of the funnel, Kitty pushing her Honda along the L.A. freeways, Kitty pulling on a pair of nylons by stages, at stop signs, as she hauled freight from one audition to another. Always with the tooth-strewn smile.

And my anthropological detachment began, albeit slightly, to fade. Then the manuscripts began arriving.

Shanghai Heart. Mum's the Word. Man With No Shadow. The woman had been writing *plays* all this time. Through all the turn-downs, all the piecework, all the third-banana bits in TV commercials ("Lookit all this sugar!" says Kitty to Annette Funicello for Skippy peanut butter), she is writing these plays: at her real-estate receptionist's desk, in the unemployment line, during gridlock . . . these jaunty, shrewd, good-hearted, yes, *smarty-pants* plays. Plays that were getting performed—storefronts, yes, but performed. And reviewed. *The Los Angeles Times* actually called her "a natural." "As a writer, Kitty Felde is a natural"—that's what the *Times* said about my pal Kitty! Hey!

So, no more Samoan detachment. If Kitty Felde represents life in the broad end of that funnel, then Tinker me no more Tinkers. Point me to the nearest storefront. These are my kind of folks.

Maybe it's too late to do anything for Shelley Long. Poor kid, she's famous. But if Kitty Felde ever shows up as the wacky roommate on *More Than Enough*—well, you can say you knew her before they shrunk the "her" and stapled it tooth-strewn onto a press release.

Here's an advance look at you, kid.

NORMAN MARK GETS THE LAST
NYAH-HAH-HAH-HAH-HAH

A tale of friendship and rivalry over twenty years with the man even Mary Tyler Moore couldn't love

My standard response to wedding invitations, of which I receive exceedingly few these days, is to demur with thanks and a preemptive gift, usually something from an airline catalogue.

Nevertheless, when the invitation arrived from Chicago not many weeks ago, I called my travel agent.

Never mind the treacheries of New England weather at midwinter; never mind the inconvenience and expense. (Well, mind the expense a little.) This one came straight from a time of madness and laughter, a time of hard rivalry and improbable friendship. It betokened one man's triumph of honor and élan in a medium (and a life) that generally recognizes neither. It reawakened memories of the miracles inherent in toasting sunsets with cheap champagne.

This one came from my incredible buddy Norman Mark.

I went.

The bride—I happened to know this in advance—was one of those frighteningly sumptuous Wagnerian cloud-striding blondes, miles of shoulder blade and cheekbone and panache and brains. Her name, as befits mythology, was Grace. The wedding consummated a twenty-five-year romance. It bracketed other marriages, children. All this was unsurprising, if you knew Norman Mark. Because Norman, who is even taller than Grace, is a man to whom exactly nothing ordinary has ever happened. He is one of the few people I know who has obeyed William Saroyan's simple injunction: In the time of your life, live.

If you live in Chicago, or if you're passing through, you can catch him most weekdays on the 4:30 P.M. newscast on WMAQ, Channel 5, the NBC-owned station. Some nights on the ten-o'clock. Some days on both. He's the entertainment reporter. Big guy. Black eyebrows. Good in a suit. A little sweaty. Machine-gun chuckle. *Nyah*-hah-hah-hah-hah! Norman Mark. Talks like this. Thinks like this. Lives like this. Million ideas. Tremendous life-force. Big star now. In Chi. Cab drivers hail *him* on the street. "Hey, *Norman!*" Autographs in restaurants. The whole schmear.

It's about time.

He's pushing 50 now—who isn't? When I met him, twenty years ago, we were young newspapermen in Chicago. It was the beginning of the final flicker of a luminous newspaper era that sprawled back to the Twenties and beyond. Chicago newspapers bore the traces of gods: Carl Sandburg, Ring Lardner, Ben Hecht, Charles MacArthur. In our time there were Mike Royko, Bob Greene, Roger Ebert. Chicago papers were lyceums for poet-journalists, men and women for whom tomorrow never existed, in Hecht's phrase—talented and often self-ruined people pulled across the sky by comets and spun around in torrents. This was before Rupert Murdoch and then the *USA Today* syndrome quieted all that.

Norman was already writing the radio-TV column for the afternoon Marshall Field newspaper, *The Daily News,* when I took over the same beat for Field's morning *Sun-Times.* I spotted him one day on a Michigan Avenue bus. He was wearing a beard and some kind of trench coat and was scowling over a thick paperback. I was 27, just up from Missouri. I thought he looked like Moses. A terrifying intellectual.

But it wasn't intellectualism that I had to contend with; it was his damned reporting. He just reported the bejesus out of the radio-television beat, both locally and nationally.

Some perspective is necessary here. At the dawn of the 1970s, nobody read a daily TV column for the reporting. It was three-dot filler stuff, press-release rewrites and Lucy phoned up to chat about her new season. Reporters got to be TV critics as a last chance before the alcohol-abuse program, or because they happened to own a set.

Norman Mark changed that. He would sit there on the other side of the plate glass that separated the *Daily News* and *Sun-Times* city rooms, with one of those old-fashioned fly-boy–style telephone headsets clamped to his skull so he could type with both hands, and he'd work the broadcast industry as if it were the police beat. *Nyah*-hah-hah-hah-hah, I could almost hear him roaring. He loved to compete. While the rest of us (there were two other good critics, for the morning and afternoon Tribune Company papers) more or less watched television and wrote opinions of what we saw, Norman was covering the industry from the inside out.

Pretty soon, the rest of us began to clamp on our own headsets. We began to cover television as a consumer issue, as a political prism, as an arbiter of statist and corporate self-interest, as a medium of public accountability. And for a long time, nobody did it better than Norman.

He cultivated sources. His sources were phenomenal. Anonymous tipsters from the stations were actually arranging to meet Norman in seedy bars, where (swathed in knit caps and raincoats) they would press incriminating documents into his hands and then vanish. Norman would write a column. The next day, three guys in black suits would fly in from network headquarters in New York, and that night a station manager would sleep with the alewives. Norman got the local stations so paranoid about leaks that at one of them the management sought to protect a Draconian interoffice memo on secretarial dress codes. A boss read the memo aloud to each secretary, then destroyed it.

But the boss reckoned without the diabolic reach of Norman Mark. The secretaries conspired to commit one line apiece to memory. Then each one jangled Norman's headset with her line. *Nyah*-hah-hah-hah-hah! Verbatim memo, right there in Norman's column!

This is the sort of competitive prowess that, in Chicago at least, was normally acknowledged among one's peers by blood-hatred. The problem was that Norman was so hard to hate. Obnoxious, loud, know-it-all, the sort of guy who would buttonhole Julia Child at a press reception to lay on her *his* recipe for chocolate soufflé. Yes. Norman was all of that. But hard to hate.

There was the laugh. *Nyah*-hah-hah-hah-hah! It was infectious. The four Chicago critics spent a lot of time together in screening rooms, getting advance looks at forthcoming shows. (It was Norman who had shamed the industry, through his columns, into *allowing* daily critics the privilege of advance screenings, without the quid pro quo of a puff review.) Norman and I discovered we shared a certain irreverence—all right, a snotty, malicious contempt—for most of what we were watching.

We began to riff out loud on the story lines. Call us rude, call us unprofessional. Confronted with the video image of

Hal Holbrook as Abraham Lincoln, poised grandly atop a marble staircase, with about eight pounds of Lincolnesque rubber cement makeup on his face, I might turn to Norman and stage-whisper, "I hope he doesn't trip on the rug and *dribble himself to death!*" "*Nyah*-hah-hah-hah-hah!" Norman would roar, while our competitors would hiss for silence and the publicist would begin to weep.

We took our insufferable behavior to the annual springtime national TV press tours on the West Coast. These are the much-remarked gothic rituals of press freedom in which sixty or seventy critics in various stages of leisurewear, sleep deprivation and cultural illiteracy are assembled in Los Angeles, festooned with nametags, smothered with press kits and stripped of their motor control by industrial-strength Bloody Marys, then herded by publicists trained at Jungle World to rows of chairs in a conference room at the Century Plaza, there to perch respectfully, front paws extended, while phalanxes of stars from the networks' newest impending catastrophes wax quotable for fifty-five minutes about the fiber content of their macrobiotic diets and their ambition to "stretch." (These sessions may have been the spiritual genesis of *Entertainment Tonight*.)

Norman used to tower damply over these timorous tourists, screaming wild bonhomie into their faces and causing moos of apprehension, while the flinty-eyed publicists stalked the perimeter, looking to cut him out of the herd. I hung in his wake, a good hick avid for corruption.

Our questions to the luminaries sometimes took on an edge. Amid colleagues who considered "How did you come to be born in Atlanta?" a fairly prosecutorial gambit, we introduced the concept of irony. After listening to Aaron Spelling natter on about how the police helicopter in his forthcoming series, *Chopper One*, would be a "fully developed character" along with the cops who flew in it, one of us raised his hand and inquired whether we could look forward to the helicopter's having a sex life.

Nyah-hah-hah-hah-hah!

It was at one such Hollywood press conference that Norman gained a sort of deification among his fellow critics. The guest of honor was Sir Lew "Low" Grade, the dwarflike British baron of crass American-style TV. Thanking his network hosts for the opportunity to meet with the Colonial press, Lord Lew was moved to a good-fellow burst of etiquette. "You must all come and see us in London sometime," he blandly remarked to the critics, lifting a glass. Norman immediately leapt to his feet and screamed, "WE'RE ALL FREE IN OCTOBER!"

Lord Lew did the decent thing. And so it was that in October 1972 a British Airways jumbo jet arrived at Kennedy Airport in New York to transport some seventy thunderstruck critics to London for a week of screenings, interviews, Daimler limousines and tickets to *Long Day's Journey Into Night* at the National Theatre, with Sir Laurence Olivier in the role of James Tyrone. Norman picked up some bargains at Marks & Spencer.

Through it all, he wrote and wrote—and made an impact. Many TV critics receive angry feedback for tough, adversarial columns. Norman is the only critic I know of who was written into an episode of *The Mary Tyler Moore Show* in order to be handed his comeuppance. Norman had taken Miss Moore to task for reverting to a goody-goody sensibility after several seasons of realistic themes. "Regained her virginity," I think was the euphemistic way Norman put it in print; privately, he was grousing to his colleagues that Mary Richards had received the first hymen transplant in the history of prime-time sitcoms.

The show's producers struck back. They assigned Susan Silver, one of their best writers, to create an episode in which a television critic named "Mark" misquotes Mary in print, then asks her for a date—and is rebuffed when he tries to go to bed with her.

Norman had the last *nyah*-hah-hah-hah-hah, however, when a network publicist phoned him from New York to admit that this time Norman had been slandered. "You have misquoted people," the flack assured Norman, "but you have *not* not gone to bed with them."

It was along about this time that a funny and transitional thing happened. My column won the Pulitzer Prize for criticism in 1973. In the culture of Chicago journalism, what that, in fact, meant was that everyone else in town *lost* the goddamned Pulitzer Prize that year. I still have a scrapbook filled with letters, telegrams and other missives of congratulation from my Chicago compatriots, many of them sincere. Many of them not.

Of all the responses to my unexpected honor, I think I respect Norman's the most. He threw a fit. He ripped off his headset phone and flung it across the *Daily News* city room. Then he went home. Then he got out his gym shoes and ran along the Lake Michigan shoreline. "I'd never even run a mile before that," he told me years later. "I ran three and a half miles that day. I just ran, and ran, and ran, and ran, and ran. And then, you know, everything was pretty much okay."

Perhaps not so okay. One could make a strong case that Norman had a Pulitzer year that year. My stuff was pretty good. But it was Norman who broke the story that the surgeon general's report on television and violence had been misrepresented to the public. The networks had lobbied for an editorial voice in the summary of the findings—to be published in the papers—and managed to tone it down from the hard line of the text itself.

In the best newspaper year I ever had, Norman scooped me. And no cigar.

It was years before I learned that Norman's anger was directed not at me but at his own paper, which had not bothered to nominate him, on the assumption that no TV critic could hope to win a Pulitzer. The paper later apologized to Norman. But apologies don't get you in Who's Who.

———

Our careers began to diverge after that—though, paradoxically, our friendship grew stronger. I left the *Sun-Times* a couple of summers later. I rented a cottage on Lake Michigan eighty miles from the city and started work on a book. That was the summer I met and romanced the woman who is now my wife. One of our indelible memories of that romance is of Norman barging in on weekends with armloads of cheap champagne, with which we'd toast the gorgeous sunsets that fired the lake and our laughing faces.

His own life had taken some nasty turns by then. The *Daily News* was dying, and so was his marriage. Norman had wed a childhood sweetheart, a good and intelligent woman who bore him two sons—he used to cite his boys when he wrote about children's television; the tenderness and intimacy he revealed were unexpected counterpoints to the bull-in-a-china-shop tone of most of his stuff. But now those boys were nearly grown, and the marriage had gone stale. Norman seemed less concerned with his own problems than with nudging me along toward matrimony with a woman, who was, in his critical opinion, a far better catch than most of the bimbos he'd seen me squiring around. *Nyah-hah-hah-hah-hah!*

I spent a final year in Chicago after that summer. Then I moved to New York and married the girl.

Norman quit his TV column. The paper, desperately cautious as it tottered toward demise, refused to let him run some well-documented columns on payola at local radio stations. Then the *Daily News* died. And the odyssey of Norman Mark began.

He did some free-lance radio and TV work in Chicago. He tried out for Second City, the famous improv-comedy ensemble, and eventually caught on with a sort of second-string group, the Reification Company.

He got an overnight gig on an all-talk radio station in town. He got another gig in Cincinnati. At the same time. He commuted between Chicago and Cincinnati, doing talk shows in both cities. Then, in 1981, came a big break.

A West Coast friend tipped him off about auditions for a new syndicated Metromedia daytime show, to be called *Breakaway*. The show was looking for a movie reviewer. Norman wangled a three-minute audition. He got the job. For a while he kept his radio show in Chicago, flying back and forth to the Coast. But after six weeks, *Breakaway* was in deep ratings trouble, and the producers asked Norman if he wanted to be the new host. It sounded like a date with a dame called Destiny.

Years later he told me about his life in the fast lane.

"For the first few months," he said, "the show was *embarrassing*. At one point we had a woman who did a combination of gossip and astrology. She would say, 'Sylvester Stallone was seen here with so-and-so, but *the stars say they're not gonna get together*.' *Nyah*-hah-hah-hah-hah!"

Still, there was the whiff of success: "I had one person for makeup. One for hair. One for clothes. And seven people booking guests! And this *incredible* pressure, where one day there was a meeting with seven people about how I said the word 'and'! They said, 'When you say "and"—lissen, we'll show you on tape!—you say, "*aaaaaaaa*nd." Hear that? It should be "*and*." Hear the difference? Sometimes you say, "*aaaaaaaa*nd." ' "

This hiatus in paradise lasted a year. With Norman as co-host, *Breakaway* tripled its ratings. So Metromedia canceled it.

Somewhere along the way, Norman's marriage had been canceled as well. He went to San Francisco to seek out Grace, whom he had met a quarter century earlier, as a college student. She was now a successful advertising executive, divorced, with a daughter. The flame was still alive. Norman and Grace began living together. And Norman became the Freelancer From Hell.

He did industrials. He did voice-overs. He landed a part in a James Bond movie, *A View to a Kill*. He was a guard. "I had a speaking line," he recalled. " 'You go this way.' They cut my hair, put me in a uniform, put me in shadow, put shades on me, cut the scene down to four seconds—and then they *dubbed my voice!*"

He got a part in the soap opera *Rituals*, Metromedia's attempts to do syndicated daytime drama. He commuted between location in Los Angeles and acting lessons in San Francisco. He filled in the empty hours as a part-time talk-show host on KGO radio. This went on for about four months.

Then KPIX, a big San Francisco TV station, lured him away with an offer to become its anchorman of the future. But after three days, it was clear that the station had no idea what to do with him.

"And so I was there six months, but I spent five months and three weeks looking for a job. It was like it all never stopped."

Nyah . . . hah . . . hah . . . hah . . . hah.

On November 10, 1985, Norman Mark's odyssey came full circle. The new general manager of WMAQ in Chicago decided he needed a strong local critic to compete with a couple of other legends who'd come of age in the final flicker of the town's great newspaper era—Gene Siskel on WBBM and Roger Ebert on WLS. Who better than Norman Mark?

And so my pal Norman went home to be a big deal in Chi. Beautiful Grace went with him, leaving behind a successful career and reestablishing herself in the Windy City. In a town that still puts media stars at the top of its celebrity list—a town, after all, of Kup and Studs Terkel and Royko and Oprah—Norman and Grace hold their own. They show up in the local magazines. Taxi drivers stop and hail them. And *everybody* is glad to get Norman's recipe for chocolate soufflé.

We got back in touch. The two of them visited us in the East. My wife, Norman and I introduced Grace to the art of toasting sunsets with cheap champagne. And then, on one of those visits, Norman pulled one of those wonderfully Norman things that reminded me how much I'd learned from him, about the time of one's life, and living.

We were all at a high-school baseball game in Connecticut. Four sophisticated grown-ups and my two small boys, on bleacher planks. Norman's idea. He'd spotted the game from the van as we tooled around the small town where my family spent weekends. My older son, then 6 years old, became enraptured with the big players and their glamorous uniforms. He wanted to meet them.

I grew intensely practical. Not now, son. There's a *game* on. My son put his chin in his hands. It was Norman who came to the rescue. For a man who had once conjured a British Airways jumbo jet and a week in London for seventy American television critics, what was a high-school baseball game? He swept my son up in his arms and bore him, clattering hugely down the bleachers, to the home-team bench. "This guy wants to meet you!" he informed the coach.

The coach did the decent thing. He shook hands with my son, and then he gave him a baseball, which my son has in his room to this day. The crowd burst into applause. Big exit. *Nyah*-hah-hah-hah-hah! For the rest of the day, I tried to act nonchalant about having a friend as wondrous as Norman Mark.

I went to the wedding. It was splendid, and the champagne this time was not cheap. I noticed that someone was weeping during the ceremony. It was Norman. He turned to Grace at the conclusion of their vows and told her with tear-streaked eloquence about his love for her at first sight, and about how he had continued to love her at first sight—at first sight every morning. . . . The elderly judge reddened, cleared his throat. Once again, Norman was reporting *all* the facts.

I had one regret about my presence at Norman's wedding: I had forgotten to bring a gift. But what, really, do you give a guy who already has the gift of life?

WHERE THERE'S A WILL,
THERE'S A MOYERS

*Never has TV news tolerated two commentators
as brilliant—or as different—as George Will
and Bill Moyers*

One night around Thanksgiving on *The CBS Evening News*,
Dan Rather threw it to Bill Moyers, and Moyers, squinting
hard into the TelePrompTer and reading in that curiously un-
conversational singsong of his, did a couple of minutes on
California youth gangs who attack homeless men—trolls, the
kids call them—with baseball bats. And for those few minutes, the entire cat's cradle of modern television news—the
computer-generated graphics, the sharply edited videotape, the
considerations of "pace" and "flow"—all of it evaporated unnoticed, collapsed back upon the most ancient and primitive
and abused and falsely devalued of all the medium's devices:
man's puny, inexhaustible voice.

Moyers's commentary detached itself from the quotidian body
of the newscast with unnerving subtlety. Its effect was similar

to that of strolling a familiar morning route to the office and finding that on this day you are obliged to step over a prone pair of legs. Moyers did not preach. He did not explicitly declare himself opposed to young people who pound transient men into bloody pulps. He conceded that the homeless were a nuisance. He explained that the young people were angry over "the way the trolls go begging while *they* have to work and pay taxes. . . . That's one way of looking at it," said Moyers evenly. "Indignation can inspire the spirit of justice, or in this case, of meanness." He closed with a quotation from Justice Learned Hand, something about the spirit of liberty as "the spirit which seeks to understand the minds of other men and women."

No videotape. No actualities. No statistics. No pronouncements from "authorities." It was almost—*almost*—what anchormen call a reader, a bare-bones news report. Almost, but not by a long shot. Weeks later, I couldn't get the damn piece out of my mind. Moyers had heightened the horror of his subject—troll bashing—in an artful way, by pointedly *under*exploiting the limits of argument available to him in the commentary form.

To put it another way, Moyers *counterprogrammed* his own environment: His cool phrasings pointedly lowered the temperature from the surrounding "rhetoric of crisis" that fueled *The CBS Evening News* that night—and indeed fuels all network newscasts every night. This "rhetoric of crisis" has been singled out by Christopher Lasch in his book, *The Minimal Self*, as one of the more numbing causes of our cultural paralysis and shriveling social consciousness. Its rampant presence—not just in the news, but in nearly all discourse—"emasculates the *idea*" of crisis, writes Lasch, "and leaves us indifferent to appeals founded on the claim that some sort of emergency commands our attention." In such an atmosphere, a few well-chosen calm words can have the effect of a pistol shot.

Not that most news executives necessarily understand this

particular virtue of commentary, this capacity to *set aside* an issue, or an idea, for special consideration away from the maelstrom. Recall that as recently as 1981 there were *no* commentators on any of the networks. CBS News did without an analyst from Eric Sevareid's retirement in 1977 until Moyers rejoined the network in 1981. ABC, having hustled Howard K. Smith off to involuntary retirement in 1979, waited until September 1984 to install George Will on *World News Tonight* (although Will had been appearing as ABC's gadabout panelist for four years). At NBC, David Brinkley's departure in September 1981 brought a halt to punditry there until John Chancellor took it up the following year.

What is it that makes news executives so edgy in the presence of commentary (or "bed-wetting," as it is revealingly known to a few vice-presidents)? A better question might be the reverse: How did the analyst ever pry his way back onto the evening news at all?

His strategic liabilities seem prohibitive: He is a dreaded talking head, encroaching upon the anchor-star at that. He interrupts the compressed, high-energy visual flow of the newscast and crowds out at least one videotaped story from that night's story budget. Finally, his is the segment most likely to alienate viewers: The mere statement of any point of view presupposes that it's in disagreement with something.

It's small wonder, then, that for a while television news executives voguishly claimed that technology had replaced the need for news analysis. Smaller, more mobile equipment made it possible—in the words of ABC vice-president Av Westin, speaking in 1980—for crews "to get out and get an automobile worker to tell us how it feels to be laid off, instead of relying on a pundit to tell us that the worker undoubtedly feels bad."

Take *that*, Howard K.

To extend that logic: Commentators are redundant with news. Information is self-referencing. Data is as data does. The meaning and weight of a story are implicit in themselves, especially if the weight can be expressed numerically. (*Percentages* of Santa Cruz kids who wallop homeless old men; the *median income* of those kids; the *rise in such incidents over the past year*; what percentage of those kids' parents identified themselves as disaffected Democrats—the factoidal yield of such a story is limitless.)

Further, since all the stories in a nightly newscast are categorically important (else, why would they be included in the limited agenda of stories?), there is no need to underscore their significance any further via the commentator-icon.

Ah, but look. It doesn't quite work that way. "Important" stories, "crisis" stories, presented in an endless context of importance and crisis, swiftly lose their defining edge of urgency; they become invisible. A good example is the African famine story (which already seems somewhat dated, out-of-fashion, to media-conditioned sensibilities). On October 23, 1984, *NBC Nightly News* created a nationwide furor by airing some BBC-produced film footage of starving children in Ethiopia. The extreme suffering it showed surpassed even the nightly pitch of "crisis," and for several weeks the nation—and its news conduits—behaved as if the famine had previously been a well-kept secret: In just over two months, Americans contributed $45 million to aid Ethiopia.

But the story had not been a secret. NBC News itself insisted—and with no little proprietary pride—that it had broadcast no less than *thirty-three stories* about African famine since 1981. But none of those reports had contained the visual evidence, or at least visual evidence with enough graphic intimacy, to implant a sense of *special* crisis in the public mind. In a way, that October BBC footage became its own commentary. That happens now and then with television news stories, but not nearly often enough: The ante of urgency has been canted so high every day that only a catastrophic infusion of crisis can seize the public's notice.

All right—perhaps we're agreed that news commentary fulfills a need for establishing some scale of urgency in the nightly flood tide of information. We might even agree that commentary is a useful device for clarification: The American Association of Advertising Agencies reported a few years ago that 80 to 85 percent of all TV watchers misunderstand at least part of whatever programming they watch—an estimated one fourth to one third of whatever they watch. If this is true, the networks don't need commentators as much as they need the Second Coming of Miss Frances and *Ding Dong School.*

Still, the question remains: What *internal* needs do the commentators fulfill? Or why, having purged news commentary, did the networks allow these troublesome characters to reestablish a beachhead?

The key to the resurgence is Moyers. CBS may not necessarily have wanted a news analyst when it rehired Moyers from PBS in 1981 (he had left the network in frustration in 1979), but it sure as hell wanted Bill Moyers. He was simply too brilliant, too good at too many things—documentaries, cerebral interviews, use of the language—even for a talent-glutted news division like CBS's to do without. Moyers's sheer marketability, then, allowed him to negotiate for exposure on the division's crown jewel, *The Evening News.*

Once established, Moyers quickly revived the classic social-justice liberalism (as distinct from doctrinaire leftism) that has been CBS News's historic hallmark from Edward R. Murrow down through Sevareid. But whereas Sevareid mostly analyzed, Moyers goes boldly further: He advocates. He does not hesitate to quote, for purposes of reprimand, from a letter signed by three born-again evangelical politicians, asking voters to defeat a Jewish incumbent and "send another Christian to Congress."

Now, there are millions of born-again posteriors that shift uneasily in their Barcaloungers upon being confronted with this sort of upbraiding. Judging from November's election results, Moyers—whose following is huge—is nevertheless out of step on certain secular issues, too.

Which may explain in large part why a certain horn-rimmed,

bow-tied apostle of nineteenth-century rationalism was ushered by the ever-competitive Roone Arledge onto the set of *ABC's World News Tonight* last September.

George ("If you know the mind of an 1847 Oxford movement Tractarian, then I'm an open book") Will is an inspired alternative to Moyers. His twice-weekly presence alongside Peter Jennings assures viewers of the widest, most highly defined contrast of sensibilities in TV-news-commentary history.

There are bracing aesthetic differences as well. Unlike the somewhat humid and TelePrompTer-riveted Moyers, the professorial Will presents his ideas in the form of quasi-Socratic dialogues, with anchorman Jennings serving as the interlocutor.

Unlike the populist Moyers, Will's pieces tend to be astringent, highly theoretical and focused (with a Henry Adams–like hauteur) upon the maneuverings of Washington insiders. And unlike Moyers, Will brooks no fanfare for the common man. On his October 30 commentary—just a few days before the election—Will icily eviscerated one of America's most beloved myths, the Sacredness of the High Voter Turnout!

"Who do we *get* when we nag people to go to the polls?" Will sneered. "We get people who do not care very much about politics and therefore do not know very much about politics. I'm afraid the rule probably is that more means worse where the electorate is concerned, because smaller means smarter. These are jarring truths, but truths."

(Yes, Andy Rooney said roughly the same thing on a *60 Minutes* spot a few nights earlier. But Rooney is a jackanapes. Will is a—well, he's a *commentator*.)

Of course, Will was not the first network alternative to Moyers. John Chancellor has lent his considerable emeritus prestige to *NBC Nightly News* since 1982. But Chancellor—perhaps reflecting his early days as a Chicago newspaperman—tends to be more the classic analyst than the engaged partisan.

Still, even Chancellor's detached pieces are worth preserving. News commentary might ultimately be likened to sex (I realize this may be a minority point of view, but there you have it) in that even when it's bad, it's better than doing without. And when its *good*—well, how many of you remember *anything* that was said on the network airwaves during the last election night? Any fact, any statistic, any exit poll. I remember . . . one thing. I remember Bill Moyers telling Dan Rather point-blank that the "overwhelming reason" white southerners fled the Democratic party—to Ronald Reagan's great benefit—was race. It was a bald, stark, dangerous, unqualified human opinion, and it rang above that entire fact-saturated telecast—all three fact-saturated telecasts—like a phone call in the night.

Man's puny, inexhaustible voice. Commentating.

III

Programs

All right, all right, so *L.A. Law* and *thirtysomething*, each of which I consign, in this section, to the Third Circle of Hell ("*L.A. Law:* D.O.A.," and, a little later on, "Trivial Pursuits") were among the bell-ringing, gully-washing definitive smash-eroos of the 1980s. What's a television critic for, if not to fling himself into the path of an advancing tank now and then?

In point of fact, I stand by my original reactions to these blockbuster ABC hits: that each panders, in its own sleek and highly programmatic way, to some of the decade's most un-appetizing social hallmarks—an overwrought and hard-burnished celebration of merciless careerism, in the case of *L.A. Law,* and its corollary, an overweening sanctification of the inner Self, in the case of *thirtysomething.*

Similarly, the flurry of formats, late in the decade, that dealt comically or seriously with the plight of men whose Women Done Left them ("The Male Eunuch"—the second component in this collection's title) struck me as elements of Yuppieology. As more power women left their power nests to don power suits and join the power workforce, dreaming of the ultimate power prize—a spot in an AT&T power commercial—their menfolk began to pout over the resulting power outage. A battalion of prime-time scriptwriters immediately landed on the scene to cry, in effect, "inner Self! inner Self!"

"Sorry, Maury" is my tender paean to that most noxious entry in the 1980s "Tabloid TV" sweepstakes, *A Current Affair*. Historians of the era will note, or footnote, that no less an eminence than Van Gordon Sauter himself, the defrocked high priest of CBS News and later an unsuccessful purveyor of "reality" exploitation programs, came to the defense of Tabloid TV last year in a cover article in *TV Guide*. It makes one wonder what might have happened to CBS News if Sauter had somehow survived. Moving from the ridiculous to the sublime, I have ventured a personal evaluation of one noble, and inevitably damaged program of that era—*CBS News Sunday Morning*, where I served as media critic for five years. I had deep reservations about undertaking the piece—"Sunday Mourning"—as the essay itself makes clear. My feelings about the program and its brilliant, bilious creator, Robert (Shad) Northshield, were deeply bound up in personal loyalties verging on devotion. Thus my judgment—that the program has suffered from its personnel cuts and its change of senior management—is scarcely objective, a fact that I freely acknowledge here. "What's worth succeeding in is worth failing in," said Robert Frost—and the consideration that finally made me feel a piece about *Sunday Morning* was worth failing in was a simple one: even in its post-Northshield era, the program is so uncannily, almost seamlessly excellent that reviewers seldom think to write about it at all. Reviewing it is like reviewing clean air. So I did it. So sue me.

"Omigod, What Hath Holly Wrought?" is a glance at a familiar network television stratagem: trying to replicate in series form the appeal of a box-office movie hit—in this case, *Broadcast News*. (Sneak preview: they failed.) "The Popcorn Pugilists" examines the widening (sorry, Roger) genre of TV programs *about* the movies. It suggests that this branch of movie criticism may have grown comfy-cuddly with its subject (the better to satisfy the demands of its format) at precisely the time when movie criticism needed every inch of disputatious distance it could muster.

Joan Rivers has returned to television since my admittedly gleeful farewell to her effulgent late-night talk show at Fox, "Thin of the Night"—a departure that made late-night safe for the remarkable Arsenio Hall. But I've included my "farewell" piece anyway. Call me some kind of literary genetic engineer: I wanted to put her between covers with Morton Downey Jr. and see whether some bizarre new life-form would emerge.

Television did some of its most desolate work, in the Eighties, on the audience least equipped to judge its corroding effects: children. A slackening of federal licensing restraints empowered toy merchandisers and their advertising firms to effectively seize control of kidvid programming content—leading to the era of what child advocates branded "program-length commercials." (It actually came to this: *The California Raisins*, a kidshow that sprang from an animated commercial about raisins.) This same new freedom from accountability allowed the networks to slash into their already minimal allotments for children's informational programming.

The cable revolution did not help. Nickelodeon, an experimental channel for innovative animation and gentle themes, promised—briefly—to be a genuine alternative to the hard-edged clatter and sell. Ho. Along came Warner-Amex, the MTV people, and ate Nickelodeon. Under its new masters the channel became *Dolla*rodeon, and its schedule shot up with the same hyperstimulants that were oozing from the networks and local stations: saturation doses of shrill, fast-edit commercials for junk food and cheap toys; promotional spots for its own programs, spots that assured young viewers of their nascent kickass sexuality and ironic superiority; and programs that featured scaled-down versions of adult greed-mongering game shows. (Typical "game": small fry crawling through vats of spaghetti sauce to beat one another to the finish line and a swag-haul of brand-name consumer goods.)

Nickelodeon had become a boot camp for the MTV generation.

The children's corner of this section begins with an appreciation of Pee-wee Herman ("The Last Human Being on Saturday Morning"). It continues with a lament for the premature junking of a certain Rad Rodent ("The Last Angry Mouse") as reinterpreted by the wondrous animator Ralph Bakshi. "But Daddy, Try to Grok the Story Line" is a purely imaginary fable of an utterly make-believe Father-as-Ditz, who essays to share a little tubeside Quality Time with his videofluent sons. The plot is utter fantasy. It can't happen here.

SUNDAY MOURNING

Kuralt & Company have yet to recover from the absence of their spiritual leader, the brilliant Shad Northshield

Not long ago, I picked up a fashionable weekly magazine and read a glossy article about the inner workings of Diane Sawyer's departure from CBS News for a fabulous new career at ABC.

Everything was fine until I got to the passage that described how CBS's president, Laurence Tisch, ordered his "exhausted beaten brass" to invite Ms. Sawyer into his office so that she could rip up her contract, write a new one "and fill in the numbers."

Fill . . . in . . . the NUMBERS?

At that point my vision went a little red. An old nausea welled up fresh. I was reliving the grotesqueness of a March Friday in 1987: a day of shock and cruelty and tears and shame, the sort of day I had heard and read about but never experienced in twenty-five years of professional journalism. It was the day of the Big Layoffs at CBS News—more than 200 people in all, a day when Laurence Tisch seemed to have misplaced his supply of blank checks, a day when many good and honorable people at CBS had their careers ripped up and stuffed down their shirt pockets.

It was a day when Tisch's corporate bean counters did to CBS News what their larger counterparts have done to the tropical rain forests: gouged an ecosystem for short-term profit. The damage was particularly acute at *CBS News Sunday Morning*. Despite a regeneration in the past year, perhaps the best program in commercial-television history has not fully recovered from the razing it suffered early in 1987. It's doubtful that it ever will.

I had always promised myself that I'd never write a column about *Sunday Morning*, for the very good reason that I worked there for five years. Even at this moment, as I break it, that promise seems remarkably sensible. Columns about one's prior employment are like serenades assayed or fights picked in barrooms: They almost never achieve their intended result, and the exercise generally leaves both participant and eyewitnesses feeling lower than floor paint. (There is the added risk here of appearing to denigrate Diane Sawyer, a former colleague who showed me kindness, humor and goodwill. No denigration is intended.)

On the other hand (*fill . . . in . . . the NUMBERS?*), I keep hearing the voice of Willy Loman's wife, and I think it applies to *Sunday Morning*: "Attention, attention must finally be paid. . . !"

Few people who have *not* worked inside *Sunday Morning*— and this includes its most devoted admirers and reviewers— have ever quite appreciated the program for the infinitely nuanced ecosystem that it is, or was. The program has been a victim, to that extent, of its own successful illusion.

Critics tend to describe *Sunday Morning* as "folksy" or "down-to-earth" and Charles Kuralt as "avuncular," and to conclude that the program succeeds because of its appeal to "the heartland." While to the show's natural predators within CBS News—and there have been a few—it was simply "that show about deer running through the woods."

This analysis hardly accounts for either of the two groups that form an unlikely but dominant bloc of *Sunday Morning*'s viewership: upper-income, upper-educated suburban managerial types and low-income urban blacks.

The program's creators described it as a video version of the Sunday newspaper—those leisurely essays, that handsome art. And there is the shrewd producer who decided *Sunday Morning* was a secular American liturgy, a ritual progression from sin to celebration, from hellfire to forgiveness.

She cited the stunning trumpet votary opening (by Gottfried Reiche, an eighteenth-century trumpeter in one of Bach's ensembles), to the welcome by the Right Reverend Kuralt, to the sermon (the often disturbing and morally charged cover story), to the bulletins and announcements (the correspondents' confab, the resident critic), to the offertory (the fine-arts or jazz piece), to the communion (the profile of someone who has sacrificed for the well-being of others), to the final prayer (the meditative nature segment that concludes the program).

My personal theory is that *Sunday Morning* is sui generis. But I digress. Let us now separate the pastoral illusion of *Sunday Morning* from its tempestuous realities.

Sunday Morning was conceived by a CBS News president named Bill Leonard. The "electronic Sunday paper" was his formulation. He put it on the air in January 1979.

But in every important aesthetic and moral sense, the program belongs to its senior executive producer of eight years (until he was abruptly plucked from the program in 1987): its auteur, its Ahab, a broadcast outlaw of magnificent gifts and calamitous furies, a fanged and profane tyrant whose name, appropriately, approximates the sound of a wolverine tearing flesh. *Sunday Morning* belongs to Shad Northshield.

Network television boasts a vast rogues' gallery of misfit managers, atavistic executives, raving idiots savants. Robert J. Northshield is to this gallery as Genghis Khan is to the Joint Chiefs of Staff. A legendary figure within broadcast circles— a bowlegged, bearded man with violent eyebrows and a taste for turquoise belt buckles and incendiary shirts—he is one of its half dozen authentic geniuses.

Yet at 66, Northshield is not so well-known outside the industry. This may be because his path to a position of ultimate visibility (news-division president, let's say) has been blocked a number of times by little pink dismissal notices, which Northshield, not an entirely unsentimental man, keeps framed in the bathroom of his Westchester County fortress.

I see that I am in danger of committing one of those affectionate sketches of a lovable rogue. (I knew I shouldn't have begun this. But *attention, attention must be paid*.)

Let us remain clear-eyed. "Lovable" is not a word that should be placed within a quarter mile of Shad Northshield. He is a man of wounding rages. To work on his "folksy" program was to suffer the constant and instantaneous danger, as one cameraman described it, of being raked by a cat. Shad's sarcasm was public, and darkly brilliant, and brutal. Nearly everyone who worked for him got raked, at one time or another. Me included. "ARE YOU SO GODDAMN ARROGANT YOU DON'T EVEN HAVE TO GODDAMN REHEARSE YOUR GODDAMN SCRIPT?" This by way of greeting in the all-ears control room after I'd flubbed a word, and I am using "goddamn" here as a euphemism. I don't even want to talk about the time I wished Kuralt "Happy Easter" one goddamn Easter Sunday.

And yet talented people wanted to work for Shad Northshield. The *Sunday Morning* staff remained exceptionally cohesive until that 1987 pogrom. Many of the original producers, videotape editors and technical crew are still with the show. These people are not masochists. They scarcely relished being victims of Northshield's tirades. It was the Dr. Jekyll aspect of the man that compelled them—compelled all of us—not the Mr. Hyde.

For this was the side of Northshield's nature that flowed through *Sunday Morning* and gave it a radiance without precedent in the history of the medium.

This was the aspect of an uncommonly well-read man, a collector of art and a lover of music from Mozart to Mingus, a political scholar and a published ornithologist, an accomplished photographer of wildlife and a journalist (he came out of the Chicago school, having reported for the old *Sun*) of exacting usage and clarity. Unifying these diverse talents and interests was an undeviating moral insistence, a passion for the authentic and the good. A passion for American excellence.

That passion had already left its mark on the American consciousness. As executive producer of *The Huntley-Brinkley Report* on NBC in the mid-1960s, Northshield insisted on giving primary coverage to two disturbing stories—the Vietnam War and the civil-rights movement. He thus helped make them unavoidable issues on the national agenda. "I believe that television in America has changed history a lot in only two instances," he said recently. "Civil rights and Vietnam. That was because the coverage was so absolutely massive."

Northshield improvised an astonishing array of rules, or aesthetics—"styles," he called them—that continue to form the recognizable design of *Sunday Morning*, even in his absence. Most of these styles amount to a shrewd *reduction* of television technique instead of a new overlay, a Zen-like paring away of artifice. ("To work on this show, I've had to unlearn every manipulative trick I'd built up over twenty-six years," a cameraman once told me.)

Interview subjects on *Sunday Morning*, for instance, face the camera, not some invisible interlocutor at a forty-five–degree angle. As a matter of fact, correspondents on this program tend to *remain* invisible; they are seldom heard and more rarely seen. And yet the writing, on this intensely narrative program, had to meet Shad's exacting standards of grammar, or else.

"This has to do with respect for the people who are watching," said Northshield. "I have no idea who they are or how many there are." He concluded with typically perfect grammar and imperfect decorum: "I never play the common game known as 'fuck the viewer.' "

Then there is the style of photographing works of art at an exhibition ("NOT EXHIBIT, GODDAMNIT!") On *Sunday Morning*, a work is first shown full frame; then its various segments are shown in close-up; then there is a final full shot. This sequence, Northshield believes, replicates the eye movements of a museum visitor. (As with many other elements of a *Sunday Morning* piece, the museum segments are accompanied by long stretches of silence or muted natural sound. No haranguing narration; no prodding, insinuating music. Another distinctive style.)

Perhaps the most famous of Northshield's styles is the endpiece, the wordless nature segment that concludes the program—"the deer running through the woods." Besides showcasing a realm of deep interest to Northshield, this segment brings each week's program out of whatever anxieties its cover story and topical pieces might have aroused and toward a climactic affirmation.

"People find something they want to find there" was Northshield's Taoist explanation of the endpiece when I asked him about it not long ago. "There's no pressure on them to think or feel anything. Certainly not anything specific."

Northshield also relieved me of a misconception about the endpiece. I had always assumed that this segment had a partly utilitarian purpose: Its length could be expanded or contracted to allow each program to finish on the dot. But, "Naw, the endpiece always ran a minute forty-five," growled North-shield, as if this was something any goddamned fool who'd done time on the program should know, which is probably true. "The 'accordion' was the IPF. That's when I'd talk into Charlie's ear: Cut it down, go long."

The IPF is Kuralt's live mid-program conversation with CBS News correspondents. Northshield invented the IPF. He also assigned it its jargony-sounding initials. I had worked on the program about three years before I thought to ask Ken Sable, the director, exactly what IPF stood for. Sable took me aside and gently explained that IPF stood for International Pig-Fuck.

I could go on serenading. Attention must be paid to the gifted producers and videotape editors who have weathered *Sunday Morning*'s many storms, and who now sustain the aesthetic link to Northshield's original vision. Virtually no attention has been paid here to Charles Kuralt, who is (as it happens) a great deal more intelligent than avuncular and who performs small miracles of technical virtuosity at will—bringing, for instance, the empathetic tonal shifts and inflections of a great jazz singer to his incomparable narrations. The wedding of Kuralt to *Sunday Morning*—an afterthought, in the organizing confusion of 1979—was a lucky stroke that surpassed even Northshield's intuition.

But this risky piece was prompted by a seeing of red, a welling up of old nausea (*fill . . . in . . . the NUMBERS?*). To the issue, then:

What happened on that March Friday in 1987 was a violation within a violation. On a day of insupportable losses to the news division, the profitable and repeatedly acclaimed *Sunday Morning* took the hardest proportional hit. Seven of the show's eleven producers were let go, a traumatizing loss.

In the same stroke, *Sunday Morning* lost its cohesion as a self-contained unit. The staff survivors were herded from their hive eleven stories above a car dealership into the main news barn across the street. There they were merged organization-ally with the Weekend News, both under the control of a ca-reer hard-news executive in her mid-40s named Linda Mason.

Northshield had already been disposed of. It was the damnedest coincidence. Howard Stringer, then the CBS News president, had pulled Northshield from the program just a few weeks before the layoffs—to develop a high-priority prime-time magazine show, you understand. A pilot aired, then the project evaporated. And Shad Northshield remains in CBS limbo, developing, developing—as if genius at that news di-vision runs as deep as its supply of Diane Sawyers.

And so it was that *Sunday Morning* began, ever so subtly but in ways unmistakable to a close viewer, to be something other than *Sunday Morning.*

The moral insistence started to waver ever so slightly. A new sports commentator named Bill Geist, who had written wonderful essays at *The New York Times*, felt at liberty to poke occasional fun at his subjects—the grammatically inept Yogi Berra, for instance, or those hard-to-figure Japanese. No one objected. Ridiculing the subject of a piece had been close to a capital offense under Northshield.

The show's passion for excellence softened a little, into an enthusiasm for trends. Fashionable people had appeared on *Sunday Morning* in the past, but now they began to appear *as fashionable people,* and not as incidental components of a larger story. The impeccable writing and editing of the scripts began to show lapses into misusage, cant, vernacular. Perhaps most confusing to a core staff that had been trained to produce seg-ments that were *intrinsically* interesting, there began to de-velop a demand for a *topical* angle to each piece, a sensitivity to the viewer's presumed question, "Why am I watching this *now?"* ("BECAUSE IT'S GODDAMN BRILLIANT!" one can hear the old auteur bellow, approximately.)

"With Shad," recalls one disaffected staff member, "you sat down and talked with him for an hour before you began your research on a piece. Then you had to call him every day from the field. Now there is no intellectual give-and-take before you walk out the door. And not much reaction afterward. In the old days, you'd work your ass off on a story, and if it worked, boy, it was such a high! Shad might say nothing more than 'Swell,' or 'It'll do,' but often there'd be tears in his eyes."

Linda Mason does not see *Sunday Morning* as being in decline, and she offers a plausible argument—buttressed by a two-to-one ratings lead over new competition, *Sunday Today* on NBC—to vindicate her hard-news reinterpretation of the program.

"We've been able, in the past two years, to engage in 'stretching,' " she offers, using without irony a word that might have made Northshield's jawline twitch. "If we continue to do the same things, we become in danger of stereotyping ourselves.

"We've expanded our horizons. We did an hour and a half out of the Reagan-Gorbachev summit. We took a look at the New South for the Atlanta convention, a look at New Orleans for the Republican one. We did an hour and a half from Japan; China, for Gorbachev-Deng."

As for the question of her divided attention span, between *Sunday Morning* and the Weekend News, Ms. Mason answers crisply, "Charles has never been happier. And I screen every piece that airs."

The staff has regained its old numerical strength. (This is a double-edged blessing, by my admittedly subjective lights, as replacements move the unit ever farther from Northshield's original vision.) *Sunday Today* has not cut into *Sunday Morning*'s absolute numbers; on the contrary, the total viewer pool available to both programs has expanded. And a new high command at CBS News seems well-disposed toward *Sunday Morning*, a significant departure from the sneering, leavened with indifference, of the Howard Stringer–Van Gordon Sauter years.

Still.

Sunday Morning is no longer what it once was, something

rare in any collaborative medium and virtually unheard-of in commercial television: a work of art founded on a single vision. It is a testament to the power of that vision that deep strains of it remain under the more prosaic stewardship of an executive who, understandably, has her own priorities and agenda.

That work of art was reduced to merely good television by corporate bean counters less interested in golden ideas than in golden hair. How ironic—how awful a testament to them— that in the end, they weren't even able to purchase the golden hair.

L.A. Law: D.O.A.

A new series by the creator of Hill Street Blues *has a long rap sheet of sins, including a television rarity— trying too hard*

It's the dawn of another typical workday at the high-powered, comprehensive-service L.A. law firm McKenzie, Brackman, Chaney & Kuzak. The subplots are still wandering into the story line, and the ambient confusion is just starting to rise from the sound track. But Arnie Becker, rakish, womanizing junior partner, has already figured out what the terrible smell is. It's Chaney, over in the corner office. Chaney croaked in the night, one claw still clutching his desk appointment calendar, like a blatant, ironic detail.

"He's dead," observes Arnie's secretary, slowly lowering her can of spray disinfectant.

"He is," agrees Arnie. "I had dibs on his office."

Bam! Opening titles: *L.A. Law*. Executive producer and co-creator, Steven Bochco. . . .

175

"Creative control" used to be the Golden Fleece of prime-time entertainment—the phantom "vision" in television. If a sensitive, idealistic young screenwriter could only find some way to wrest creative control from the bad network vice-presidents, then he or she could instill *content,* could essay *dramatic shading,* might even venture a teensy step in the direction of *values*—certainly *production values.*

It was a comfortable myth; comfortable because it would never be tested. Looming like Cybill Shepherd's kneecaps in the path of such righteous impulse was an impediment of diabolic cunning: that bureaucratic answer to the Undead known as the *writer-producer.* So long as the best TV screenwriters were rewarded with an administrative stake in their projects' ratings success, with all the incremental wealth that the "producer" mantle guaranteed, they would be highly disinclined to venture out beyond the safe, soggy boundaries of the unthreatening, the formulaic, the vanilla.

Then five years ago that comfortable myth was—aiiee!—fulfilled. *Hill Street Blues* flashed onto NBC like a meteor to wipe away the brontosaurian limits on action drama's capacity for realism, complexity, authentic dialogue, moral ambiguity—to say nothing of plausible tenderness, earned affection, humor and grief. Chief among its creators at MTM Enterprises was Steven Bochco, a brash and brilliant young producer who had risen through the ranks of salaried writing jobs at Universal Studios and NBC. At MTM, the New York–born Bochco welded the contradictory mandates of writer and producer into a seamless artistic function. He limned cops-and-lowlifes dialogue with the ear of a young Dashiell Hammett. He orchestrated interweaving subplots like William Saroyan. All the while he fought, as a producer, *on behalf of* the show's birthright—to take thematic chances, spend money.

He was personally rewarded with six Emmys (*Hill Street* won a total of twenty-six during his tenure there), a Peabody, a shower of humanitarian awards and, more important, the

Golden Fleece itself: At the age of 38, Steven Bochco, poet and protector of prime time, gained unfettered access to creative control.

What lessons are to be learned, then, from the early signs that Bochco's new *L.A. Law* is a disagreeable mess, bordering on a monstrosity?

The ambient sound divides like a cell; divides again as the denizens of McKenzie, Brackman, Chaney & Kuzak (oops, make that McKenzie, Brackman & Kuzak) struggle with their responses to the death of the senior partner. Through the obligatory murmurings—"What's going on?" "Mr. Chaney's dead." "Oh, my God!"—there emerge a few wisps that hint at this law firm's prevailing regard for the moderating virtues. "One minute," a voice is heard to drawl from the gaggle, "you're hip-deep in the tax code. The next—" there is a snap, as of fingers.

"The guy's so stiff you could put him in a museum," a cop joshes, and someone else says, "His feet are, like, frozen." A jocular voice asks, "Can we have a little *reverence* here?" There is a close-up of the corpse being hauled away, lurching and yawing. "Turn him, *turn* him—no, the other way!" "Be careful, you're gonna lose him!" Wittily, Chaney's mortal remains go *clunk* against a doorjamb and sag like yesterday's enchiladas suizas to the carpet as a secretary's voice, off-camera, answers a ringing phone: "Mr. Chaney's office—no, I'm sorry, he's not available right now."

Clearly, these are not the offices of *Owen Marshall: Counselor at Law*. Perry Mason would probably flee this place in tears. But, hey, we're still just in the amenities stage of this two-hour pilot episode; we're getting *acquainted* with these people. The serious slime is still a couple of commercial breaks ahead.

A Bochco-induced sense of extremism, of set-piece scenes jacked up to their ultimate shock-value payload, quickly begins to insinuate itself. ("Spiking," this is tenderly called in the business.) We meet Kuzak, the ensemble's designated empathy figure (it helps to have a scorecard, or a press release), as he broods double-breastedly over the arrest charges filed against his thuggish, Method-actorish client in a jail cell. Kuzak is played with moist and cow-eyed passivity by the alarmingly well-groomed Harry Hamlin.

Is Kuzak's client a wrongo, a bad apple? Just listen to Kuzak, reading from the rap sheet:

"Says here she was beaten, raped—*and when her wig fell off during the assault, she was tossed into a Dumpster,*" (My italics; I love the wig part. *Quel* pathos.)

The client is somehow unmoved by this remembrance of things past. Twisting his mouth into a sneer the approximate shape of an L.A. freeway cloverleaf, he avers that it wasn't that way at all. "She followed me outta a liquor store," he leers. "Sez she'll do the three of us for fifty bucks." As the hisses and catcalls begin to cascade from America's living rooms ("Minimum wage! Minimum wage!"), the wastrel sinks deeper into perfidy: "You talked to my *father* yet? For a thousand bucks she'll fold like a deck chair."

"That's doubtful," ripostes Kuzak, with icy civility. "She has . . . *acute leukemia!*"

Yowee! This is better than Martina versus Chris Evert Lloyd. Just when our necks are starting to get sore from all this back-and-forth swiveling, this ground-stroke rally of one-down-manship, we are mercifully wisked back to the plush offices of McKenzie, Brackman & Kuzak, where a working luncheon has been convened to indulge a little trendy cynicism.

A secretary (need one bother to say "comely"?) passes a wrapped sandwich to Arnie (Corbin Bernsen), he of the upwardly mobile nostrils. "This is *tongue*, honey," cracks Arnie over his shoulder. "Are you trying to tell me something?"

More subplots rush, like so many white blood cells, into the story line. In a courtroom, a flinty judge summons the bickering prosecutor (female) and public defender (male) to his bench to ask the legalistic question "You two hot for each other, or what?" (Spike No. 1.) "I'm mad 'cause I lowered my standards," retorts the prosecutor. (Spike No. 2.) "Yeah," snorts the defender, "along with your skirt." (Spike No. 3, but don't start counting your pulse rate yet—the judge is about to announce that he needs a potty break.)

Lawyers (Kuzak included) spin deals over drinks, furtive as Florentine courtiers. The patriarch of the law firm, Leland McKenzie (Richard Dysart), nudges Kuzak to see to the defense needs of the millionaire's son turned wig snatcher and Dumpster tosser. Kuzak is a silent (but acquiescing) partner to a brutal courtroom cross-examination of the thug's victim— who, it turns out, not only was raped, beaten, de-wigged, Dumpsterized and leukemia-ridden but is *black*. (Spike!) Kuzak's associates seek to portray the woman as a terminal thrill-seeker—"Gather ye rosebuds while ye may, Miss Moore!" (Spike!)

And meanwhile, the viewer's sensibilities scan this sordid little universe of preeners, posturers, viperous shysters and zomboid exploiters for—a hero. Or, absent a "hero" (quaint term!), a locus of sympathy, some avatar of hope. If not Othello, then at least Daniel J. Travanti. And scan and scan, but no such figure emerges from the sulfur. *L.A. Law* seems truly a vision of urban, professional America as unremitting hell.

Instead of finding hope, we get relief from the mendacity in the form of black humor—or what Bochco apparently flatters himself is black humor. Arnie and his hired private investigator, a punk-cropped Valley toughie in a satin tank top that delineates some Serious Prime-Time Nipple, are perusing some covert photographs of a divorce-seeking woman's husband and his doxy.

"And here's the pièce de résistance," snickers the gal gumshoe, handing over a glossy. "George and his honey poolside on a chaise lounge, engaged in a sex act usually described by a two-digit number." (Spike! Spike!)

A moment later, the femme fosdick has turned philosophical. As Arnie prepares for lunch with his soon-to-be-devastated client, she probes the ineffable: "I swear I don't understand you, Arnie. You take this poor woman to some snitzy restaurant. You slap *these* on the table. She goes into the ladies' room and ralphs up fifty bucks worth of lunch all over the velvet wallpaper. What's the point?"

It is a question that must have occurred to more than a few viewers by this time. Is Bochco asking us to take these dreadful people seriously or for laughs? The tone veers drunkenly between the two attitudes. In the two-hour episode's most gratuitous and painfully off-key scene—Chaney's funeral—one colleague ends his groping eulogy with the archly written line "If I had to describe him in one word, it would be—'fiduciary.'" The succeeding eulogist, a newly hired secretary, reveals herself to be . . . a transvestite. She met Chaney in a gay bar. *L.A. Law* is at this point trafficking in what someone considerably to the left of the late Meese Commission—the oversigned, for example—might unflinchingly term "smut."

Black humor, properly sustained, artfully rendered, is a welcome device for a prime-time series. But it is a testimony to this pilot episode's ultimate soullessness that the satiric tone is contradicted—subverted—by a recurring streak of white-knuckled Liberal Oblige. This violent mood shift occurs mainly when the Women of the Firm are onscreen. Jill Eikenberry as counselor Ann Kelsey gets to declaim a lot of feminist-idealist sentiments on the order of "I am not against earning a buck, Leland, as long as we don't sell off our humanity in the process." (Meanwhile, the episode's "little" women—Arnie's divorce client, for instance—have to content themselves with more plebian sentiments, such as "Chew on those numbers, you impotent piece of snot.") The I-Am-Woman fugues are no doubt traceable to Bochco's cocreator on *L.A. Law*, Terry Louise Fisher, a veteran of *Cagney and Lacey* and no stranger herself to the delights of creative control.

So benumbed was I at the end of this two-hour crawl through the swamps of hip cynicism—and so put off by the facile last-minute anointing of the schlemiel-like Kuzak as a Really Good Guy at Heart—that I reached into antiquity for possible parallels. I flipped on a cassette of the original episode of *Hill Street Blues* to see whether Bochco had suffered similar catastrophes in the early stages of his great masterwork.

I found no such problems. True, certain Bochco tendencies had not yet been smoothed into their eventual subtlety—characters took turns hogging center stage for long set-piece turns, as when Belker complained that he had not been allowed to bite a suspect on the leg. There was the now-famous vignette of unbridled horror, the stark shotgunning of two highly sympathetic officers. There were oversimplifications of personality.

But at the center of that first *Hill Street* stood Daniel J. Travanti as Captain Frank Furillo, an unmistakable rock of benign authority and (dare I write it? It's the *d* word) decency, and, however compromised he was by the frailties of the flesh, duty. And around Furillo swarmed a myriad of grubby, irritable, violent, tender and comical people—citizens of, and vulnerable to, a society that was both monstrous and radiant. In *L.A. Law*, by contrast, the monsters have taken over—both on the outside and in the inner circles of the ensemble cast.

What has changed in the five years between the premieres of *Hill Street Blues* and *L.A. Law?* It is possible that Steven Bochco, with his undisputed ear for the rhythms of American life, is responding to some wrenching downdraft in the country's capacity for redemption? Has he thus created a greater—if infinitely darker—masterpiece than the series that won him fame? (And if so: Is he accountable, even granting his genius, for the act of pandering to the dark appetites?)

Or is the explanation for *L.A. Law* more limited, more narrowly behavioristic in scope? Is it a simple testimony that *too much* creative control, even in an industry as rudderless as network television, results in a tarnishing orgy of hubris? A tendency to reach ever more wantonly for the next spike?

It's hard to say for sure. But in either case—to borrow from the eloquence of Kuzak's client-thug when he heard that Miss Moore had leukemia—that's too bad.

Sorry, Maury

Fox's A Current Affair *reflects the sordid sensibilities of King Rupert, while wasting the talents—and hairdo—of its anchor, Maury Povich*

"*S*ay a prayer for Sarah—that she is in the world someplace!"

"Tonight, a live interview with Virginia LaLonde—just out of jail today for hiding daughter Nicole in a custody case. . . ."

"Father Tormenta, do you see any conflict between your role as a priest and your role as a professional wrestler?"

The iconographic symbol of Rupert Murdoch's latest piece of journalistic turpitude, *A Current Affair*, on Fox Television, is for some damn reason a translucent pyramid. Something to do with psychic power and Egyptians and sex triangles and other standard news concepts, no doubt. But if you watch the program (starring . . . oops, I mean *anchored by* Maury Povich) for any prolonged period of time—say, two nights in a row—it isn't hard to think of a more explicitly representative design.

That would be a line drawing of a mollusk. Or perhaps a boiled potato reclining on a couch. Either would symbolize Citizen Murdoch's celebrated esteem for, and vision of, the American audience, whence derives his long-held journalistic mission to stoke that audience's burning involvement with the Great Public Issues of the Day.

Perhaps a *mashed* potato would be more closely evocative, or the mollusk should be depicted with an itty-bitty horoscope on its spandexed lap.

And isn't that a coy title, by the way? *A Current Affair*. Ooh-la-la! Ladies—*ladies*! Mr. Povich is a Serious Anchorman! And besides, he's *married* (to NBC anchorwoman Connie Chung)!

Vintage Murdoch, to find some smutty trope on the phrase "current affairs"—the concerns of politics and social policy—to identify his first national venture into video news.

Back when Murdoch was still an Australian, and while he was still gorging himself exclusively on American print-journalism properties, I used to get a strained chuckle or two at parties by floating a mock rumor: Rupert was poised to take over *Screw* magazine and turn it into a *sleazy tabloid*. With *A Current Affair*, he has actually performed the analogue: He's taken the trappings of local television newscasts and turned them into something lurid and trivial.

Right from the program's opening graphics (it's syndicated weeknights in twenty-five major markets), there is no possible room for doubt as to its, well, its intentions.

Fade in on smoke wafting across the purplish screen, curling tendrils of smoke, tendrils of *blue* smoke. Cigarette smoke? Cigarette smoke from the nostrils of someone's inamorata having a postcoital puff? MAURY, WHERE ARE YOU?! Ah, but now comes rolling and tumbling that translucent pyramid, rolling and tumbling right out at us from deepest computer font—to be bolted to the show's title with the electro-replicated vibrato of a flung knife striking a breastbone.

Then Povich appears. Nice casting here. You're doing Tempestuous News for career matrons who put on their faces while riding the commuter bus, you don't want to play it too gigoloish, too John Tesh. You go more for the chief of surgery at Shopping Mall View General Hospital on the soaps. A little-weathered-but-still-boyishly-tousled type, who'd have the class to sweep a gal away for drinks at the Coach and Dragon instead of trying to hustle her into the nearest Ramada Inn. That's our chap Maury: strictly business, yet having a hard time keeping down a wry twinkle. He is seated behind a medium-range, land-based anchor desk—hey, this is a *news program,* after all—all jawline and cheekbones, the world-weary rumpled elegance of a disinherited Polish prince.

"Tonight," Povich might begin, with the sidelong baleful nod of a man about to announce the defaulting of the Brazilian economic system, "the bizarre story of those rattlesnake murders in New Jersey. . . ." And: "By *day,* he tends to the needs of his flock. . . ."

Povich (who in a sojourning bicoastal career has actually performed credibly as a local-news anchorman) presides over one of the more—oh—surrealistic news-gathering menageries in the annals of man's quest for information. Say what you will about *A Current Affair* (and the bill of particulars is longer than a sleepless night), the program, by God, *deploys.* It *reaches the scene.*

It is the Cable News Network of crime-blotter stories, the *60 Minutes* of slime. Take a few lousy nude photos of your drugged psychoanalytic patients, seduce a couple of women in your congregation, and you can pretty well count on having some case-hardened cookie in bulletproof lip gloss shoving a Fox microphone in your face and asking you just what this is all about.

Credit here is due the ferocious mobilizing instincts of *A Current Affair*'s production crew. The entire staff numbers only about forty, sopping wet—and that includes executives, producers, reporters, crew, videotape editors, even secretaries—

a hopelessly, laughably inadequate garrison compared with the hundred-plus phalanxes of any medium-size local-news department.

But how they scramble! Hopping whirlybirds from midtown Manhattan to the New York airports on minutes' notice, whisking about the country for same-day coverage of fast-breaking trash, the reporters doubling as their own writer-producers . . . the energy and sheer technical competence of the *Current Affair* staff are its most appealing resources.

Too bad those resources cannot be used for good rather than trivial.

Did some bridegroom in Los Angeles have the transcendent pig luck (and requisite vulgarity) to be videotaping his own mother as she awoke in her hotel-room bed *at the precise instant an earthquake erupted in Southern California*? ("Hey, that's exciting, Mom—you got to be in a *California earthquake*," says the guy, taping away. *"OOOOOOOOH! Where's a good place to go?"* squeals Mom, flailing about in her nightie. "So, Mom. Tell me," the guy croons on. "How do you feel about your first earthquake experience?") Well, damned if they don't all show up for a live interview on *A Current Affair*: Mom, the bridegroom, the bride, the videotape, even old Dad, looking stunned and humiliated, but still not about to blow this chance for a little national airtime.

In these situations, Povich demonstrates a fairly impressive talent for deadpan camp. "Were you angry with your son at all for keeping the camera rolling?" he reasonably asks the mother in this Dadaist farce. "No, not at all," she replies in her fascinatingly competent broadcast-interview voice. "He was given a great opportunity, and I wasn't about to interfere with it. . . ."

Or, say, another newlywed couple get so biliously drunk on champagne at the reception that they crawl on to their honeymoon flight in a haze of hell-raising riot and proceed to gross out their fellow passengers so foully that true nastiness ensues. Hey! Primo candidates for *A Current Affair*, where they grinningly own up to wry Maury regarding their scabrous behavior.

Again, Povich's craggy, ever-so-slightly-weathered presence is of the utmost importance to the mix. No flaxen-maned young steroid-enhanced mannequin could successfully anchor *A Current Affair*. What's essential here is the legitimizing counterweight of *authority*.

Rupert Murdoch's vision of American life is so sulfurous, so marinated in morbid contempt for the common man, that he needs a figurehead with some hint of savoir faire—some air of irony—to mask the program's essential condescending cruelty. The locus of identification must be with the bemused anchor, not with the parade of mountebanks, Tammyfayes, buffoons and monsters who pass before his squinty gaze.

Thus, last fall, when Robert Bork's Supreme Court nomination was in the balance, it was Povich's chuckly reaction that leavened a series of "man-on-the-street" interviews that portrayed Americans as jovial know-nothings on the Bork issue. ("He looks like King Tut from the old *Batman* series." "It's vague, it's really vague. I read in *Time* magazine that he was dressed up like a monk or something." "I know they keep interrupting my favorite shows—Bork doing this, Bork doing that. I think they should have a certain time for the Bork shows.")

Not even Povich, however, can always save Murdoch's lumpenprole formula from revealing its concocted underpinnings. The program's lurid worldview has been imported from the tabloid pages of *The New York Post* by such Murdoch minions as its former metropolitan editor, the Australian Steve Dunleavy. Now, as a reporter for the show, Dunleavy helps invest *A Current Affair* with the paper's demimonde fascination with crime, sex and celebrity glitz.

One of the regular contributors on *A Current Affair* is *Post* gossip columnist Cindy Adams, a woman of such hard-shell vacuousness that her lacquered beehive hairdo seems to be some sort of self-induced parody of her prefrontal lobe. Doubtless with the gleeful encouragement of Murdoch, Ms. Adams fancies herself the type of gal who can get in there and mix chummily with the stars, then bring their impossibly glamorous world down to the beetle-brained terms of the average Joe and Jane. (While interviewing her Good Friend Jill St. John, Ms. Adams popped the question that must have been on the lips of every woman in America—"What do you do with your eye makeup and hair when you're fishing up in the Rockies with Bob Wagner?")

During last December's summit meeting between President Reagan and Soviet General Secretary Mikhail Gorbachev (which necessitated the dispatching of Povich to Washington so that he could introduce a segment about a smut-dealing psychiatrist while framed inspirationally by the Capitol Building), Ms. Adams was thawed out from her cybernetic freeze unit in order to have a little Neanderthal fun at the expense of the two First Ladies.

It was Ms. Adams's witty conceit to portray the ceremonial encounters between Nancy Reagan and Raisa Gorbachev in terms of a heavyweight-boxing match.

"Well, as First Ladies go, these two are the top contenders in the world," Ms. Adams brayed over videotaped footage of the two women. "The two heavyweights, Nancy R. and Raisa G., weighed in this morning at the White House. . . . So far, they're equally matched in hair tints . . . but Nancy does cop a few extra points in furs. . . . As for Raisa, she's the first First Lady of the U.S.S.R. not to look like Buddy Hackett. . . ."

And so on in this sidesplitting vein. The real problem was that once Ms. Adams built up a little cruising ballast, she was next to impossible to hush up. Povich finally managed to wrench the conversation toward a pair of incredulous guests standing by in a studio: Sally Quinn, the Washington bête noire novelist, and Sheila Tate, former press secretary to Mrs. Reagan. Small veins popped in the temples of these two sophisticates as they strained for every forgotten dictum of Junior League scene-rescuing lore.

Ms. Quinn made a nice attempt to guide Adams's gibberish into a discussion of how Raisa Gorbachev had been obliged to learn the nuances of state ceremony on her own, without the guidance of a secretary or public-relations staff. But not even Miss Manners herself could have peeled Cindy from her comic premise.

"Oh, they're like two gladiators! They're squaring off! They're like Schwarzenegger and Stallone!" she yammered as Ms. Tate became intensely interested in her hem and even Povich began to make little involuntary grunts of animal warning. "It's like Raisa is made of pure, untempered steel! And Nancy is not exactly a Twinkie! You know, we used to say about her in the old days, if she fell down, all she'd break was her hair. . . ."

Well, one could only feel sorry for Povich's discomfiture, but what goes around comes around, as they say. In consenting to front for a communications mogul whose contempt for the common man is already the stuff of twentieth-century legend, one risks getting stained by the occasional detritus from the pig's bladder.

And—speaking, as we seem to be, of Rupert Murdoch— from where exactly does he derive his peculiar passion for portraying proletarian life in its most prurient, puerile terms? A somewhat worked-over question, admittedly, after nearly a decade now of acclimation to the man's sordid publications.

Yet, as one watches *A Current Affair*, some fresh clues do emerge.

In his 1941 meditation on the leering vulgarity of British twopenny postcards, "The Art of Donald McGill," George Orwell thought he had located, amid all the renderings of chamber pots and women with stuck-out behinds, a hidden affirmation of a working-class moral code.

"What they are doing," Orwell wrote of the cards, "is to give expression to the Sancho Panza view of life"—to the little fat man in all of us, the "unofficial self, the voice of the belly protesting against the soul. . . .

"It will not do to condemn [the cards] on the ground that they are vulgar and ugly," Orwell warned. "That is exactly what they are meant to be. Their whole meaning and virtue is in their unredeemed lowness, not only in the sense of obscenity, but lowness of outlook in every direction whatever. . . . They stand for the worm's-eye view of life, for the music-hall world. . . . Like the music halls, they are a sort of saturnalia, a harmless rebellion against virtue."

What the Australian Murdoch has mainly done, it seems, has been to appropriate this hallowed, and peculiarly British, "Sancho Panza view of life"—but without any trace of the essential compassion for Sancho Panza. His print and broadcast versions of those old twopenny postcards retain the leer (and add the menace) but omit the underlying smile of affirmation.

Murdoch is free to litter the American landscape with his twopenny postcards, of course—God knows there will always be a receptive clientele. What seems regrettable is the complicity of men and women who have some claim to the standards and disciplines of legitimate broadcast journalism. They have become willing minions in the ongoing creation of Rupert Murdoch's odious pyramid.

THE MALE EUNUCH

A gaggle of new shows about abandoned men make
up in bawls what they lack in, uh, . . .

Attention! Attention, Jackie Collins! You have been granted literary amnesty! All of your cheap, tawdry, sleazy, cynical, hard-edged, ball-busting potboilers about Hollywood sex life have been reconsidered in light of recent efforts and found barely palatable after all! Please proceed to nearest word processor and begin emergency draft of new tell-all miniseries to be called. . .

Hollywood Men Without Mommies!

I mean, suddenly they're all over Beverly Hills, apparently. Schlimazel chic. Bigger than the Brat Pack. Six-deep at the Polo Lounge. De-phallused phalanxes of Lonely Guys. Tragic dweebs in their Missoni jackets, blubbering into their seafood stir-fry—their women done gone and left them, *oh*, yeah. (How did the caption of that wonderful *New Yorker* cartoon go? "Would you please have the orchestra play 'Tea for Two,' and I'll just have tea for one, thank you.")

You think you've been hardened to every shock, every depravity the sexual revolution had to offer? Well, brace yourself, pal. Get ready to simper with the . . . *Men Without Mommies!*

Listen to a few titles out there: *Empty Nest. Dear John. Men. Raising Miranda. Pussy Whipped.* (All right, I made that one up to see if you were paying attention.)

Consider a few of the plot premises: Guy's wife leaves him for his best friend. Guy's wife leaves him to find herself. Different guy's wife leaves *him* to find *herself.* Divorced marriage counselor, a guy. Bunch of guys seeking out one another for guidance and support.

Need a hankie, guy? How about a guy wire, to hang yourself?

You can see why we need a badass bassoon blast of Jackie Collins, just to sound a needed note of butch fatalism amid the reedy woodwinds. These newly rampant schlimazels, these Men Without Mommies, are all so picturesquely *chipper*, so goddamned *adorable* in their coping, so *competent* in their nurturing of various leftover children, so . . . so *Alan Alda* about it all, that what they need is to be turned into Collins characters for about ten hours over five nights, so they can go out boozing and whoring and looting and burning and pillaging and sending out anonymous letters drenched in chicken blood to certain parties. Not that I *or* Jackie Collins would necessarily recommend such behavior to viewers watching at (broken) home.

I mean, what's the fun of being abandoned by Mommy, if you can't have a good time?

But *noooooooooo.* These prime-time putzes have all been stun-gunned into a kind of moist domesticity. So beatific! So self-denyingly dutiful! What sort of composite portrait of post-marital American man, exactly, are we getting here? Is it the martyred self-image of their many male creators? Or is it a subtle lampooning from the jaundiced viewpoints of the several women whose credits adorn a few of the shows? (Who knows, after all, better than Mommy?)

The scary thing is that from series to series it's almost impossible to tell a difference.

Take *Men* (please), a Universal series scheduled as a mid-season replacement on ABC. *Men* is about these four . . . guys, who are pals, see, and who have to constantly adjust to today's ever-changing social trends. (No snickering, please, this is an *hour-long drama*, dammit!) They *cope* a lot with the contemporary problems they face. They seek out one another for guidance and support. They have these regular *guy* names, like Steve and Charlie and Paul and Danny. They have subplots. They trade likable banter, and they have meaningful male raps while playing roundball down at the Y. They wear circle glasses. They play song trivia, screaming stuff like "Cozy Cole, 'Topsy, Part II,' 1962!" They live in a world of poker night and pizza cartons and laundry baskets, and each of them is capable, at any second, of fixing the others with a sincere kind of look and saying, "Hey, guys—this is as good as it gets."

Except it isn't as good as it gets. Lurking Hydra-like in the background are Mommies, and Mommies are always spelling trouble for the guys of *Men*.

Take Paul (please). Paul, the point-of-view character in the series, is the very model of the modern major schlimazel: the sort of guy who goes through life getting drinks spilled on *him*. Paul has very primo Mommy problems: His wife, name of Claire, has left him, but he's still in love with her, so they keep on having lunch (*lunch!*), and one day Paul tells the other guys he's gonna get back with Claire, and he gets all set to surprise her with the Big Question at lunch, but Claire has a surprise for *Paulie*—she's engaged!

So does our Paul do what any red-blooded guy would do—brain her with a breadstick, stun her with a soul kiss, drag her across the restaurant floor by her coif, take her to a mountain hideout and threaten to blow up the Grand Coulee Dam unless she plights her troth to him?

Well, not exactly. What he does is assume this sort of sickly piano-keyboard grin (the pain! the inner pain!) and start bobbing his head up and down about what a wonderful piece of news *this* is, and how Claire can always count on his friendship, etc. One got the impression that if Paul had happened to have a cask of brandy strapped around his neck, he'd have offered Claire a celebratory sip. Back with the guys at Schlimazel Central, Paul lets off steam by acting out "Big Girls Don't Cry" and playing a little cutthroat trivia. . . .

Look: This is the Lego approach to television entertainment. Every frame of *Men* is a perfect little interlocking plastic cube of color-coded nuance and sensibility. Every character is a Type, balanced by some equal and opposing Type. (Mommy-addled Paul gets upbraided by the womanizing Steve.) Every little stopwatched subplot crisis has been machine-calibrated to some male-issue trend as predigested by Donahue, Oprah, the "About Men" column in *The New York Times*. And every microsecond rings perfectly false. I've known men. I've worked with men. *Men*, you're no men.

Robert Guillaume, on the other hand, might very well be the black Bill Cosby. The former star of *Benson* has a new sitcom (midseason replacement, on ABC) with his own name in the title, à la the Coz. He works in a healing profession (marriage counselor, in this case). He lives in an overlighted, squeaky-clean Coz-house and is equipped with great clothes, an adorable son, an adorable daughter ("Hey! Guess what! I got a part in the school play!") and a lovably indigenous old dad, who is in charge of steaming about the premises and issuing such funky aphorisms as "Just tell 'em they too *ugly* for anybody else!" and "If I'm lyin', I'm flyin'!"

The difference, in *The Robert Guillaume Show*, is that the Ur-Coz is divorced. Abandoned by Mommy—a fact that has left

194

him Wary of Commitment but otherwise incredibly chipper and sage and that has not noticeably damaged the adorable children one iota. (The Stepford-like resiliency of the broken-home kids is a spooky sort of subtext in nearly all these shows. Mommy's departure leaves the spawn a little glum, to be sure, but almost never knocked off their perky one-liner aplomb. Are they all planning make-believe careers on *HBO Comedy Hour*?)

The one stroke of boldness in *The Robert Guillaume Show* has Edward, the Guillaume character, falling rather hesitantly in love with a white woman. Dramatically speaking, this match is as contrived as everything else about the show, but at least the *Guillaume* creators have surpassed their *Cosby Show* prototype in implanting the condition of blackness in America as a central theme. Hey—one is not asking for *A Raisin in the Sun* here, but Cosby's hermetic pretense that racial consciousness is no longer even a teensy irritant in black middle-class America has long since grown threadbare.

Richard Mulligan's wife/mommy made her departure the old-fashioned way: She died. (What kind of hellhag could willingly abandon good old Richard Mulligan, who has more adorability tucked into the various folds, furrows, dewlaps, tics, winks, moues and crow's-feet of his ungulate mug than might be found in Robert Morley's entire midsection?) So the silvery-thatched star of NBC's *Empty Nest* is left to pitch unbearably adorable soliloquies at his adorably droopy Saint Bernard, Dreyfuss (not to be confused with Paul on *Men*). "I don't date," his Harry explains mournfully to anyone who will listen, including the woman he's dating. "My wife just died." "Mom just died," his two grown daughters, Regan and Goneril (just kidding), remind him at every opportunity. Mom died eighteen months ago, or nineteen months before the actuarial chances of this series begin to plummet.

Harry is not so Mommy-deprived as to be totally insensitive to his new potential love interest, however. As he points out to his daughters, "She's the only living, caring being in my life right now who doesn't drink from a toilet." HIT THE LAFF MACHINE! *Empty Nest* is written and produced by Susan Harris, the creator of *Golden Girls*, which serves as its Saturday-night lead-in. Is Susan trying to tell us something? If so, what? And why?

Women—dare I say Mommies?—were also the primary suspects in the perpetration of an even ghastlier atrocity called *Raising Miranda*, which was recently canceled. Produced by Jane Anderson and Martha Williamson and written by Ms. Anderson for GTG Entertainment, *Miranda* got read its rights on the CBS airwaves last fall. It should have remained silent; its words are about to be used against it.

"Yooo will still be yooo and yooo don't have to change yoo-hoor dreeeems," trills the treacly theme song in part, which serves as fair warning. See, this married guy thinks things are great. Wants to take the family on a drive to the lake this weekend. But wifey-poo has to go workshop-ing. (UH-OH! TIMMM-BERRRRRRR!) Next thing you know, Dad is on the receiving end of a long-distance call, and you can read the whole story in his anguished expression, etc., etc. Sadness, perky daughter, wry neighbors and strong primary colors ensue. Let's see, have I left anything out? Noooo, don't think so. . . .

So rampant is Men-Without-Mommies mania that even Officer Crockett jumped onto the blandwagon—and then apparently was pushed back off. *Flipside*, a Don Johnson Company pilot so bad that not even a loaded AK-47 could induce anyone to extend it into a series, is about a British rocker who is abandoned . . . but you must be way ahead of me by now. Rumor has it they wanted Ringo Starr for the lead; they got Trevor Eve. I SAY THEY GOT TREVOR EVE—never mind. Suffice it to say this would have been the sort of series where the laugh track gives off a scandalized "Ooooooooh!" when the

6-year-old lisps, "David Bowie puts on a better live show than you, so there!" and a startled "Awwwwww!" when the selfsame moppet gurgles, "I love you, Dad!" Miami Nice.

Yet be of good cheer. The Men-Without-Mommies movement has not been a total washout. The infinite number of schlimazels on their infinite number of word processors have produced their *Hamlet* (all right, their *Cats*): *Dear John*, a state-of-the-art professional network situation comedy on NBC. Here is a series so refreshingly playful and well acted that one forgives its formulaic slickness and almost wishes it weren't lumped in with such insipid fellow travelers.

Generated by the same smart people who created *Taxi* (Ed. Weinberger, Bob Ellison and Peter Noah are the adroit writer-producers), *Dear John* is television ensemble comedy at its manners-and-morals best. The fall guy here is played by the estimable Judd Hirsch, whose comedic timing and prowess have deepened over the years. Hirsch plays the Everyman marital victim with a stony fatalism that recalls Buster Keaton; Hirsch's anthracite eyes have seemingly sunk ever deeper under his thatchy brows, giving him an appropriate look of conditional paranoia. (He is also allowed to utter the single slyest line of any character in any of these travesties—"Hi, honey, I'm hooome!")

Dear John works because it obeys one of the oldest and simplest (and most elusive) rules of make-believe, whether it be sitcom or fiction or opera or bedtime stories: *Character is plot.* The writers actually seem to respect the fragmentary lives they have sketched out and nudged into motion here; so do the actors and the director. Jere Burns, as the ineffable lady-killer Kirk, is destined to be a big star; Jane Carr projects the right mix of sanctimony and salaciousness as the voyeuristic therapy-group leader; and Isabella Hofmann underplays her natural glamour as John's lonely-but-reserved potential love interest.

To put it another way: *Dear John* surmounts its Men-Without-Mommies premise because it doesn't really *need* the premise. We'd follow these characters into whatever predicaments caught their fancy, because they're captivating, diverting people; they're not forced, like so much wet pasta, through the grinder of High Concept.

And because the central character, Judd Hirsch's John, is allowed to retain his essential humble, decent dignity. No bathos, no mugging with a Saint Bernard. And there's the essence of it all: It isn't Mommy that's the crucial missing ingredient in most of these new series. It's manhood.

Omigod, What Hath Holly Wrought?

With one exception, TV's Broadcast News *rip-offs are babbling (James) Brooks*

Success-maddened morning anchorqueens leap from commandeered stretch limos to drive their spike heels deeply into the modest dreams of struggling underlings. Brassy blonde magazine-show star bitches skewer their scandal-ridden subjects with the Big Question, *live in prime time,* while their horn-rimmed Harvard M.B.A. superiors wince and clutch their guts. Frenzied floor directors scream, "Five! Four! Three . . ." as the program's star ambles haughtily toward the set, tossing her mane, while back in the control booth, production staffers wear baseball caps and squirt water pistols authentically. Peevish newsguests draw real side arms and ventilate one another on-camera ("Can I just get this in before the break?"). Real-life telenames are dropped: Oprah! Pauley! Donahue! Vera Similitude!

Not even the nation's high schools are safe from the tidal wave: New, maverick journalism teachers abolish the old student paper and usher in the Minicams as their ecstatic students dance on tables and scream, *"Give me video or give me death!"*

James L. Brooks, James L. Brooks, what have you wrought?

This new season, you can't turn anywhere on the tube without bumping into a knockoff of *Broadcast News*. (Deck the fall with bows to Holly.) And Brooks is the guy to blame. The writer-director-producer of 1987's cinematic hit has handed television an almost idiot-proof blueprint for turning its eye upon its favorite subject—itself. Finally.

Despite television's resounding success at self-reference in commercials ("I'm not a doctor, but I play one on TV"), in sports and in convention coverage and on the postmodernist/ MTV fringe, the art of mainstream metafiction has proved elusive. Tantalizing, but elusive.

The movies, of course, have been teasing the medium with prototypes for years: *Network, China Syndrome, Eyewitness.* But TV's attempts at self-dramatization have mostly produced self-conscious, or fringy, clunkers. (Anyone here remember *W.E.B.?* Or *Max Headroom?*)

It remained for the old CBS hand Brooks, and his rich, Dickensian consciousness, to prove that a mass audience would identify with the TV newsroom as a teeming and layered social universe—Mary Richards's WJM, but adultified and tinged with roman à clef. And now the smaller minds, conditioned to dumbing down big ideas for the tiny screen, are beginning to hum feebly with a cicada chorus of "Oh, *I* get it. . . ."

Not that all of this fall's several variations on the *Broadcast News* theme *do* get it, exactly. Nearly all of them miss the subtle essence of Brooks's alchemy—a merciless parody of "the industry," tempered by an extraordinary tenderness toward the human beings who populate it.

Even less forgivably, and despite their showy grace notes of

Inside Atmosphere, these new series are remarkably erratic models of TV news's complex inner dynamics. A fascinating paradox, really: Here now are the networks in effect blandly ratifying in prime time every venomous charge of malevolence and avarice leveled against their news divisions in recent years (now that the mass audience is in on the little joke, why not exploit *that* marketplace reality?) and yet still getting the nuances wrong. (Did I say "idiot-proof"?)

This failure is not total. One standby series in particular— ABC's *Studio 5B*, ready as a winter replacement—radiates with wonderfully perceptive glimpses into the Cheshire-cat surrealism of a network-news ensemble. But in too many cases the writers have simply squandered their chances at comic authenticity in favor of the very stereotypes (the craven executive producer, the anchorwoman as airhead, or spoiled shrew, or both) that have been diverting popular attention from the deeper, institutional problems of network news.

Opportunities go flying in the soupily written first episode of *Murphy Brown*, CBS's sitcom vehicle for Candice Bergen and her heroically resilient kneecaps. (CBS, of all networks, should have plenty of file material for news-division send-ups.) It may have been someone's idea of subtle irony to cast a ventriloquist's daughter as the star reporter of a network newsmagazine program, but if so, the iconoclastic daring (as well as the logic) ends there.

This show falls back on such hoary devices as the Star's Grand Entrance, presold by some elbow-in-the-ribs set dialogue; viz.: "At ten o'clock, Murphy Brown is gonna *get off that elevator*, late as usual! She will *insult at least three people*, grab a cup of *black coffee* and *bum a cigarette*. Then she will *lock herself in her office* until she comes up with the *perfect piece for next week's show*, AS USUAL!"

Wow! say we credulous couch potatoes. That Murphy Brown must be some pumpkins! And sure enough, Ms. Bergen—last observed (as they say on *Unsolved Mysteries*) actually covering the Muhammad Ali–Joe Bugner fight for NBC Sports in 1976—does her drop-dead damnedest to sashay niftily through the minefield of such material. Phyllis George had better odds. Bergen plays a sort of Diane Sawyer type (the insouciance, the kneecaps) implanted with the world-weariness of Tina Turner (she's just back from a stay at the Betty Ford Center), the interviewing skills of a *Contra*gate prosecutor (she won't compromise!) and the moral absolutism of Tipper Gore—she's going to ASK THAT BIG QUESTION, *live in prime time,* of her scandal-ridden newsguest even though her horn-rimmed Harvard M.B.A. boss has *promised the guy she'd lay off*!

The newsguest is one Bobby Powell, and the scandal is that he may or may not have slept with a married woman who happens to be running for vice-president of the United States. The dilemma—ready?—is: Will Murph or won't Murph ask the forbidden question? ("He wants to tell his story with some kind of dignity," Murph's ratings-corrupted boss explains—and show me a non-ratings-corrupted boss in one of these shows and I'll show you a case of scriptwriter malfunction.)

Plot-logic problem: Since there is no Bobby Powell "story" apart from the Question (he is presented in the episode as utterly without a history, apart from the scandal), what would be the point of interviewing the big bozo and not asking it? I pondered this question right up until the moment that I recalled the Barbara Walters interview with Donna Rice on *20/20*—and then kept right on pondering. Didn't wash in life, doesn't wash in art.

Plus, the interview is live. Why would anybody dodging a Big Question go on *live* television? Plus, there's the question of the boss's agreeing to terms, and then whimpering when Murph asks the Big Question anyway. Look, "terms" are agreed to all the time with TV interviews. But with a nobody, a male bimbo? And when the terms are violated, why would our craven exec-producer go to pieces? This guest isn't Henry Kissinger; he's not coming back anyway. Tough titty, Bobby-cakes! Next case!

These little missteps may seem trivial (Good Lord, people, we're dealing with a trivial *medium*), but, toted up, they weigh against that minimal bubble of authenticity that must surround even a bagatelle such as *Murphy Brown*. Hey, the mass audience has *wised up* about the TV-news biz. They watch *Entertainment Tonight*. They read the TV column in *GQ*. (So do certain scriptwriters, apparently: A gag on *Murphy Brown* involving the pronunciation of the word "Shiite" has appeared in this space—*twice*, it mortifies me to admit, most recently in the December 1987 issue. Glad to see my unyielding crusade for excellence is having its impact on the industry.)

Meanwhile, over at Roosevelt High, the new journalism teacher is happily liquidating 500 years of Western typographic tradition in order to bring *Broadcast News* values to the *Fame* generation. *TV 101*, also on CBS, is a vision of what might gestate if *West 57th* mated with *Ferris Bueller* (discounting idiocy due to inbreeding, of course).

Sam Robards, son of Jason Robards and Lauren Bacall it says here for me to mention, plays Kevin Keegan, a hard-consonanted but softhearted type of Lonely Guy who's coming back to his alma mater after a shaky marriage to revitalize the old school's creaky journalism course. (Shall I pause while you read back over that sentence? Isn't the typographic tradition *fun*?) He encounters token resistance from *his* former J-teacher, Emilie Walker—the first prepubescent high-school faculty member in history, if we are to believe the fawnlike features of actress Brynn Thayer.

"Kevin, these kids watch too much TV as it is," recites Emilie in the least convincing Passionate Declaration since Ali MacGraw in *Winds of War*. "They don't need to be producing more of their own."

Kevin has been waiting for a line like that one. "Well, that's where you're *wrong*," he declares, whipping out his Minicam as Miss Walker grows wide-eyed. "Look how you're acting! You know why? Because you're *on the spot and you can't hide*!

That's what I wanna do! I wanna get these kids in front of a lens where they can't hide what's goin' on inside! That sense of reality is something the old student paper couldn't touch in a million years! All I need is a chance to make it work!"

And before you can say "This is Fawn Hall reporting from the White House," the *101* kids, refugees all from Benetton, are fanning out adorably through the halls and byways of Roosevelt—discovering toxic waste, producing *PM Magazine*—quality light features on school boredom, generating electronic graphics. When the druggie pal of the class's Alienated Kid dies in a van crash, you just *know* the Kid is gonna do a heart-wringing stand-up in front of the van, affirming pro-social attitudes. The school principal here takes the place of the craven executive producer—he's obsessed with "community standards" instead of ratings, but the venality's the same.

TV 101 skips and gambols fetchingly, trilling its Pied Piper tune that literacy is yesterday's fad and video is, like, where it's at right now. "Together I hope we can make it cool to be informed," Kevin earnestly tells his class. I believe this was intended as the show's pitch for a Peabody.

Still awaiting an airdate is the best *Broadcast News* knockoff of them all, a series that also manages to be a dead ringer for *L.A. Law*. It is called *Studio 5B*, it is sitting on ABC's storage shelf, and it offers a most sophisticated, and mordant, glimpse inside the sulfurous inferno of the network morning shows. (Could this be why it is sitting on ABC's storage shelf? *Naaaaaah. . . .*)

"We got *Oprah*, we got *Donahue*, plus cable, Carson—we are in a *war* here," the producer character rails during a routine morning staff meeting. (Wow, that must be one *looooong* morning show!) What this means is that damn near anything goes, including the scheming anchorwoman's cynical plan to put a recently paroled child molester on the air, *live* (anytime you hear the word "live" on one of these shows, get ready to duck), alongside the still-fulminating father of the girl the fiend abused.

Wendy Crewson plays the anchorbitch Carla Montgomery in a way that suggests the term "evil" might not be purely a biblical abstraction. David Hartman in a tailored minidress could not wreak one tenth the damage this woman connives as she purrs sweetly on the air and makes subordinates eat humble pie behind the scenes.

Much of *Studio 5B*'s strength lies in its accurate portrayal of newsroom sociology: the obsessive office politics, the abject desperation of young women seeking entry-level jobs ("bookers" are the *Front Page* cub reporters of the Eighties), the parallel desperation of producers seeking a chance to get on the air.

On the other hand, the show's technically savvy writer, Judith Parker, has fallen short of the human charm with which Brooks infused *Broadcast News*. None of the characters on *Studio 5B* seems fully equipped with a soul—as in *L.A. Law*, they are interesting mainly for their rich variety of neuroses. The conclusion of the pilot episode was needlessly sordid and implausible; it reduced an otherwise inventive story line to conventional bloody melodrama. Still, the series has substance and promise. If it wasn't so classy, it would be a smart pickup for Fox Television.

Broadcast News has given the networks a fertile premise, one that holds some fascinating potential. As real television news strays closer and closer to entertainment, and entertainment ventures farther and farther into "reality programming," we may soon find ourselves viewing a program whose authenticity is completely unfathomable. Even to the producers.

TRIVIAL PURSUITS

Despite lofty aims, ABC's thirtysomething
is really aboutnothing

Welcome to totally rull life. ABC's precious little pasta-link of a series designer-labeled *thirtysomething* (alternative title: *skinnywhitepeoplefromhell*) is pouting its way toward the triumphal windup of its first season. Like its success-clenched characters, the program can find, perversely, plenty to pout about.

'Cause, see, it's got IT ALL! Rully! Ratings, critical prestige, the thanks of a grateful baby boom—POUT CITY! As Michael himself might huskily verbalize it, asked hyperanalytically by Hope why he can't enjoy the things he has, " 'Cause I might *lose them.''*

Well, hey. Not rully. Not if the people meters and the pop-cult press can help it. So far, *thirtysomething* has rully, like, MADE IT! Quickly renewed for '88! Awesome numbers and demos! Great "buzz" factor! (People are talking about it.) *thirtysomething* has won everything but the Overachievers' Citation for Uncommon Narcissism with radicchio cluster.

Isn't this what we fought the Battle of Grenada for? So that the next generation could be totally free to deal with the concept of preweaning?

Let us not minimize the achievement of creators Edward Zwick and Marshall Herskovitz: With *thirtysomething*, they have accomplished the nearly impossible task of flattering the least flatterable generation in American history. (Not entirely beside the point, it is also the most desirable generation in the history of television audiences.) The subtlety of this accomplishment has not been properly appreciated.

Let us now praise famous yuppies.

The characters in *thirtysomething*'s ensemble are a markedly waspish lot—in all senses of that term. Even the Jewish characters. Their abiding petulance has been owned up to, often uneasily, even by the show's most breathless boosters. Camera shots track across vast geographies of listless (but great!) bodies, to settle upon angst-ridden faces gazing pensively into the Zeitgeist. Sensitive guitar music accompanies a wife's tearful revelation that she's *cleaned house three times today*! ("I don't want to hear this," her best friend from college is sure to pipe up—"it's too hurtful.")

Unmarried women in wine bars wonder if they should have arguments with someone who wears polyester shirts. ("They're not even blends?" their companions ask, incredulous.) There is much talk of sex ("Total stress!"); there is some modified upscale stripping (down past the Princeton sweatshirt); there is upscale kissing. The kissing scenes are augmented by a sound effect suggestive of, say, a 1967 Château de Fargues being s-l-o-w-l-y uncorked. Children appear, children named Ethan and Brittany. A site must be found for Brittany's theme birthday party. The republic holds its breath.

In its thematic concerns, at least, *thirtysomething* is scarcely the breakthrough concept that some have credited it with being. It is to some extent the old *Dick Van Dyke Show* as rewritten by the Ephron sisters. This is scarcely a critical flaw. The denizens of Ephronland cannot consume enough anthropology about themselves, as Diane Keaton and the nonfiction best-seller list will attest.

Michael and Hope Steadman, *thirtysomething*'s central couple, are the sort of black-belt strivers who can seamlessly free-associate the killing of a cockroach into an 20oververbalized referendum on their entire domestic financial structure:

She [*stalking the insect*]: There's a baby in this house! I will not have these disgusting, disease-ridden invertebrates running through her apricots and tapioca—HA! [*Smash!*]

He: Aaah, my racquetball shoe! [*They kiss*] Listen, I'll call the exterminator tomorrow, they'll spray the place with carcinogens.

She: They'll come back with mutant strains.

He: So we'll spray again.

She: Janey will grow up stunted.

He: So we'll move.

She: We can't afford to move.

He: We can't afford to live here; what's the difference?

Try introducing a neutral topic to the Steadmans over the baked Brie at the next gallery opening.

Michael, played with snail-buttered sincerity by Ken Olin, is a young advertising executive. (A master touch, since advertising is the semiotic that unifies the characters' essential concerns with those of its target audience.) He wears kick-ass raw-silk jackets to show he's Arrived and adorable canvas sneakers to show he hasn't forgotten his Values, and he speaks in this eensy-teensy little Sincere Voice in which every hand-stitched sentence ends in a gasp of angst-laden air.

Michael's wife, Hope (played by the scarcely less adorably named Mel Harris—don't these people ever LET UP?), is the kind of woman whose genetic fate is to be Rully Nifty, so why fight it? Aerobicized to within an inch of her skeletal structure (*no raisin bread!*), blessed with a brave crooked grin that only enhances her snookums good looks, tossing off ironies like disposable diapers, Hope is the June Allyson of the junk-bond age. Don't take her lightly; she has an outlaw streak a mile wide. ("Who's dealing with dinner, 'cuz . . . *I'm not dealing with it!*") But overall, she exists to psychoanalyze her and Michael's way through the thicket of upscale America's Big Issues: Is backpacking viable without a good baby-sitter? Is wallboarding the sun-room rully worth $5,000? Should one nuzzle one's spouse's hair after mousse has been applied?

Orbiting Michael and Hope's mortgaged milieu is an assortment of case histories who seem to have bolted en masse from an Oprah Winfrey panel on white anomie. There's Elliot (Timothy Busfield), Michael's adorable but hypermasculine creative partner, who spends his time at the office dream-sequencing about his impending divorce and twirling a Nerf basketball the same shade of orange as his hair and beard (no symbolic comparisons implied, surely). There's Elliot's neglected wife, Nancy (Patricia Wettig), a Joan Kennedy look-alike, who must amuse herself with brittle bons mots in posh bistros. ("I'm not gonna eat any animal where I have to eat its house too," she announces, disdaining the soft-shell crab.) There's Melissa (Melanie Mayron), the screwed-up single gal. ("How'm I ever gonna have a baby? I'm *dating* babies.") And— let's rully hear it, you gals in the audience—how about a big welcome for Gary, the de rigueur Peter Pan Bachelor Guy, portrayed with such shoulder-ringleted infantile perfection by Peter Horton that you start looking for the little green slippers and the gossamer wings.

Tickled into dramaturgic action, what these various types do mostly is behave—and speak—prototypically. (Since behavior, for this particular demographic pool, is virtually indistinguishable from speech, the *thirtysomething* crowd tends to speak *quite a lot*.) "I blew off the Teller account," Michael is likely to whisper as he pecks the missus in the evening, a refreshing Eighties variation on the old Van Dykean "Hi, honey, I'm home!" To which Hope might well respond, "Why do you have that look on your face?" Which will prompt Michael to huskily aver, "I *don't* have a look on my face," and so on, into the very abyss of transactional analysis.

All of which is accurate and contemporary—*rully* accurate and contemporary, let us hasten to acknowledge—but it veers frequently into unwitting Feifferesque excess. Creators Zwick and Herskovitz, in their zeal to render a video verbal verité, may have triggered the next prime-time megacrisis: gratuitous dialogue. Imagine Crockett and Tubbs this coming fall, in the midst of a perfectly respectable firefight, pausing to deal with their commitment to their total relationship. Imagine the *Tour of Duty* gang forming a male encounter group.

Frankly, a little hyperverbalism in prime time is just what the analyst ordered, from one's retrograde linear point of view, anyway. In palmier moments, one likes to imagine *thirtysomething* as the long-awaited antibody to the MTV virus.

But there's a flaw built into *thirtysomething*, and it is, regrettably, the obvious one: The show's famous "little moment" situations—the microprocessed plots—simply do not support all the wonderful grace notes, the dead-on scripting and the menus and the clothes. Although the characters display tons of fashionable irony, the show itself seldom risks ironic distance from the characters.

To put it most brutally, their pathologically petty self-absorptions—Gary's horror of "commitment," Nancy's shattered dream of illustrating children's books, Michael's goddamned wallboard fixation—are presented at face value. Almost never is there more than the subtlest whisper of satiric edge. It is in this sense that *thirtysomething* shamelessly flatters the legendary narcissism of its thirtysomething core audience.

One can expect some argument on this score. Didn't *Newsweek* hit the mark in its rhapsodic review last December when it paused to worry that the show's "mirror" reflects something "by and large remarkably unflattering to the very viewers it most wants to win over"?

Naaaaaaaah! Au contraire, as they say down at the Rolex repair shop. Those viewers GOTTA LOVE IT! *thirtysomething* is the culmination of the yuppie civil-rights movement. At last, the mass media is portraying their grievances seriously. When Michael puts his chinny-chin-chin on his hands and gurgles, "I'm depressed about everything in life not ever being exactly the way you want 'em to be," the huddled masses out there in their condos aren't hurling sun-dried tomatoes at the screen; they're shouting, "RIGHT ON!" Michael has been to the mountaintop! And skied down it! Can I get a rully neat *hallelujah*?

Here's how the program calibrates its scale of values to the prevailing mood of the times: In the first episode, the overmastering issue seems to be whether Michael and Hope can find a suitable baby-sitter in time to go backpacking with Gary and his ex-girlfriend. (Trust me.) There is lots and lots and lots of over-verbalizing on this matter, and a funny little set-piece spoof of the baby-sitter interview.

Weaving among the many subplots, meanwhile, is a moral dilemma confronting Michael back at the ad agency. Elliot has designed a campaign for an important client— a rip-off of a currently successful campaign. Needless to say, the client loves Elliot's approach.

Michael is *sincerely* troubled by this. "What are we doing here?" he asks Elliot huskily. "Why did we start this business?"

"To do our thing," Elliot husks back. And then: "We won't always have to deal with sleazeballs like this. [*Pause*] Someday we'll be dealing with a higher class of sleazeball. [*Pause*] We'll come back to it [viz.: the moral issue] another day. Right now, we've got two wives, three kids, four cars, two mortgages and a payroll." Elliot sits back: "That's life, pal."

And bango, as they say. So much for *that* little distraction. Rationalized in their compromise, the guys return to more pressing considerations—Michael's choice of sleeping bags, Elliot's secret choice of sleeping partners. As for the workplace (which is as close as any of the *thirtysomething* crew gets to public life—politics and civic affairs being total abstractions, mere fodder for bons mots), well, it's the old ends-and-means game, pal. Ciao!

Flattering to the arrested-adolescent id? A little. I'd say that if the movie *Wall Street* is an indictment of baby-boomer values, *thirtysomething* is the editorial reply. Fine; so be it. Television entertainment need not be a call to moral regeneration (not that it ever is), but let us at least be clear-eyed as to the intent here. *thirtysomething* satirizes its audience the same way the Gridiron Club satirizes the president and First Lady: ve-rrrrr-y gingerly.

And yet there is the occasional, the all-too-occasional, hint that somewhere down deep the show knows better. Toward the end of one episode, Elliot turns to Michael and remarks, apropos of nothing in particular, "Maybe our wives are secretly the same person." Then he thinks a bit and adds, "Maybe *we're* the same person." Another thoughtful beat. *"Maybe we're only leading one life."*

To which this jaded (and admittedly fortysomething) observer can only append: *Rully.*

THE POPCORN PUGILISTS

Those proliferating movie critics love to slug it out—even if there's nothing to fight about

Ebert and Siskel had just been *At the Movies,* and Siskel was about to unsheath the terrible sword of judgment upon a vehicle of dubious pedigree entitled, with perhaps unwitting irony, *Out of Bounds.*

"When it comes to deciding thumbs-up or thumbs-down on this picture," Siskel informed Ebert with the sort of noisy irritability that has become a convention among Movie Guys, "I have to put mine down!"

As studio patriarchs and investment lawyers the length of Marina del Rey pitched forward in front of their deck-top Trinitrons, feebly clawing for their nitroglycerin tablets, the camera shot shifted and Ebert's Buddha-like visage filled the screen.

"I have to think! Gene!" screamed Ebert—Movie Guys scream

more than the cast of *Friday the Thirteenth's Mediterranean Vacation*—"That what we're up against in this one! Is our old friend the idiot plot!" Ebert began making jerky, geometric movements with his arms, like a third-base coach signaling a passing Coast Guard cutter. "This movie is so filled! With opportunities for this kid to solve all of his problems! That it's very frustrating! For us to sit there watching him make one mistake after another!"

By this time, Siskel had his dukes up—one means, literally had the old meat-hooks up and doubled, and was swinging rhythmic little shadow punches, not too far from the Ebertian schnozzola.

"You see!" Siskel shouted in a barroom-clearing baritone. "It's a great moment that they always blow! *Have* the kid go into the police station! And then! As a writer! Figure out a situation where the police don't *believe* him! And then deal with that!" Siskel threw a few more punches. "Make the script tougher on yourself!" he bellowed. "Rather than make it easier on yourself! 'Cause if you make it tougher on yourself [*Schoop! Schoop!* went the dukes], you're gonna make it tougher and more exciting for the audience!"

It was another Ebert-Siskel donnybrook, I thought gleefully—just the kind of hammer-and-tongs dustup that has always made their original Movie Guys show so mesmerizing to watch. You might not always be able to remember what Gene and Roger *said* about a movie; you might not even recall which way the thumbs pointed. But one thing, bud: You knew you'd been witness to a no-holds-barred, down-and-dirty, Chicago-style *interface*.

And yet, and yet. Something seemed missing from the unpleasantries, something essential. I couldn't think what it was, though, because now Roger and Gene were looking at *Heartburn*.

"You see! That didn't get me at all!" Siskel was frothing at Ebert as the film clip dissolved. "What we are really hungry for in this movie! Is some *genuine confrontation!* As we would expect from anyone in real life! Here are two of our greatest actors! So let's strip away the jokes and let 'em go at it!"

Ebert wasn't about to take this lying down. "I didn't know! When this movie was over! Why their marriage had a film made about it!" He yelled into Siskel's face. "It started at the end! And worked backward! This movie doesn't have an ending! It doesn't have a conclusion! It doesn't have a place it was going that contained something it wanted to say about these two people!"

Yow, I thought—the fat's in the fire now. This *has* to be the segment of *At the Movies* we've all been waiting for; the one where the usher has to come running down the aisle and hold the two of them apart until the men with tranquilizer darts burst through the lobby. . . .

Except that *they weren't arguing*! That's what was missing from this renewal of the Siskel-Ebert weekly feud: *disagreement*. In fact, on every one of the four films up for review on this edition of *At the Movies* (an early August show, not long before the boys departed from the Tribune Entertainment Co.'s syndicated program and took their act to Disney's Buena Vista Television), the two thumbs, the pudgy and the slim, ended up pointing in the same direction.

You wouldn't have known it from the body language, mind you—all those flailing elbows and blazing eyebrows and exclamation marks; all that palpable sense of *arena*, of smoldering syllogism and the manly art of a posteriori. But these guys, these original Movie Guys, were doing *Auld Lang Syne*.

Is that what happens when Movie Guys run out of movies to disagree about—they keep on going through the motions of disagreement? A small point, arguably, in the issue-laden universe of television, but perhaps not an infinitesimal one.

Consider (a) the proliferation of Movie Guys to *three sets* this fall, a 50 percent increase over the summer in defiance of any discernible plea from a market in which 75 percent of Americans see zero movies in a given year. (By the way, why are there no Movie Gals? No Movie Black Guys? No Movie *Brats,* f'gawdsakes, given the great mucilaginous pubescent skew of the product?) Consider (b) the current state of aesthetic crisis in American moviemaking, a situation that would seem to call for more than a cloned and rigidly formatted response from national video criticism. And consider (c) the provocative clues this adversarial motif offers about "content" on television in general.

The proliferation problem may be laid directly at Siskel-Ebert's invisible but restless feet. They move around a lot—from the Public Broadcasting System to Tribune Entertainment and now to Disney—and every time they move, another set of Movie Guys springs up in their wake, like little dragon's toothlets, all genetically coded with the casual duds (why are Movie Guys so sweater-vesty, so open-collar?), the viewing screen, the orchestra seats, the balcony. (Why not a Movie Guy 'n' a Movie Gal *making out* in the balcony? Perhaps the Playboy Channel could test-market this concept and save itself from oblivion. I suggest Mel Tormé and Shannon Tweed.)

At PBS, the current Movie Guys are Jeffrey Lyons and Michael Medved, a duo who combine the semiobligatory pumped-up decibels with a good-vid smilingness that would win points on the parallel bars at the Winter Olympics. Lyons-Medved are not without their moments of insight, but they can't quite pull off the old proletarian cut-and-thrust with the aplomb of the originals. A key tip-off is that while Ebert-Siskel lock eyes with each other during conversation, Lyons-Medved look at the camera, suggesting the programmatic hiss of the Tele-PrompTer.

But if you think, as I do, that Lyons and (particularly) Medved occasionally come off a little too meticulously produced, *do* catch the latest set of Movie Guy replacements for Siskel-Ebert at Tribune Entertainment. They seem expressly selected to test the credulity limits of Rupert Pupkin, the mega-nebbish show-biz addict in *The King of Comedy.*

"A thorough nationwide search" is the way Tribune Entertainment's publicists described its quest for the ideal new team of cohosts. (They didn't say which nation. Consternation would be my guess.) What they came back with were two of the more spavined war-horses of the mainline mass-cult H'wood-to-B'way bromide beat: Rex Reed, whose Oscar Wildean aphorisms were saucy enough twenty years ago, when the heartland still thought Charles Nelson Reilly a bit of a caution; and Bill "Good News" Harris, who has combined an uncanny resemblance to a cartoon symbol for automotive rustproofing with an unfailing instinct for the great sycophanatic middle (producer for *Good Morning America*; writer for Rona Barrett, if that is not an oxymoron; celebrity admirer for five years on Showtime).

What these two iconoclasts have allowed themselves to front is a weekly production so humid with added-on audience-vamping devices ("Six rotating features!" "Actual in-production shots!" "The Dog of the Week!" "Stories that haven't even broken yet!") that Reed's famously pouting lower lip seems to have taken on a terminal curl.

And the repartee? Pigeons must come scuttering off the production-studio roof in horror when Harris ventures, "I thought for the money, people will love it," and Reed parries with "Well, *I* thought for the money they should have *thrown in some Excedrin*." Or when Harris offers, "I wish they'd let Tom Cruise grow up," and Reed zings him with "*I wish the people who made this movie would grow up!*" The most appalling evidence of Reed's vanished prowess came in this setup for a Dorothy Parkeresque mot that simply wasn't in storage when Rex reached for it: "I don't think I've seen anything this moronic [dramatic pause] . . . in a long, long time."

Which brings us to point b, the very real likelihood that Reed *hadn't* seen anything that moronic in a long, long time. The aesthetic corruption of the American movie—fed by crapulous conglomerate pricing structures, the overweening egos of artist-directors, the cult of pandering to unformed adolescent

217

tastes, the non-narrative infestation of MTV's influence and a hundred other intertwined pathologies—is one of the few truly compelling pop-cultural stories of the decade. Considering the movies' deep historical resonances in the American mythos, it is probably the *most* compelling story of them all—more worthy of concern, perhaps, than television's continuing and relatively tame depredations.

A number of the nation's best print reviewers have lately examined this crisis in searing, impassioned essays: David Denby in a landmark article for *New York* magazine; Tom Shales in *Esquire*; Kenneth Turan in a fashionable gentlemen's gazette whose initials currently escape me. If the defilement of American movies is really this severe, and the forces that fuel it really so pervasive—if the most thoughtful critics are currently yelling "Fire!" in our less and less crowded theaters—then isn't there something a little overripe in the very notion, the very idiom, of the TV Movie Guy?

I will grant that Ebert and Siskel seem at times to grasp the ghastliness inherent in what they're covering. They alone (Siskel in particular) seem capable of honest outrage and of turning that outrage upon the movie audience itself, for its doltish complicity in its own debasement. I am less sure of Lyons and Medved; and as for Reed and Harris, they appear, in the context of the times, as two happily doddering Catskill gaffers, dusting off their hoary one-liners over hot pastrami at the Carnegie Deli, while a few blocks down Broadway the stone griffins of Fox's Theatre clunk heavily to the pavement.

Which brings us to point c, this curious and recurring sense of the adversarial motif in Movie Guy shows, even when the Movie Guys are not actually being adversarial.

Watching Ebert and Siskel wave their arms and pump their fists at each other even as they agreed wholeheartedly on everything, I recalled a penetrating essay by Michael Arlen some years ago on the subject of Norman Lear's comedies. What was it, Arlen set himself to know, that was so fascinat-

ing about these comedies?—allowing Arlen's critical judgment that it wasn't the comedy itself, which he esteemed not
bad, exactly, but surprisingly contrived and second-rate.

Arlen's conclusion struck me as ingenious at the time, and
it holds up well in the present inquiry. It was *anger*, Arlen
declared, "the constant and steady presence of anger . . . a
curious, modern, undifferentiated anger, which serves to provide the little dramas with a kind of energizing dynamic—
sometimes the only dynamic."

Attributing this dynamic to what he called the new contemporary consciousness of the media—a commonality that seems
to have been created largely by television itself—Arlen reached
a rather harrowing conclusion: "Now, maybe, we are trading
dizzily into a new phase, where both act and motive have
blurred or receded and what we are left with . . . is the strange
dynamic of a ubiquitous, unfeeling, unknowing, discursive
collective consciousness . . . connected to nothing."

Sam Donaldson sparring with George Will on *This Week With
David Brinkley* about—what? Anybody? The glib jackanapes
from *The McLaughlin Group* thrashing out at one another's stands
on—on what? And what stands? And the Movie Guys, sometimes agreeing, sometimes disagreeing; thumbs-up, thumbs-
down; flogging the rotting movie industry or fawning over it.
It's tableau that matters, son, in today's television world,
meaning in today's world—tableau, not content.

Which is perhaps the real reason—though no Movie Guy
has mentioned it—that the movies are worse than ever.

THIN OF THE NIGHT

Noxious fumes are spreading from the West!
Joan (Princess) Rivers challenges Johnny (King) Carson.
Can we sleep?

The Joan Rivers partial meltdown in Los Angeles last spring
was a warning that must not go unheeded. The debacle, from
which noxious fumes are still spewing, suggests that it's time
to reexamine our nation's long-standing commitment to the
television talk show as a cheap alternative source of . . .

Of what? Entertainment? Ideas? Satori? Sedation? Grooming tips? Autohypnosis? Whatever the depressing answer might
be, consider me on record as favoring a total moratorium. Tell
me where the next demonstration is going to be; I'll show up
with my "No TALKS" placard, willing to chain myself to the
nearest junior assistant producer in charge of working the
"APPLAUSE!" sign.

I'm prepared to hand out literature on street corners on this one. Head up coalitions. Bang on motel doors in Corn Belt towns late at night, shouting at the encyclopedia salesman inside to switch off Johnny and commit himself to a safer, saner video environment. Like *Herbalife*, on the cable channel.

You think I'm being some kind of alarmist here? You think Rivers was a freak accident, a once-in-a-lifetime fluke, something that could have been avoided with the proper protective backup systems, say a layer or two of sealing wax around the lip fault line?

You line up pro–talk show? Oh, the shortness of American memory.

Doesn't anybody remember *Thicke of the Night*? Or *Not for Women Only*? How about Jerry Lewis, a catastrophe-in-the-making that was averted only by massive volunteer infusions of ennui? *Joanne Carson's* (yes!) *V.I.P.'s*?

Even a partial list of disasters and near disasters should be enough to make the blood run cold—a symptom common to those who have actually witnessed a talk show: Peter Bogdanovich subbing for Johnny Carson. The guy with the hand puppet. Igor Cassini. Bess Myerson. Les Crane (assisted by the Elliott Lawrence Orchestra). John Davidson. Tom Cottle, "the Sensitive Shrink." Jim Peck (assisted by the hypnotist Elroy Schwartz). The Bakkers and their evangelical wardrobe from North Carolina. And speaking of the Christian Broadcasting Network and its adoration of secular humanism's socko style, let us not forget Pat Robertson and his *700 Club*, the veritable *China Syndrome* of talk shows; the one that might not stop penetrating until it reaches the presidency.

And if that grim recitation fails to stir you, consider this scientifically verifiable fact: Once you put one of the damn things on line, it takes on the half-life of an isotope. It cannot be counted on to disappear in the lifetime of your children, nor your children's children.

Griffin, Douglas? Sure, they've been quiescent lately, but who knows when they might flare up again—or worse, fuse into one ball of mega-blandness that could engulf North America and the NATO countries in a spreading cloud of torpor?

Cavett, Philbin, Bill Boggs, Joe Franklin—still active, though the needles barely flicker above trace level. David Brenner is in final start-up stages. Somewhere the evacuated plant that was Snyder still seethes, waiting, waiting. Somewhere David Frost, again, eyes Richard Nixon, again. Somewhere Morgan Fairchild prepares to do a guest stint. And Ali MacGraw. The New Osmonds. Consumer advocate David Horowitz. Do I have to go on like this, fill your mind with nightmarish scenarios? Do I have to remind you that no treaty or agreed-upon set of safety standards specifically exempts a talk show featuring an unshielded Howard Cosell?

Are you starting to comprehend the ghastly dimensions of the crisis? Are you willing to admit it's time to call a halt? Or do you stubbornly continue to point to *Larry King Live* as proof that the talk show can exist harmoniously in the environment?

(I'm specifically exempting David Letterman from this category, by the way. Letterman is a traditional talk-show host only in the way that Claes Oldenburg is a traditional manufacturer of clothespins.)

King is the exception that proves the rule, say I. Find me another, and good luck in avoiding the mention of Dr. Ruth.

While you're thinking, and however much you might like to sidestep the example, let us review the particulars of the Joan Rivers meltdown.

Here is the logic of the American talk show truly extended to its penultimate noxious horror. Here is the final spasm, the inevitable fumy consummation of a thirty-six-year fool's paradise of an experiment that began in May 1950 with the premiere on NBC of a strange amalgam of vaudeville, singing and self-conscious show-biz chatter called *Broadway Open House*. It starred, among others, Jerry Lester, Morey Amsterdam and the statuesque Dagmar. Sylvester "Pat" Weaver, one of broadcasting's genuine deities, created that program. It was the scale model of his greatest invention: *The Tonight Show* premiered four years later and began to implant the idiom of Las Vegas hip into American mass culture—an idiom that, in time, even the Christian evangelical right would goofily embrace.

In fact, one might argue that the TV talk show did more than rock and roll to revolutionize (read: secularize) America's image of itself. After all, it reached moms and dads as well as the kiddos with its images of cool, got-up glamour figures trading self-worship and ironic japes about the semisacred and, later, the taboo.

Thus the atoms of megalomania were tucked into the very architecture of the talk show. Danger signals began to flash as early as Jack Paar (who himself may not be finished *yet*; who knows), but America was bedazzled, and the new form began to burgeon toward critical mass.

It's even possible to grant the talk show a golden age, or at least an age in which its essential semiotic—the nightly domestication of the gods—served a truly novel function, a function wedded to television's form. Oscar Levant free-associating, Paar's eyes brimming, a hint of genuine hostility between Johnny and his starlet guest, the young Dick Cavett obviously bristling as he interviewed a Pentagon-issued general—hell, even Don Rickles "dropping in" on a Carson show, Johnny thunderstruck in close-up—these were authentically riveting moments of television; truth and the hint of danger arising from a contrived context.

Who can chart the exact time when it all started to corrode; when the needles began to register "diminishing returns"; when the chatter turned stale and the confessions merely turgid— when the American ear hardened against shock at the off-color and the gratuitous, and the new, young comics were merely competent; when, finally, in the memorable analysis of the

writer George W. S. Trow, the trivial was raised up to power
and the powerful lowered to the trivial, and the middle distance fell away?

When the anarchy loosed upon the world became mere.

And a rough beast slouched toward Carsonland to be born.

Joan Rivers was encoded into the final logic of the talk show
from the very incubation. This appetite encased in sequins is,
in certain metaphoric aspects, less a distinct personality than
a force of physics—an inevitable, geometric expansion of original vulgarity that has swollen in proportion to certain vac-
uums.

Carson, who was so brilliant for so long, could not have
foreseen it; he was too close. But there was nothing left for
the talk show save the all-consuming, the curiously lifeless
and impersonal, the seemingly automated virulence of Rivers.

Rivers's comedy is the comedy of aging-airhead affluence
and the edgy contempt that such a parasitic existence breeds.
Like her prototypical fan, seen braying at her vulgarisms in
cutaways during those ineffable specials on cable TV—a
leathery matron of certain years, besotted on Vegas and time-
share condos and the odd high-cultural foray into dinner
theater—Rivers has grown nastier, more bloated in temperament, in direct proportion to her rise in wealth and status.
Rivers likes to claim, in her more pretentiously heartfelt moments, that she owes her comic perspective to Lenny Bruce.
Sure, and Nancy Reagan owes her social ideals to Woody
Guthrie.

In fact, the locus of Rivers's comic persona is in the very
stratum of overripe, privileged fatuousness that Bruce de-
spised. Bruce shook his fist upward in nothing-to-lose defiance at a puerile ruling class. Rivers *represents* the ruling class.
She can make cruel jokes about Karen Carpenter's death by
anorexia before an audience of college students; she can flounce
around at a White House state dinner and brag, "No scum
here tonight!" She can smirk, as she did immediately after

jilting Carson for the next brass ring, that her ratings on *The Tonight Show* were higher than "the regular host's."

And then, when cornered, she can commandeer six pages in *People* magazine to bleat girlishly, under her byline, that "the way Johnny found out about my new talk show was horrendous. *I* wanted to be the one to break the news to him— and had planned to do it first thing Tuesday morning."

Please.

Rivers consolidated her lug-wrench grip in show business over twenty-one dogged years as a *Tonight Show* guest (and later guest host, to employ that sublime oxymoron). This was all due to a generous bestowal of grace and goodwill by Carson. In return, Rivers not only insulted her benefactor but attempted a quick raid on his key production talent on her way out. If there is any rational explanation for the mass audience's toleration of this woman, it must reside in their vestigial, innocent wish to believe that all public boors and roughnecks are really sweeties deep down. (See the Lite Beer commercials.)

In Rupert Murdoch, Joan Rivers has found her divine afflatus—her twin of voraciousness, an inspired and untoppable companion in her ransacking spree through television's vast mall. Here is an American patriot freshly minted, a new citizen newly sworn to uphold and defend the Great Et Ceteras of American life.

As the new owner of the Fox Broadcasting Company, Murdoch—whose imprint on print journalism is such that if the world should end, many fear his papers would overreact— will continue in that same public-spirited tradition this fall: *The Late Show Starring Joan Rivers* will be offered live to non-Fox stations, beginning at 11 P.M. in the East. Thus, in angling for an extra measure of "edge" against *The Tonight Show*, Rivers will be in direct competition with local television newscasts across the country.

So if you're bored sick with all that informative news crap and the Jeffersonian hopes that vaguely underpin it, Rupert

Murdoch and Joan Rivers have their own designs upon your brainpan.

And the final desiccation of the talk show will commence. Seriously, if anyone is trying to organize a moratorium on the form, can we talk?

THE BEASTIE GIRLS

*For a certain breed of fan, TV and life
slowly begin to merge*

When I first heard about the people who wanted to save
Beauty and the Beast from cancellation on CBS—the Helper's
Network people—I admit it: My first reaction was to begin
daydreaming about my next cuticle transplant.

Call me jaded. Call me hard-boiled. But I have a tendency
to get a little . . . Robert Mitchum when I hear from fans who
are grieving because their favorite television show has been
taken off the air.

What the hell did they expect? A lifetime commitment? It's
over. Hey. Don't get mixed up in prime time, doll. It'll sell you
a bottle of fabric softener and then put rings around the collar
of your heart. You wanna get involved, go buy *Wuthering
Heights*.

Which is not bad advice, as far as it goes. And it's a handy

227

ironic shield. One needs a coating of irony in the TV-criticism business. It protects one from having to think too deeply about certain things—for instance, about the people who are perhaps the most, well, poignant victims of commercial television.

Not the couch potatoes, the eight-hours-a-day hard users who care too little about the garbage that washes over them. No. The others: the fewer in number who have the curse of empathy, the unfortunate capacity to reach out and *engage* some new TV program; who discover meanings or resonances in it that may not have been fully apparent to the assembly-line workers who slapped it together and shipped it out on the airwaves. The others: those who make the mistake of caring too much. The Devoteds.

The Trekkies are the most notable example, of course. *Star Trek* lasted four seasons on NBC; it died in 1969. In its best year, *Star Trek* finished fifty-second in the Nielsens, behind something called *The Iron Horse*. Yet its fans never stopped caring. They formed clubs. Had conventions. Newsletters. Just a few nutty devotees. An insignificant crumb of the Nielsen Index. Only enough to support five big-budget *Star Trek* movies, the most recent of which came out this past summer.

There have been other . . . Devoteds. For Lawrence Welk. For *Dark Shadows*. For *Kojak*. For *Cagney & Lacey*. Last fall, a national movement formed to save *The Equalizer*—like *Beauty and the Beast*, a casualty of CBS's audience flowcharts. Pickets. Mass mailings.

Who can *care* that much? About some prime-time television show? Best not to think about it too deeply.

So, okay. I finally picked up the telephone and dialed the number of Kimberly Hartman, the California woman who has made a kind of theological study of *Beauty and the Beast*.

Perhaps you recall the network history of *Beauty and the Beast*. It turned up on the CBS schedule in the fall of 1987, one of those bold-stroke new concepts from the young network president, Kim LeMasters. (As was *The Equalizer*, come to think of it.)

B&B starred Ron Perlman as . . . Vincent, a sort of wised-up MGM Lion with the heart of Leo Buscaglia who lives in a secret society down in the sewers under Manhattan—we're talking *real* underclass, pal—headed by a kind of benevolent Ur-Koch called the Father. Your basic ethical Utopia without central heating, where citations from Shakespeare and Frost are part of the rap, and the word "quest" gets used a lot.

It costarred Linda Hamilton as Catherine, the Beast's mane squeeze, the ultimate Eighties career woman–criminal law-yer–rich girl–princess type who can't tear herself away from the big lug. (Which just goes to prove that if you're single and straight in New York, the women will overlook just about anything.)

However, *B&B* didn't exactly rewrite ratings history. So much for bold-stroke new concepts. It did not make CBS's fall 1989 schedule. Not really *canceled*. "Pulled off for retooling" was the curiously air-transportation–sounding line. (The show is scheduled to return any minute as a midseason replacement.)

But all along, almost from the outset, there has been this . . . following. This network of *B&B* groups. Like, for in-stance, the *B&B* International Fan Club, of Cedar Rapids, Iowa. Or Condos and Caverns, of Snohomish, Washington. Or the Sororal Order of Cat Kissers, of Milwaukee. Not to mention the Ron Perlman Research Library, of Omaha. Or *Pipeline*, the monthly *B&B* newsletter. And on and on.

Kimberly Hartman and her Helper's Network is more or less the unofficial umbrella for all these groups. She operates out of Fullerton, California. And as soon as I dialed her number, I realized that I was in the Land of the Devoteds.

The first thing I got was eight minutes of Kimberly on tape. Kimberly is the voice of the Helper's Network Information Hotline. "I encourage you to have pencil and paper ready," she said at the beginning. A fair warning, I quickly discov-ered.

I learned that the Helper's Network has outposts in New York City, England and Canada. I got the latest *B&B* news: Ron Perlman would be appearing the next week on *CBS This Morning*. "We think it will be Wednesday." I learned that something called the Creation Convention was going to salute *B&B*. And that there would be workshops (*workshops*?!) scheduled in San Jose, California; Minneapolis; and Arlington, Virginia. And that the Helper's Network of Canada was planning its first special event; a human chess game with a fully scripted *Beauty and the Beast* story line. The *B&B* album—Perlman doing music and poetry from the series—had sold a quarter of a million copies and was climbing the charts. The first videotape had sold 200,000 copies and more were coming. *Beauty and the Beast* novelizations were now a reality.

There was some more assorted lowdown—"filming on the two-hour season premiere is well under way"—and then finally Kimberly signed off: "Keep writing and keep the faith," she urged. "Vincent and Cathy are alive and well."

I left my name and number at the beep, and within minutes Kimberly herself phoned me back. Right away I was given to understand that this was no loopy, lovesick dame I was dealing with. In a competent voice, Ms. Hartman identified herself as a theologian, a student of philosophy and science, and a "fantasist." "*High* fantasy," she specified. "Fantasy that addresses the larger issues: the fight between Good and Evil. The Nature of Beingness. What Existence is. Is there a God and in What Form is He?"

She came upon *B&B* quite by accident, she assured me, and was immediately struck by the profundity of the mythopoeic references within the dialogue. It was a real intellectual rush. "Not only was it a lot like the literature I like to read," said Ms. Hartman, "but it espoused the values I espouse."

I asked her to elaborate.

"My entire life's purpose is to gain and share information," said Ms. Hartman. "That's why I call my organization the

Helper's Network. In *Beauty and the Beast*, 'Helpers' are people in the aboveground world who help those in Vincent's world below. Grocers who give surplus food, doctors who give surplus medicine. The people down below, like Vincent and the Father, are dependent on the world above. And that's what I do, I run an information network about *Beauty and the Beast*. A hot line. And I publish a compendium, a list of the literary references within each *Beauty and the Beast* episode, complete with bibliography and index.''

We are basically dealing with an actor in a lion suit, I wanted to put in here, but instead I asked "Why?"

"People's lives have been changed by this show," declared Kimberly, and now her voice was a little less disinterested. "Our world is very callous. Very human and subject to evil. The world as we know it has a tendency toward evil. Or at least indifference. All that is needed for evil to triumph is for good men to do nothing. But the main theme of *Beauty and the Beast* is to find one's inner strength and to look beyond appearance to the person underneath. The whole idea behind this show is changing people's lives. Letting the person realize they are a worthwhile person. I've talked to psychologists and therapists who've used this show. It works on so many hierarchical levels.''

I asked her to name me a hierarchical level.

"The first level is the romance between Vincent and Cathy,'' said Ms. Hartman without a moment's hesitation. "It has become a truism in this culture that sex is not the same as love. A man can confess undying love the night before, kick you out of bed the next morning and then go out and brag about his conquest. Vincent and Cathy's romance feeds a need for commitment. For a love that is everlasting. There are a lot of people out there who are not married. They're dumpy, nondescript. They don't have any real interests. They're not a person. They're drifting through life. They say, 'My gosh! If these people who live down below can work toward making a Utopia, so can I!''

My conversation with Kimberly Hartman up to this point had been quite detached and intellectual—a lot more detached and intellectual than I'd expected, to be absolutely frank—but then I happened to ask whether *Beauty and the Beast* might have struck any personal chords with her.

Kimberly hesitated a beat or so before answering. "No one has ever asked me that question before," she finally said. "I have cerebral palsy. When I get tired I limp and my eye will wander a bit. I can't open a doorknob with my right hand. I was always a bookworm. My nickname was the Cripple, and that's what I had to deal with. But I became a very strong person. What's often called a 'survivor.'

"I discovered science in high school. But in college I discovered that science can't give us all the answers. So I went heavily into philosophy. I was everybody's mother confessor. When the captain of the football team and the head cheerleader were doing their thing, I wasn't invited. I knew what it was like to be an outcast, to be excluded. Ron Perlman knows that too. He was a fat kid in school. His nose and chin were out of proportion."

I asked her whether she had ever felt like Catherine, under Vincent's spell. Again, there was silence while she thought.

"I met my husband at a science-fiction-and-fantasy convention in Denver," she said after a moment. "He came up to me—I was struggling with my suitcases—and said, 'Pardon me, you need any help?' We *talked* and got to know each other. His mother told me afterward that he called her in Albuquerque and said, 'I have met the woman who will become my wife.' He's a computer-systems analyst."

Kimberly's words were coming rapidly now.

"On *Beauty and the Beast*, people *talk* to one another. They talk about feelings. They try to aid and abet one another. Vincent will never change. He will never become the handsome prince. But he said, 'Don't deny who you are! Don't deny what you can do in the world!' I believe in that—as a theologian and a philosopher and a fantasist. I work at least four hours a day on the Helper's Network, getting people to come together and discuss *Beauty and the Beast,* discuss their feelings, discuss how the show has changed their lives. I think the show is going to survive. I think I'm going to run the Helper's Network for another twenty years, at least."

The next day I got Vincent—Ron Perlman—on the telephone. I asked him what he thought of Kimberly Hartman and her Helper's Network. Perlman thought a little bit. Then he thought a little bit more. Then he said: "It sort of represents a vast sentiment that is quite overwhelming. I've not gotten involved personally with these folks. I don't know—there's something so great about having unsolicited response to your work. I felt, the more I stayed away, the more I would allow them to do their own thing without my influence." Perlman thought some more. "Therefore, this has made my enjoyment of their labors all the more rich and rewarding."

Check.

It was not long after this uplifting conversation that the rumors began leaking out, rumors about certain technical adjustments in the two-hour episode of *Beauty and the Beast* that will reintroduce the show this year. Raw adjustments would micro-manage a couple of problem areas at once: namely the need to write the pregnant Linda Hamilton out of the script while at the same time spreading the show's tents a little to include viewers from, shall we say, a slightly more action-oriented perspective.

Not to put too fine a point on it, the changes would involve the impregnation of Catherine by Vincent, her capture by the evil Gabriel, the birth of the baby, the murder of Catherine, and Vincent's vengeance-maddened pursuit of Gabriel over several episodes.

I steeled myself and called Kimberly Hartman again. Her voice remained calm and professional. "If the worst-case scenario happened," she told me, "I still have faith that the creators of the show loved it enough not to violate its essential spirit. If Bobby Ewing can come back on a more reality-based show like *Dallas*, then they can bring Catherine back to us in this fantasy series, even if only temporarily.

"I'm just about to record a new Hotline message," Kimberly went on. "I'm telling people not to lose heart. To go, as Vincent says, with courage and care. We cannot do less."

As I said, a certain layer of irony is helpful when one thinks about the people who are wounded by their capacity to care about a television show. But in Kimberly Hartman's case—and in the cases of all the Kimberly Hartmans—I find that I can't summon that shield. I have this retrograde impulse to blurt: Keep the faith. You are alive and well.

The Last Human Being on Saturday Morning

Well, Pee-wee Herman sort of qualifies, anyway

I began to suspect something chronic, something *Pee-wee*, when the 6-year-old started flitting around the living room at about triple speed and flashing his profile at everybody.

There was no mistaking the symptoms. The child was giving attitude.

Then he wiggled his eyebrows at me one day and said, in this strangled duck voice, "Rainy days are *special* days. There's a lot of *special stuff* we can do when it's *raining.*"

When he put on an outfit he'd outgrown two years ago, I knew it was time for some crisis intervention. Some de-Pee-weeing.

Thank God, my kid and I have always been able to dialogue with each other. We have this honest and open, really caring type of relationship. In lots of ways we aren't like father and son; we're more like, I don't know, friends.

I sat him down opposite me for a little nonjudgmental interfacing. When the floor lamp had stopped vibrating, I looked him in the eye and said:

"Just tell me one thing. Is it—is it Pee-wee?"

"Today's secret word," the kid gurgled, "is 'back.' Heh-*huaw*!"

We're liberals in our household. I don't mind saying it. We like to keep open minds. We read female minimalist fiction, and we applauded—*applauded*—what Jesse did on Super Tuesday. We try to keep on the cutting edge, and if that means exposing our kids to new concepts, new trends, we say, "Hey! Whatever!"

But honest to God, I never thought it would come to Pee-wee Herman.

You've seen him—*don't say you haven't; the demographics have you nailed*—in his itty-bitty gray suit and red bow tie, copping those coy profiles like some fast-forward send-up of Johnny, the Philip Morris bellhop. (You never heard of Johnny? You never heard of Philip Morris? *You never heard of bellhops*? Getouttahere, kid, you're too young to be reading men's magazines. Go watch Pee-wee Herman.) You've seen him do the pogo on MTV, then on HBO. You've seen him dish it with Letterman. You probably caught his major Hollywood star vehicle, *Pee-wee's Big Adventure*. And now—heh-*huaw*!—you've sneaked a peek (YES! ADMIT IT!) at Pee-wee in his second season as the Buster Poindexter/Max Headroom axis's emissary to kidvideo: the homunculus-king of *Pee-wee's Playhouse* on CBS.

Chances are you know the Pee-wee legend: a performance creation of a 35-year-old Paul Reubens (himself a performance creation of Paul Rubenfeld), spawned in the postmodern, postlinear, postprandial phosphorescence of the L.A. punk/

improv clubs. A two-time winner on *The Gong Show*. (You never heard. . . ?) A quintessentially Eighties avatar of neo-infantilism, the performer serenely subsumed into his make-believe persona, the artist as his own imaginary friend. (I think, therefore I am . . . Pee-wee!)

Pee-wee is the only Saturday-morning kid's show featuring a certifiable human being, however broadly one chooses to apply that definition in Pee-wee's fast-edit case. About all the show has achieved so far is six Emmys and the Television Critics Association Award for outstanding achievement in children's programming.

And there's more: The essence of Pee-wee, the whole Pee-wee Weltanschauung as it were, taps even deeper nerves in the nation's psyche.

CBS audience research shows that an impressive—one strains to stop short of the term "frightening"—percentage of Pee-wee's Saturday-morning viewers are, ah, how shall we say it . . . *grown-ups*. Like about a third? (Dig it: About 5 million little nippers tune in, aged 2 through 11; they are joined by something over 2.8 million men and women eligible for driver's licenses and enlistment in the Armed Forces.)

But not just any grown-ups. Not just the chronological technicalities one glimpses in the Morton Downey audiences and on the freeway after 4 A.M. No, we are talking intelligentsia here. Culturati.

Rolling Stone has committed a Pee-wee cover; *Vanity Fair* has made Pee-wee pow-wow. That naughty gazette of the avant-garde, *Metropolitan Home*, found the show to be (brace yourself) "hot"! Even the august (actually, the *summer*, heh-*huaw*!) pages of *Artform* have pronounced, Pee-weewise: In a humid exegesis, wonderfully titled "Pee-wee Hermeneutics" (heh-*huaw*!), writer Glenn O'Brien limned the metaphoric payload of Pee-wee's anthropomorphic toys and declared the Playhouse to be "the Sistine Chapel of nurseries."

Heh-*huaw*!

Thus, Saturday morning's peewee-eminent role model to the

nation's children, the Backbone of Our Future. In Pee-wee-ness lies the salvation of the world. Or something. Ah, for the innocent days when G. I. Joe and Masters of the Universe spoke to children's more traditional, life-centered fantasies.

I decided that what my kid needed was the benefit of some of this grown-up insightfulness.

Perhaps if I sat with him as he watched—not just as a father and nationally prominent media critic but as a *pal*—perhaps I could more or less subtly put some of the program's more sophisticated semiotics into a child's perspective and defuse some of his imitative compulsion.

Only if that failed would I consider ripping out the television set by its connective-cable roots.

I flipped on a *Pee-wee* segment (a half dozen episodes have just come out on video) and plopped down companionably on the sofa beside the lad.

"Anything you don't understand, son, just fire away and I'll try to field it on the fly," I offered heartily.

The first thing I keenly noted was that the program's opening was an incomprehensible blur. It was impossible to make head or tail of the rapid-fire images—Pee-wee flitting here and there, my hastily scribbled notes point out—or the maniacal theme song, speeded up to such a pitch that it could have contained dangerous subliminal messages, for all I knew.

I was trying to recall whether I had Tipper Gore's phone number on my Rolodex when the child, the nubbin, spoke. "Don't try to break it down frame by frame, Pop," he lisped. "It's very Dada, very surreal. Just let it wash over you."

Pee-wee leaned into the camera for a profile close-up that made his face look like a polished albino hazelnut. "I'm gonna go play with my *toys*, heh-*huaw!*" he screeched, and skipped away.

"Boy, there's a knockout line," I muttered, " 'I'm gonna go play with my toys.' Who writes his material, *Dennis Miller*?" I

238

glanced down to see if the kid was responding to my helpful irony.

"Gosh, Dad, don't you know an existential burst of pure freedom when you hear one?" he asked, squirming on the sofa. "Pee-wee isn't doing stand-up shtick; he's projecting this wacky aura of the child eternal, the child immune."

"Sit up straight," I pointed out helpfully.

On the screen, Pee-wee was making hissing sounds at a robot who seemed to have a ghetto blaster for a stomach. Then a trio of flowers sang a song to Pee-wee, who bobbed his head. Then Pee-wee talked to a fat woman on a picture-phone apparatus, using a fruit-cocktail can as the receiver.

Here was an area where I felt I might be of some help. "Pshaw," I whispered, leaning close to the little scamp's ear, "you can't *really* hear someone through a—"

"Isn't the whole anthropomorphic overlay a cosmic gas?" chirped the moppet. "See, Daddy, everything has a face on it! Pee-wee's chair! The windowpane! The picture-phone! The globe! It's so wacky!"

"Globes can't really—" I began lamely.

"We little kids love anthropomorphism," the sapling went on. "It reinforces our inherent faith in a magical and benign universe. And don't you just love Gary Panter's supercharged set design? I hear it costs $325,000 to make each episode. Serious prime-time-production simoleons. Can I have an oatmeal cookie?"

"No," I explained.

Other characters had appeared inside the Playhouse. I could make out a sort of cowboy. Cowboy! *There* was a piece of iconography I could relate to.

"Son," I began, draping an arm around his shoulder, "did I ever tell you about the Durango Kid? Now, *there* was a . . ."

Onscreen, the cowboy, whose name seemed to be Curtis, was telling Pee-wee, "I showed you mine! Now you show me yours!"

"DEGENERACY!" I screamed, leaping from the sofa. "GET ME TIPPER! GET ME JIMMY SWAGGART! I'M GOING—"

"*I'm going door-to-door to make you this incredible offer!*" screamed a salesmanoid on the screen before Pee-wee slammed the door in his face.

"Harmless layering of plateaus of meaning, heh-*huaw!*" my toddlekins reassured me, shooting me a bit of wacked-out profile. "It mostly goes right over our little heads anyway, except that it reinforces the 'lodge' aspect of the show. Would you like me to explain the 'lodge' aspect? Daddy, is the world round or flat?"

Before I could answer, a purplish face had filled the Playhouse screen. Purplish face, lipsticked, wearing a turban. Well, at least the program featured a rough balance of male and female role models.

"*Mekka lekka hi, Mekka hiney ho!*" said the face in a resonant basso profundo.

"Oh, God," I murmured, hiding my face in my hands.

"Relax, Pop," chirped the papoose at my elbow. "That's only John Paragon as Jambi. It's all very postsexual. Try to focus on the essential innocence that's being projected here. Daddy, is there really a Mr. Kite?"

For the rest of the program I sat in a kind of reserved silence—perhaps "catatonia" would be nearer the precise medical definition—and more or less let the *Playhouse* wash over me. Supra-absorbed the information is what I believe I did.

I gazed in terrible serenity at the refrigerator food that wore sunglasses, at the tennis-playing dinosaurs, at the—I don't know, at all that stuff. When Mrs. Rene the Fat Lady sat down on the chocolate cake that Pee-wee, rendered invisible by the wish-granting Jambi, had slid under her derriere, I even managed a wan half smile as my heir and descendant dissolved into feet-kicking horselaughs beside me.

When it was all over, and to my immense gratification, my child had a question for me.

"Daddy," he whispered, turning bright eyes up at me, "is there really a Pee-wee?"

It was the moment I had been waiting for.

"Heh-*huaw!*" I explained.

"But Daddy, Try to Grok the Story Line"

If you think kidvid is still Popeye, Mighty Mouse and Tweety Bird, you're missing the frightening realities

Well, well, well, what have we here—Saturday-morning cartoons, eh?" Chuckling absently to myself, feeling in the pockets of my frayed cardigan for matches to light my favorite calabash, I shuffled into the living room one recent weekend at dawn—stirred from sleep no doubt by the faint ululations of galactic electro-thermoblasters emanating from the television set, over a musical score that seemed, to my sleep-thickened ears, rather more twenty-four track than was wont for kidvid.

My spawn lay about the floor, lizardlike in their cathode raptness. The screen seemed momentarily wracked by some sort of interference—riotous ribbons of color, luminous as supermarket food, interspersed with some underlying pulsation of blinding white. A thunderstorm in the air no doubt; atomic

242

testing. Disdaining lumbago, I flopped amid the spawn, sensing their unstated plea for Quality Time.

"What is that darn cat up to this time?" I demanded heartily of the room at large. "Got the mouse cornered in the old haunted house, I'll bet a nickel. Well, he better watch out for the old exploding-cigar trick—right, gang?"

Thaddeus (not his real name), the eldest, shifted his gaze to catch my fatherly wink. For the first time, I noticed that he affected pajamas imprinted with the likenesses of armed men.

"We're watching Voltron, Defender of the Universe," Thaddeus said with what may or may not have been a soupçon of condescension. "There are no mice," he added after a moment's pause. "There is a Robbeast," he said, helpfully.

I looked back to the television screen. The shimmering multicolored iridescence had resolved itself into five distinct figures, hurtling through a field of wildly veering shapes—asteroids? There was a cutaway to a nightmarish mass of porcine pinkness. Beams of light flashed from its extremities. This was not Porky Pig. A voice from the TV set—a manifestly nonstuttering, abjectly *adult* voice—said: "Our robot attack fleet is taking heavy losses. Open fire on those sensor satellites."

"Here's where the individual units form Voltron," hissed Thaddeus. I noticed that he had arisen semiconsciously from the floor and had assumed what I later came to think of as a bureaucrat's attack stance.

The five distinct figures onscreen—spaceships—arced and merged. In a trice they had melded into a single form: a heroic humanoid shape with the helmet of a Visigoth and a torso that generated shards of white light. The pinkish porcine mass receded, spinning.

"No bulldogs named Spike?" I asked in a hushed voice. "No woodpeckers not realizing they're standing on thin air?"

"What I love is the color-enhancing," said Thaddeus. "It's all Japanese, of course. They program their hand-drawn color cels into computers. Notice how hot the colors are? Fluorescence. Plus they can superimpose action over a generic shot of, say, the cosmos—it knocks down the per-frame drawing costs. And check out the faces close-up. Non-Asian. The Japanese know what's exportable."

From the set, a voice said, "That means we can get on with the work we were sent here to do." Another voice said, "Yes— to find new little worlds for the people of our overcrowded galaxy."

Another voice screamed, *"How can you know this? You're three years old!"*

Thaddeus turned to me with a smile of beatific compassion. *"Mistah Magoo—he dead,"* lisped the youngling. "Pop—you know how you like to write about television blurring the boundaries? The new kidvid is blurring the boundaries between what's kid and what's not, iconographically speaking."

"Not to mention what's quote *television* unquote and what's not." It was "Yannick," my 6-month-old. "Drive out to Toys "Я" Us and check the inventory. It's like walking into the video screen. The whole Saturday-morning high-tech superhero thing started with *products*. Mattel. He-Man and the Masters of the Universe. A toy until autumn 1983. Then Group W syndicated a cartoon version directly to stations—an end run around the networks after they dragged their feet. More than a quarter million in production costs per half hour. Now cleared in 166 markets. Bing. Revolution."

"Autumn 1983—that was *eight months before you were born!*" I drew the cardigan tightly about my shoulders.

"Hey, it's a faster track nowadays," said Yannick. "I believe you were warned about the flash cards. Anyway, along came Voltron. A St. Louis outfit imports it from Japan, edits out *some* of the violence, drops in a score straight out of *Star Wars*, and bango—we tots are falling all over one another. First-run syndication in seventy-six markets. And wait'll you see what's coming off the drawing boards these days. We're talking Robotix; we're talking Tranzor; we're talking SilverHawks and She-Ra, Princess of Power. . . ."

I sat heavily on an ottoman and tried to get my bearings. *A neonate who reads the trades.* But before I could give utterance to a thought, Thaddeus tapped his digital watch. "Hate to interrupt, but it's *Thundercats* time," he said—more to Yannick than to me. He hit the remote switch.

The screen filled with muscular figures clad in leotards and amulets. One of them, a hypervirile male with flaming red hair and the yellowed irises of Michael Jackson in the final frame of *Thriller*, began swinging a broadsword at a spectral presence with red eyes, horns like serpents' heads and the face of a gaping skull.

"Fifteen years ago," I whispered to myself, "I made a modest but tony reputation suggesting that *Popeye* contained disturbing elements of violence. . . ."

Both moppets turned to me with looks straight out of *Village of the Damned.*

"You speak to us of violence," intoned Thaddeus, lifting an arm to point at me. "You, whose own generation received its moral instruction from Wile E. Coyote. Hobbesian man, the predator-absolutist in the war of all against all. Which generation went on to enrich the world with MTV, covert aid, John McEnroe?

"The symbolism has changed now, Father. Our Saturday-morning values are grounded in the good of the several. Ignore the firepower. *Teamwork.* That's the operative concept these cartoons are implanting in our young, impressionable brains."

"But—but *electro-thermoblasters*?" I managed.

"Tut," said Thaddeus impatiently. "Spaceships zapping spaceships. Robots taking out robots. Show me one malleted magpie; show me the first face-blackened Fudd."

"We admire your prophet—what is his name? *Weinberger*?" put in Yannick.

Thaddeus, my firstborn, placed a small, comforting hand on my knee. "If you wish to worry, Father," he said, not unkindly, "know that the terms of kidvid anxiety have grown more complex. Consider the iconography of Voltron. A superhero who is in fact a machine—nay, the aggregate of five ma-

245

chines. Consider similar series in the current plethora of such fare: the Autobots in *Transformers,* the GoBots in the miniseries of the same name. Is it entirely well that we of the two-to-eleven demographic, who are still struggling to sort out the metaphysics of our being, are asked to identify with a system of disembodied circuits?"

"Read your Sherry Turkle," put in Yannick, turning from his teething ring. *"The Second Self: Computers and the Human Spirit.* She fears for our engagement with machines. She writes of 'the nervous preoccupation with the idea of self as machine.' "

"Just to put a little exegesis spin on all this," said Thaddeus, gesturing toward the screen, "consider the counterweight of a series like *Thundercats.* Never mind the swords and the grinning skulls. We progeny aren't unduly traumatized; we have a prior, innate knowledge of evil and need to experience its ritual vanquishment. Read your Bruno Bettelheim. Concentrate instead on the thematic development. Do you notice anything unique about this particular strip?"

I tried to focus all my concentration on the TV screen. *Quality time,* I kept murmuring. *Perhaps they will spare my life.*

"Why, now that you mention it, Thad, I *do* see—yes! The animation flows seamlessly; it's not at all disjointed, like Fred Flintstone."

"Oh, that," shrugged Thaddeus. "Yes, they used a lot of cels; that's their big selling point. The animation is American, for a change. Telepictures Corp. Classy. They use fluorescent paint. Well, it ought to look good with a fifteen-million-dollar production budget. But I wasn't talking aesthetics. Try to grok the story line. It's a saga, like the Diaspora. The guy with the sword is Lion-O; the sword is Thundera, an all-knowing intellect that carries the power of the universe. See, for reasons that are never quite fully explained, the planet of Thundera has exploded, forcing an exodus of Thundercats in these giant spaceships. Well, they keep getting attacked by the Mutants—Reptilians, Monkians, Jackalmen. But as long as Lion-O keeps possession of the magic sword. . . ."

Thaddeus's voice continued to drone, but I was no longer listening. I had gotten up from the ottoman and padded over to the large picture window in the living room. Drawing the curtain back, I squinted into the morning sunlight, unexpectedly bright, as if rendered with fluorescent paint.

"It's a beautiful day," I said quietly, to no one, "in the neighborhood. . . ."

THE LAST ANGRY MOUSE

Ralph Bakshi's Mighty Mouse *may have been hip, cool, even brilliant, but that wasn't enough to save the day*

We interrupt the current renaissance in children's television to bring you this special development at CBS! We have Ralph Bakshi, cult cartoonist extraordinaire and creator of the highly acclaimed *Mighty Mouse: The New Adventures*, standing by in his Westchester, New York, studios. Mr. Bakshi, can you give us some sense of what has happened?

Bakshi: "It's over for the mouse."

Ladies and gentlemen, you've just heard it from the man perhaps closest to the rad rodent himself: For the second and perhaps final time in a video career launched some thirty-four years ago, cancellation has come to the caped caterer of kiddie catharsis and, more recently, an icon of ironic asides to the popcult-addled parents of those madcap moppets. . . .

What the. . . ??!! Has Bakshi, that pasha of postmodern pop-cult, finally managed to work the *entire outside world* into one of his auto-referencing scripts? Has he somehow bent external reality into the ultimate hip, knowing crisis situation for the mouse—*actually getting canceled by his own network?*

Well, you see, the fact is that—er—Mighty actually *did* get canceled by his own network. As of September, the most raved-about series this side of Pee-wee Herman's in what has been, by acclamation, a new golden age for kid video, is history on CBS

The reason? O irony! (Tight shot of the mouse, little crosses for eyes, a stubble of whiskers, a couple of rips in the cape, slinking toward the horizon!) Low ratings! Drubbed on Saturday mornings by something called *Animal Crack-Ups* on ABC.

And, as if to add insult to injury—or irony to insult—consider the official postmodern postmortem. We're talking about a kid show widely celebrated for its campy, topical appeal to adult, baby-boomer audiences, right? Well, cut to a line drawing of a faceless CBS network bureaucrat commenting: "The baby boomers were watching, *but the 2-to-11s weren't.*"

It all started to happen about two years ago. The Dark Ages of kidvid were collapsing under the weight of their own greed and unparalleled cynicism. The networks' traditional child audience for Saturday-morning shows had been fragmented, flimflammed and, finally, frazzled: fragmented by a new universe of competition from syndication, cable and VCRs; flimflammed by a craven marketing strategy of programs based on war toys and homicidal dolls already for sale in stores; and frazzled by the sheer accumulating repetition and sterility of it all. By 1987, children's audience surveys began to track a crisis of historic scope: Not only were the network numbers getting thinned out by the competition—the entire *pool* of young viewers was evaporating! Hey! Come back here! What the hell was going on? (One syndicated programmer, in a burst of unconscious self-parody, actually blamed a run of good winter weather—goddamnit, the little buggers went out and played!)

Heeeeere I come to save the dayyyyyyyy. . . .

Actually, it was not Mighty Mouse but Pee-wee Herman who first hit upon the magic formula for the Saturday-morning renaissance: Stop treating the little ones like miniature adults (*Masters of the Universe, G. I. Joe*) . . . and *start* treating their parents like overgrown toddlers!

Pee-wee's Playhouse premiered on CBS in 1986 and quickly blossomed into the kidvid equivalent of fusion at room temperature: a breakthrough formula in which ultra-hip adult comedians and artists milked the faux-naïf elements of their acts to charm Dad, Mom, Sis and Junior all at once. While the moppets marveled at the talking easy chair and the dancing vegetables, the old boomers could chuckle knowingly at all the buried ironies, the sly references to TV past.

When CBS research showed that almost a third of Pee-wee's viewership was over 18 years old, the stampede was on. Boomer sooner!

Last fall, NBC, which had been heard rumbling about getting out of kidvid altogether, sprang forth with *The Completely Mental Misadventures of Ed Grimley*, an animated version of Martin Short's gloriously childlike nebbish from *SCTV* and *Saturday Night Live*. While the kiddies are cackling, ironists of a certain age will recognize the hip voices of *SCTV*ers Catherine O'Hara, Andrea Martin and Dave Thomas, not to mention the face of Joe Flaherty, who introduces a segment each week.

Steven Spielberg, a boomer-moviemaker who knows a thing or two about childish fantasy, entered into an agreement with Warner Bros. to update Warner's old Bugs Bunny–Porky Pig vehicle, "Merrie Melodies." The new series will be called *Tiny Tune Adventures* and will be available for syndication in fall 1990.

Even PBS hiked its hoopskirts and pranced into the fray. It showcased pre-boomer Ringo Starr as Mr. Conductor (No snickering! This is not ironic!) in a rather enchanting ensemble series aimed at 4-to-7-year-olds called *Shining Time Station*, which premiered late last year.

And then there was *Mighty Mouse.*

When it hit the air in the fall of 1987, Ralph Bakshi's studiedly disheveled updating of the old rodent had all the earmarks, or the mouse-ear marks, of blockbuster success. Here was a legendary cartoon character, a favorite of children since his comic-book creation in 1944 and a *preestablished* video hit (from 1955 through 1966, something not even Pee-wee can claim). Now he was being reinterpreted by a living legend of hip animation.

Every cool guy and gal knows that the fiftyish Ralph Bakshi was the first animator to produce a feature-length X-rated adult cartoon—*Fritz the Cat*, in 1972. A kind of bebop isolato—his artistic models, he says, include such grand loners as Kerouac, Charlie Parker, Melville and Jackson Pollock—Bakshi had abruptly walked away from his lucrative commercial toon work for five years of serious, private, righteous painting. ("It represents a certain search for America" is all he will say of his subject matter.)

He came back two years ago because he sensed (thanks, in part, to the success of *Who Framed Roger Rabbit*) that animation's time had come round again. "It's one of the few mediums left," he says—thinking a tad wishfully, as things turned out— "that haven't been tainted by committee meetings. Animation is like jazz: It works best when it's left alone."

His instant success with *Mighty Mouse* incorporated some of the irony to which he is so addicted. The young Bakshi was among the group of Terrytoons animators who first brought the mouse to television a generation ago. Now he was investing Mighty with a kind of overarching self-consciousness— Meta-Mouse, as it were—festooned with a permanent ironic smirk regarding his own TV existence. That's almost *too much hipness*, as David Letterman himself might say.

(Literally almost too much hipness. Alerted by Bakshi's X-ish reputation, certain media watchdogs, or watchmice, began monitoring every sequential second of *The New Adventurers*—and finally pounced, shrieking. They'd spotted a scene in which the mouse lovingly sniffs a flower and then soars off in an ecstasy of might. *Cocaine! cocaine!* howled the watchmice, but it was never proved—the animation cels in question, presumably, having been scrubbed clean of the stuff.)

And sure enough, the fashionable critics just went nuts. They quivered with knowing glee when a Salvador Dali landscape showed up in the background. They tee-heed when Mighty did a dream sequence reminiscent of Jackie Gleason-as-Ralph Kramden. They swooned when he turned toward the viewer to deliver a self-reflexive throwaway line: "Thank goodness Bakshi finally let me get a nap in," or "Today, kids, we're going to tell an imaginary story. You see, none of it ever happened; it's what we call a cautionary tale."

Before long it seemed that everybody who was anybody was grooving on *Mighty Mouse: The New Adventures.* Everybody, that is, except . . .

(Looking back, you could almost see it coming. . . .)

. . . *Except* the audience for whom the series was scheduled and putatively intended: the children.

Have you ever watched a small child who suspects that the grown-ups are communicating in code, over her head? We're not talking irony here, pal. We're talking anger. Legitimate, rational anger. And damned if the little tykes didn't eventually stick it to Mr. Bakshi exactly as they'd stuck it to the vulgarian Toys-From-Hell sharks who'd preceded him: They quietly went elsewhere. Good Lord, they went to *Animal Crack-Ups.* Is there a moral here?

Yes. Moral: Children are children. Many of today's yield seem perversely bent on remaining children, irrespective of the current American entertainment-advertising-merchandising axis's unceasing efforts to relieve them of that nonproductive state and get their little wazoos out there in the big Shopping Mall of Life.

Irony—or, let's say, the false approximation of it dangled

by the vid-hucksters in front of their marks—is not a mind-set that children find very much suited to their worldview. They naturally tend to be much more responsive to myth, to fable, to stories that evoke and resolve their many fears and conflicts and curiosities.

Does this mean that the current kidvid renaissance is a fake? That hip adults have no conduits to childish innocence? That *Animal Crack-Ups* and interactive robots are the only realistic ploys in the bleak, bleak game?

Obviously not. Pee-wee Herman is a case in point. Herman, who started out as a boomer playing to boomers by lampooning the hidden child in all of us (and continues that conceit on his Saturday morning show), has somehow crashed through his own artifice and into a genuine communion with child-hood. His *Playhouse* is so crammed with the sumptuous cluttered *stuff* of kid fantasy that his small viewers can ignore— or forgive—his more sophisticated tropes. Similarly, Martin Short seems instinctively to understand and respect the wells of ingenuousness that nourish much of his humor (although the network obviously didn't understand it, as it axed the show recently in favor of a new one with John Candy). And as for Ringo Starr—well, since when has he been accused of forsaking his Yellow Submarine?

Now, having bashed Ralph Bakshi for his fatal hipness, let us take a little time to consider all that was admirable in his *Mighty Mouse* and all that remains hopeful in Bakshi's offerings for children.

There's an irony—what else?—in the mouse's demise, and it's this: Bakshi was *after* something in this series that the others are not, something quite genuine in its curious way, something heartfelt and bold, something admirable. He was—as he always is—after a kind of social reckoning.

Not long before the official cancellation of *Mighty Mouse*— at a time when Bakshi already knew the fate of the series—I asked him what had changed about animation in recent years.

"I don't think it's changed enough," was his reply. "It's stopped talking down to kids; I think that's good. But I also think that more issues that are pertinent to how we live should be discussed. The stories should be more *outrageously* funny. What we need is a sense of outrage.

"What we do with *Mighty Mouse*," he went on, "is make fun of television. We show television's weaknesses. Television has produced a kind of coma that the whole country is in. Let's take the discussion about George Bush and the kinds of assault rifles he says people need in order to hunt. I'd like to do a *Mighty Mouse* about this. I've *always* thought that animation was best served when it looked at our foibles. In fact, I've been trying to get *Mighty Mouse* on at night."

And there it is: In his heart, Bakshi never really intended for children to be the mouse's primary audience. What he seemed to be pushing for was an animated editorial cartoon—not a bad idea on its own merits, but not exactly suited for Saturday at noon.

However—and here comes the final irony for this month, I swear it; yubba-dee, yubba-dee, yubba-*that's all, folks!*—*however*, Ralph Bakshi is capable of creating absolutely fabulous television for children. And not just capable: He's done it. It's there, on cels, awaiting its turn on the schedule. *Tattertown* is its name.

That's not the irony. The irony is that *Tattertown* is owned by Nickelodeon. Nickelodeon is the MTV-owned cable system that embodies everything Ralph Bakshi loathes about television. It is a crass, strident, grossly overcommercialized travesty of a children's channel that portrays its young viewers, in programs, promos and ads, as dumb-jock, good-time–Charlie consumeroids—the junior varsity of the MTV generation.

Quite predictably, Nickelodeon—after braying last winter about how thrilled it was to be working with one of the greatest animators of our time and how it was going to broadcast thirty-nine half-hour episodes of *Tattertown* in prime time—has since had second thoughts. "Nothing specific" is now the muted explanation from its high-octane president, Geraldine Laybourne, by way of the channel's promotional department. And *Tattertown* sits.

Which is deplorable, because here, truly, is Bakshi at his lyric best. If *Mighty Mouse* was his muckraking *Journal*, *Tattertown* is his Rosebud—a Hobbit-like, serendipitous dreamworld that has gathered its contours and its characters over twenty-five years in Bakshi's imagination.

Nickelodeon actually brought itself to squeeze out one episode of *Tattertown* last Christmas. A promotional cassette of excerpts also exists. Watching it, I felt suffused with an old, mostly forgotten childlike sense of having entered an enchanted cave, filled with jazzy music, fabulous shadowy characters, endless surprises and excitement without menace. Bakshi himself has done most of the animating, filling the screen with cartoon styles that range from the Thirties and Forties through his own contemporary vision.

Bakshi has explained *Tattertown* most eloquently: "It's a place where everything man ever has made, and everything he has ever lost as a kid, has gone. We don't know where *Tattertown* is, but everything lives, everything fits, everything laughs and grumbles and grumbles."

Yes. And the irony here is that we'll continue not to know where *Tattertown* is—as it's gathering dust on some shelf because Nickelodeon won't bankroll its exquisite laughter and grumbling. Not when it can keep churning out the hard-sell yuks on the cheap.

This looks like a job for Mighty Mouse. But you already know what happened to him.

IV

Laughs

If television is in fact an Industry, comedy in the 1980s was its industrial waste. Comedy clubs proliferated like McDonald's franchises around America in the decade— hey, Yuppies in Oklahoma City needed a little chic abuse, just like everybody else—and created what amounted to a cheap labor force for the middle-management types at HBO, Showtime and other cable profiteers.

A new American dream began to play itself out in the late-night hours: That any boy or girl, no matter how humble their origins, no matter how vacuous their sensibilities, could grow up to be a television stand-up comedy jerk.

By decade's end, the opportunities for this fulfillment were proliferating. In November 1989 HBO launched The Comedy Channel, a 24-hour cable network that featured nonstop comedy. And the inevitable MTV announced plans to begin a similar operation, HA! The Comedy Network, in April 1990. Comedy-club performances would figure heavily in the new channels' content.

Befitting the political times, the material was supply-side (call it a kind of Laughter Curve) and, befitting the political times, it required victims—preferably the oppressed and the defenseless: Gays, blacks, immigrants, all got their gratuitous knocks from the video-processed likes of Andrew "Dice" Clay, Sam Kinison and, working regressively below his level of talent, Eddie Murphy. Ridiculing the homeless, an activity for which public horsewhipping might be an appropriate response in an honorable society (but then an honorable society would not tolerate massive homelessness in the first place) was a ticket to yuk-yuk adoration—as was the profanation of the sacred, a legacy of TV's omnivorous appetite for topic. I suppose that the nadir, for me at least, was the night I watched some famous cable channel or other as some faceless butterball in some god-forsaken comedy dive beckoned his wife from the audience. She pranced up to the stage with a baby in her arms and handed it up to its comedian-father. Cradled in her father's arms, the tot, bemused by the floor microphone on its stand, reached out a tiny hand to touch it.

The father ad-libbed a fellatio joke.

It was at that moment, I think, that I began to wonder seriously whether this culture had entered a period of profound and irreversible decadence.

(Not that the audience seemed to mind. The audiences, as captured in cutaways for these sadomasochistic sessions, never seems to mind. Why do cable-channel comedy audiences always seem to resemble a bunch of actors and actresses *portraying* a studio audience? Nerdy, pasty-faced, standard-issue white people in their casual-wear sweaters and little suburban mustaches, caught by the camera in mid–yuk-yuk from an unflattering floor-level shot, they seem not so much to be laughing as to be *working at laughing.* Yes, indeed, television may very well be an Industry.)

This overview necessarily overlooks some extraordinary comic talents who blossomed in the 1980s: Billy Crystal, Jay Leno, Judy Tenuta, Tracey Ullman, even John Candy used television to reveal vast repertories of characterization, social satire, and— at least in the case of Leno at his best—a smidgen of political barbs.

But these performers, like Steve Martin and Lily Tomlin a decade before them, face the brute fact of diminishing returns. If TV in general depletes material, TV comedy vaporizes it. Comedians in general try to top themselves; comedians on TV have no choice. The warm-spirited *Mary Tyler Moore Show,* the crown jewel of television's Golden Age of Comedy in the 1970s, would not have stood a chance in the hard-edged 1980s—nor did Mary herself in a couple of comeback attempts. Measured against the dirty-sox snortings of Fox Television's *Married . . . With Children,* MTM's literate, intricate ensemble humor seemed almost childlike.

Similarly, NBC's *Saturday Night Live* exploded network television's limits of the permissible when it hit the air in 1975, with its explicit lampoons of sitting Presidents and recognizable network stars, its mockery of TV commercials and of sexual taboos. Five years later, *SNL* was effectively over, its shock value absorbed into the fabric of viewers' expectations. The program lingers on the air, part of the late-night woodwork; its humor for most of the decade has depended on the show itself—on in-jokes based on the viewers' familiarity with the cast members' personas and the reputations of its celebrity guest-hosts.

At the very least, the dog's breakfast of "stand-up" wit in the Eighties represented a 180-degree reversal of American humor (not to say the American character) at its most robust: The nation's comic spirit has always sprung from the unsinkable common man, firing his satiric harpoons into the flanks of the mighty and the pretentious. (One can see how this in-surrectionary sass might run counter to the interests of the same large corporations whose cameras conferred legitimacy on the scrofulous comics of the 1980s. It would be interesting, in fact, to trace some connective lines between the straw-man Common Schmuck as evoked by the Comedy Showcase min-ions and by the sleeker advertising campaigns in network prime time.)

It's hardly a coincidence that Roseanne Barr, the biggest network comedy hit after Bill Cosby, was a graduate of the stand-up comedy circuit. "A Most Uncommon Common Man" is a look at the spuriousness of her network persona's mock-proletarian pose. "Mother Knows Best" suggests that while *The Cosby Show* slid into a self-satisfied decline late in the de-cade, a somewhat less-acclaimed sitcom, *Kate & Allie*, was qui-etly dealing with riskier, more authentic themes.

"Dabney Coleman, World's Greatest, Uh, Jerk" is my ap-preciation of a consummate TV comic actor. Coleman's case is a peculiar one: Although he is widely praised as one of the most technically accomplished comic actors now working, his shows keep getting canceled, and pronto. It is just possible that Coleman, whose characters always radiate a kind of cra-venness with a cockroachean shell, reminded his viewers a little too uncomfortably of some "reality" beyond the borders of the cathode screen.

WHEN THE LAUGHTER WAS REAL

TV rendered unto Caesar what was Sid's. Gleason and Kovacs cracked wonderfully wise. Once, children, comedy was really funny

" '*H*umor'?" muttered the slubberdegullion heap of old Jeremiahs who had once been the toast of fashionable salons wherever media criticism was essayed. "*Did I hear someone say 'humor'?*" A red eye opened from the folds of rheumy somnolence and swept the pages of the special humor edition that swirled around him. A hush replaced the ambient sound of cultivated aphorism. Male models, clad in the very latest fashion, half-turned in his direction, projecting a sort of four-color alertness muted by a pouty sensuality.

" '*Humor,' is it? I'll tell you a thing or two about 'humor!' I'll tell you about television's—*" The tatterdemalion apparition had arisen now and was gesticulating wildly. Chairs scraped; there was a shuffling of bylines edging their way back toward the table of contents. Suddenly a woman's voice—possibly that

263

of Veronica Geng—screamed: "Oh, my God, stop him, some-body! He's going to explain humor!"

"Worse than that, I think," breathed Wilfrid Sheed, an oasis of calm in the general panic, as the figure leapt atop the hot hors d'oeuvres table and brandished a revolver. "I'm terribly afraid he's going to tell us about a—"

"*Golden Age!*" roared the specter.

"—Golden bloody Age," moaned Sheed.

Call me a schlemiel. Some years ago—never mind how many—television comedy was funnier than it is now. There was—how might one phrase it?—a Golden Age; yes, that's it, a Golden Age of television comedy. I should hasten to add here (although why should I? I've got a gun) that this claim is not part of some overall deification of the past. The 1978 Yankees would have beaten the 1927 Yankees, the big bands are finished, how about those bioengineering labs?—and so on and so on. But TV comedy as it once flourished is deader than last week's *People* cover, and we will never see its like again.

Now I suppose you want to know why. Don't stop me if you've heard this one.

There was a great deal of speculation over that very question, some of it even bearable, when Jackie Gleason resurfaced in New York in 1985. The Great One had been brought up to Manhattan from Miami for a press conference at "21" to announce the discovery of sixty-seven episodes from *The Honey-mooners*—episodes that had not aired on television since their original live transmissions within *The Jackie Gleason Show* on CBS from 1952 to 1957. (The archival film had been in Gleason's personal vault all this time.)

Gleason himself had no doubts about whether the age he'd helped render golden was irreclaimable, nor about the reasons why. Just a shade aghast, behind his signature red corsage, at encountering a press contingent the size and intensity of a CIA-backed counterrevolutionary force—David Hartman was there with *two Good Morning America* potted plants—the silver-haired vaudevillian nonetheless disposed of modern TV comedy with brutal aplomb.

"They're taking actors," Gleason told the glassy batteries of entertainment reporters, "and making comedians out of them. Which is a strange thing. I know of several comedians who became good actors. But I never heard of a good actor becoming a good comedian."

What? He'd never heard of Alex Karras? Just kidding. A deft point, Jackie's. A nice little eulogy for *Silver Company, Three's Spoons* and all those soulless little mutants from the networks' genetic-engineering catacombs; all those photogenic, "Q"-factored young sitcom faces as innocent of mirth as oranges —*sorry, Mr. Carney, we're looking for a sidekick who's a little more . . . oh, James Arness.*

Gleason might have elaborated that "good comedian" meant—and continues to mean—"good *physical* comedian," an almost completely vanished art within the modern situation comedy. For all its MTV-inspired access to physical movement, modern TV curiously elects to display its principal comedy characters mostly as friezes—their arms uselessly at their sides, in the stock medium–close-up shot, trading those little T-shirt captions of payoff lines while the laff cassette supplies the response.

Gleason might have quoted, to good effect, from James Agee's famous 1949 critique of movie comedy: "To put it unkindly, the only thing wrong with screen comedy today is that it takes place on a screen which talks. . . . Because there is a screen, talking comedians are trapped into a continual exhibition of their inadequacy. . . ."

O return, return! Recall the young Gleason and the young Carney in their maddened chases about the Kramden kitchen, a whole physical-language system of pride and comeuppance, hubris and deflation, appetite and denial. Gleason riding for a fall with his eyes bugging out (you could almost see the springs), pushing his great belly in front of him like an upthrust ego—in pursuit of Carney, his inadvertent agent of doom, a dissolving picket fence in a windstorm, his elbows and chin an arsenal of harpoons aimed unconsciously at his pal's righteous blubber. And Audrey Meadows, who could stand still better than anyone in TV history, providing the essential counterpoint of defeated sanity.

What video comedian of the unconstrained past decade used physical bulk as eloquently as Gleason? Not John Candy, for whom it was a one-joke prop. Not Belushi, for whom it was a blunt instrument. Gleason elevated his belly to the status of a flawed moral premise—in his more ambitious sketches, to a tragic flaw.

Recall the young Caesar, whose *face* was a universe of nuanced movement: those eyes swollen nearly shut with *knowing*, that quivering chevron of a mouth—all of Caesar's tics and grimaces like a Morse code Mayday in the presence of Carl Reiner's lascivious, insinuating forehead. Recall Kovacs, sleepily, engineering his gigantic physical puns and his abstract-expressionist camera tricks, all those gags calculated to subvert the unstated expectation of what was about to happen. Recall all this, and then recall the funniest line you ever heard from the lips of Valerie Bertinelli. I'm talking Golden Age here. Don't anybody try to leave. I've got a gun.

This lost paradise of physical, extra-verbal TV comedy illuminates a related facet of those great times: universality of theme.

Ron Simon, a curator of The Museum of Broadcasting in New York, believes that sitcoms began to lose their hold on Americans' imaginations precisely as they began to be liberated from what seemed at the time to be the stifling bonds of escapism.

"In *The Honeymooners* you see the classical, the pure structure of TV comedy without the ingredient of social awareness that *All in the Family* ushered in," Simon told me recently. "Certainly the Norman Lear comedies were a great innovation of the Seventies. But now there are so many different channels, and Lear's innovations have been copied and syndicated so much, that maybe they've lost the edge that they had back when they were new. The thing about Gleason and his contemporaries is that they weren't allowed the social awareness. So they became timeless."

There are other, somewhat more ancillary theories. John Markus, the gifted 29-year old head writer on NBC's salutary *The Cosby Show*, has made himself a student of the sitcoms of his infancy, the Fifties and early Sixties. "The legacy I can feel is that of *real time* unfolding," Markus says. "Real time and real life do not have the frenetic pace that producers have been forcing into their shows, thanks to videotape-editing techniques. A Gleason sketch . . . *unfolded* . . . with a natural sense of building toward some kind of payoff. Viewers could savor that buildup. Nowadays, the premium is on punching that joke into the formula *right now*—before the attention span fades."

Perhaps these various theories—Gleason's, Ron Simon's, John Markus's—are but separate threads of a single unifying truth: that comedy on television has passed its vital peak because it has become a captive of its own freedom. Such a theory would explain, for instance, the several tortuous incarnations of *Saturday Night Live*, as well as its recent resurgence—the show has lately broken free from its shock attitudinizing, its defiant ca-ca and druggie jokes, in favor of more deeply layered character studies that owe their structure (if not their politics) to the mid-Fifties, the Golden Age.

But what of Eddie Murphy? And what of his echelon of current superstars—video comedians who have pushed the definitions, the stakes of TV comedy far beyond anything ever envisioned by the likes of Gleason, or Benny, or Berle or even the early Joan Rivers? (The late Joan Rivers is another matter.)

There is no need here to restate the enormity of Murphy's technical gifts—the elastic voice, the flawless sense of speech pattern, the onstage air of command. But Eddie Murphy lacks greatness. His lack is partly concealed by the raw talent; but it is the same lack that is far more visible in the vulgarian Rivers or the numbingly plugged-in David Letterman.

What limits these comedians—what anchors them forever in the transient sensibility of their times—is their identification with power. They have shifted the locus of American humor from its historic, democratic roots to a place where it doesn't belong, to the viewpoint of the ruling class. To watch Murphy hilariously sending up black pimps and the rest of the underclass; to watch Rivers forage into the very infrastructure of womanhood and triumphantly spotlight its symptoms of decay; to watch Letterman endlessly include us in his private-public contempt for the medium that has made him a star—to watch all this is to watch power corrode and feed, as it inevitably does, on its own roots, on itself.

The best contemporary comics on television, then, seem to have gorged themselves on the temporary spoils of a national binge, an experimental delight in flexing muscle, throwing weight. They have plundered the defiance of Lenny Bruce without taking his enormous risks; they have aped Lear's social anger and turned it back on the very groups whom Lear *perceived* as angry. They have taken comedy's essential rueful, deflating, inclusive chuckle and twisted it into a sneer.

Which is what I mean about the Golden Age and how things are different today. Okay, you can all go now. Look. The gun was empty the whole time.

THE LAST ANGRY MAN

Today's political satirists are pale imitations of the masterful Mort Sahl, who at 57 still rages at the night . . . whenever he gets the chance

Observe, on the public channel, the television political satirist (the only one we have these days) as he begins his routine.

He stands with heels together, this bow-tied man, inside a circle of crimson footlights. The camera pullback reveals a piano—blue, festooned with white stars. Already, a motif: The Satirist has wrapped himself in the iconography of the flag. This is not a promising sign. But let us hear him; he has bowed to the opening applause and has begun his patter:

"... This audience will give the same support to Gary Hart as *B'nai B'rith gave to Jesse Jackson.*"

The voice really is exceptional: a sawtooth baritone that dips into the nasal when the political satirist holds on to a vowel. This voice will lead you to the italicized punch line as surely as a German shepherd will lead a blind man through rush-hour traffic.

"Gary Hart's support is strong with people with children in *Montessori school*. . . ."

Well, um, what's on HBO? (What's on the *ceiling*?) But wait. There comes the sound of human laughter. People are actually haw-hawing at these lines? Knees are being slapped? Could the laughter be, as they say, "enhanced"? No. The pullback has now brought a studio audience into the video frame.

"How about Reagan standing on top of the Great Wall of China *remembering when it was built, now you can't top that*. . . ." (The voice plunges to low-diaphragm, superitalicized stress for punch line, hurrying into quick, hyphenated kicker over incipient laughter.)

The faces behind the political satirist are—scrubbed. The slapped knees, plump. One notes lipstick; one notes combed hair. One notes sensible reading glasses dangling from neck chains. All the faces have little croissant-eyes of mirth; little Reagan chuckle-eyes; this TV studio audience is having itself a whale of a time!

Now the political satirist has moved over to the piano keyboard. He is playing a tune standing up while he sings to the camera over his right shoulder. The camera zooms in. The tune is that hit from the late Thirties "It's De-Lovely," but the political satirist, that slyboots, has changed the lyrics:

Those cute boom babies were sweet and clean,
But in college they set fire to the dean—
Now they're Yuppies, yeah they're Yuppies,
  See the Yuppies!
They wore long hair and they wore no shoes,
Now they're driving big BMWs,
They're the Yuppies, yeah the Yuppies,
  See the . . .

Not, taken in sum, your fugitive scream of social outrage that has sent fire-eyed visionaries to rot in the gulag.

The political satirist's name is Mark Russell. Six times a year he does half an hour of this stuff out of Buffalo for the Public Broadcasting Service. Buffalo must be naturally rich in studio audiences. As for the 52-year-old Russell, he is just about the hottest TV political satirist in captivity (so to speak)—not to mention the only one.

Holder of the Distinguished Chair in Wryness on the late, Unlamented *Real People*. Frequent appearances as humorist/commentator on *Good Morning America*, with special assignments at the political conventions. A major piece of TV talent.

And as relevant to the tides of political dissidence in America as, say, the Michael Jackson public-service announcement is to the war on drunken driving.

To be quite fair about it, the printed page does not do justice to a Russell performance. The man's timing, and especially his voice, do lend a certain test-tube élan to a lot of his doggerel. Listening to that voice self-inflect, after a while one begins to wander away from Russell's content ("The Yuppies care. *They* care. They want a world made safe for new and improved pasta machines") and into reverie.

Why is this man video America's satirist laureate?

And—where, dammit, has one heard that voice before?

Shelley Berman!

Of course! It all comes back! That world-weary nasal curl at the bottom of a vowel; that grating tic, "Youuuuuu seeeeeeeee," that hovered after a payoff line—it's all Berman, that wonderful Fifties monologuist whose albums made neurotic, Kafkaesque anxiety such fun for beleaguered intellectuals.

Having located Russell's voice in Berman, one finds it suddenly easy to jigsaw in the other Fifties components of his persona (because they *are* components and not the self-created idiom of a true original).

The keyboard, clearly, is from Tom Lehrer, the Harvard mathematician whose sublimely morbid compositions ("Poisoning Pigeons in the Park," "The Masochism Tango," "The Vatican Rag") were simply too hot, too demented, for consumption on Dinah Shore's medium.

And the milieu—however scrubbed, however neutralized—is from Mort Sahl.

Sahl! God. Whatever *happened* to Sahl, anyway? Why isn't Sahl up there, in that famous red V-neck sweater, a newspaper folded under one arm, sweating and giggling ("Ha!ha!ha!ha!ha!") and baring his teeth and launching that comedy-of-consciousness ground fire of his, a patter that seldom built to any single, identifiable, rim-shot *gag line* but scooped the listener's sensibilities along in its surging, dangerous digressions?

Clearly, American big-scale television is satisfied with (if not downright grateful for) a "political satirist" who can skillfully evoke the *mannerisms* of those transformational comics of the Fifties, comics whose imprint still resides in the country's memory. But not the content. Not the ideas. No hint of sleepless nights, please; no lunatic sense of laughing-so-I-will-not-cry. Just—gags. Oh, those Yuppies.

I saw Sahl onstage not long ago in Washington. The truth is that Sahl, now 57, has not "gone" anywhere; he has been working steadily over the past thirty years—writing movies, doing the college circuit and club dates and an occasional doomed kamikaze rush at the one forum he truly loves and covets, the broadcast airwaves. In these futile assaults—radio shows on both coasts, the odd summer series—Sahl has usually proved his own worst enemy, it must be said. His unfortunate obsession with the role of Jim Garrison, the New Orleans district attorney, in the matter of John F. Kennedy's assassination carried Sahl far beyond the reasonable tolerance of any mass audience—even of his considerable, persistently adoring fans.

But the night I saw him, Sahl was as taut and polished as he will ever be. His Jesse Jackson gags probed deeper, more complex nerves than Russell's Jesse Jackson gags: "You know what kind of people call Jesse Jackson 'Reverend'? The same kind of people who call Dan Ellsberg 'Doctor.' ''

Merely isolating a Sahl "gag," however, tends to distort the man's comic approach. His routines do not translate to excerpts, to sound bites. (This may be the real reason why time-conscious television cannot contain him.) His routines are densely interwoven, picaresque journeys of Sahl the detached observer and Sahl the solipsist, the observer-of-himself-thinking.

On this night, Sahl's self-contained comic world enveloped a White House dinner that President Reagan had thrown for visiting Middle Eastern dignitaries. As his small audience (an audience not radically distinguishable from Russell's Buffalo gals 'n' guys, interestingly enough) sat with their lips curled upward, alert for the chance to chuckle in unison at a punch line, Sahl led them, with hardly a pause for transition, into Oz. In place of gags, isolated moments of revelation swam out of the verbiage and hovered briefly, brilliantly; the Hoosier vulgarity beneath the surface of White House protocol; the studied, comic patter of Great Power adversaries making small talk; the incidental absurdity of a marine harpist, a female sergeant major, playing Stephen Foster favorites somewhere on the perimeter—many things. Many startling, gorgeous, dangerous things. And always Sahl, like the ghost of Walt Whitman lurking in Abraham Lincoln's Washington, observing and observing himself observe:

"Reagan says to Shamir, 'HOW'S THAT STEAK?'

" 'Best I ever tasted!' Shamir holds it up. 'Is it aged?'

" *'We try not to talk about age around here!'*

"I was standing next to Shamir and Weinberger, and Shamir was accusing the United States of training the Saudis. He said to Weinberger, 'Your pilots take the Saudis up from 9 to 1, you take a half hour for lunch, and then you go back flying from 1:30 to 5:30.' Trying to defuse the tension with my wit, I butted in and asked, 'Why don't they take an hour for lunch?' And Shamir said, 'Because they'd have to *retrain the Arabs.*' ''

A few minutes later Sahl wandered into a reminiscence of Reagan at the 1980 convention of religious broadcasters: "Reagan was there . . . affable grin . . . 'You know, I never did believe in evolution. . . .' The crowd: 'That's fantastic! Who invited him? He might be elected? Okay!' . . . the crowd so enthusiastic, *they'd yell up requests to the stage. . . . 'Tell us about the world being flat!' "*

At the end, the audience clapped politely as Sahl tucked his newspaper under his arm and strolled offstage under his trademark Zen tag line: "Thank you for your individual perceptions." The coiffed audience looked relieved and grateful: They had seen a celebrity, and it was finally over.

A planned interview with Sahl went awry that night. He had got wind of a question I asked of the nightclub manager—"Did you take a chance booking Sahl?"—and chose to interpret it as a sign of hostility, a reference to what Sahl believes is a general media distortion of him: as washed-up, as has-been, as yesterday's comic on the comeback hustings. (In fact, my question had to do with the strategy of booking a comedian into a club known almost exclusively as a jazz spot.) The demons that fire Sahl's dangerous genius still deny him, perversely, the access he seems to crave.

Russell, who has that access, is less troubled by the demons. He acknowledges his debt to Sahl with a detached, professional candor.

"Mort Sahl was an enormous influence on me," Russell says. "I became aware of him back in the late Fifties, when I was just a piano player around Washington. His targets became my targets. His attitudes became my attitudes."

That homage might seem a shade overstated to anyone who has seen Russell only on television. In his nontelevised lecture appearances (upwards of one hundred a year at $8,000 to $10,000 a pop), Russell is in fact capable of drawing real blood. The compromises he makes in exchange for video access are self-inflicted; they seem not to hurt a bit.

"The really biting stuff belongs in the shadows," Russell

argues. "It belongs in the cabarets. It's just not a mass-media kind of thing. You can't expect to see it in the mass media."

Somewhere in the shadows, Sahl bares his teeth—but with no TV camera to record the moment, it did not happen. Thank you for your perceptions.

MOTHER KNOWS BEST

Why is Kate & Allie *America's most honest family show? 'Cause Cos &* Crew *have traded substance for sweaters*

A preternatural quiescence has lately descended upon the Huxtable household, site of *The Cosby Show* on NBC. Just an enormous amount of *beaming* is going on. Whole herds, crofts, entire *agricultures,* of nifty sweaters are being worn. Doorbells tinkle; phones ring; moppets tumble into view, beam, have their transient concerns wryly attended to, trip happily away— to change sweaters as often as not.

Well-being is exuded, verities affirmed. There is benign musing. "Dr. Haynes is a *very, very, special person,*" Bill Cosby as Dr. Cliff Huxtable muses to his wife, Clair, referring to a demi-character who is otherwise nothing more than an absentee plot device. Clair leaves the household for a few days to serve on the committee planning a celebration for Dr. Haynes. Cliff's father arrives to help Cliff take care of things. "Who

276

are *you*?" Cliff asks kiddingly, answering the doorbell. "Your father!" answers Cliff's father. "Can't be. My father ran away with the circus when I was born," joshes Cliff. "He's back!" ripostes the father. "Omigoodness," sighs Cliff, patting his nifty sweater with absent contentedness, or contented absentness. "Well, you don't *smell* like you've been around elephants."

Moppets tumble in. "Granddad!" they cry. Granddad has brought chocolate-chip cookies. "May I have one?" the moppets ask. There are kisses. "You may have one," says Granddad.

The phone rings. It's Clair. A Huxtable moppet answers with a mouthful of chocolate-chip cookie. "I have a chocolate-chip cookie," she mlumphs into the receiver. "Well, Dad said I could." There is a pause. "Mom wants to talk to you," says the moppet as the laugh track titters. Cliff clears his throat and takes the receiver: "Hi, dear. Yeah, I know it's close to dinner. But . . . but . . . but . . . but. . . ." Cliff turns to his father. "Clair says Mom wants to talk to you." Cliff's dad takes the phone: "Hello, Anna. Yeah, I miss you, too. Yeah, I'll put him on." Cliff takes the phone: "Hello, Mom. Yeah, I know it's close to dinner. But . . . well, Dad brought the cookies." Cliff turns to his dad: "Mom wants to talk to you." Cliff's dad takes the phone: "Hi, Anna. Yes, but . . . but . . . but. . . ."

Fade to the first commercial, and a change of nifty sweaters all around.

Twenty-odd more minutes of this sort of salubrious byplay and one realizes with a kind of mind-restoring jolt that—migod—*the final credits are rolling.* Time's up! Show's over! Wha' happened? Nothing—nothing but the byplay! The beaming, the nifty sweater-wearing, the musing, the affable asides . . . the cookies . . . that's the whole dang deal, Jack.

An incredible achievement, when you think about it. *The Cosby Show* has been credited with a lot of things in its three award-winning seasons: turning NBC's entire prime-time schedule into a winner, rehabilitating the image of the black American family, fueling the success of Cosby's No. 1 best-seller, *Fatherhood*. But nobody, I think, has grasped the show's most remarkable feat of all: It has died and gone to heaven.

Narrative . . . conflict . . . plot development . . . the very *notion* of "plot" . . . subtly, imperceptibly, *The Cosby Show* has shed all these qualities like mortal remains. It has purified itself into an absolute state of transcendence. It just *is*. No longer must Americans trouble to watch *The Cosby Show*; now it seems sufficient to merely *believe* in it for thirty minutes each Thursday. (In that sense, the show is more than heavenly; it is positively Republican.)

And—hey—that's fine. Given an age in which *all* video narrative is rapidly dissolving, absorbed on nearly all fronts by the solid-state ambience of video attitude, I'll grant *Cosby* its feel-good rights in a spectrum shared by the brooding bitchiness of *L.A. Law*.

What seems less than tenable, though, is the Huxtables' continuing claim as the definitive television family when it comes to Confronting the Hard Issues. Not to appear disrespectful about it, but there are no Hard Issues in heaven.

In opting to position themselves as the happiest darn family in television history (no small aspiration, given the Cleavers and the Care Bears), Cos and his ménage, and their writers and producers, are in danger of disregarding Tolstoy's famous warning. ("Happy families are all single-concept vehicles," Tolstoy wrote in *Anna Karenina*. "Every semi-happy family is fat city, plotwise.")

Let us now praise the semi-happiness of *Kate & Allie*.

Kate & Allie has burbled along on Monday nights for four seasons on CBS, enjoying good notices but hardly a fraction of the accolades showered upon *The* (often-deserving) *Cosby Show*. The consummately wised-up urban actresses Jane Curtin and Susan Saint James play a couple of dehusbanded moms left in charge of their children—one teenage girl apiece and one small boy—all of whom share living space and nuclear-tipped wisecracks in an apartment in Greenwich Village.

The creator of the series is Sherry Coben. One of the reigning smart ladies of contemporary sitcom, Coben must have shared a crazy salad or a funny sauce with the Ephrons Nora and Delia: Kate and Allie's world abounds with exes, exes' new mates, new mates' exes and other casualties of secular humanism. Coben's brand of comic make-believe draws from the bruised but resolute consciousness of women for whom the doorbell has tolled with grimmer tidings than chocolate-chip cookies (ARE YOU PAYING ATTENTION, YOU FECK-LESS HUNKS OUT THERE?)—but who persevere, by their wits and their wit.

Granted, the series is squeaky-squeaky upper-middle, the kids well fed and their arms unpunctured; granted, the sweaters, while not exactly in the Huxtables' price range, are color-coded to the set. Granted, the plots click digitally along on hairbreadth edits, and the dialogue is so tightly compressed it makes the Federal Express commercials sound like a Harold Pinter play. At least there *is* a plot. And regularly it probes the marrow of familial/sexual anxiety and grief.

A recent segment called "Jennie and Jason" pushed Allie's (Curtin's) daughter, Jennie, straight to the brink of her first coital experience. The episode opened blandly enough in the apartment's common telekitchen, with Jennie and her new beau, Jason, being waved off to the movies by the two moms. One quick edit later, it's late at night and Jennie has tiptoed into the bedroom of sleeping Emma, Kate's daughter.

"Em," whispers Jennie urgently, "Jason wants us to go to bed together." "S' get in," mumbles semicomatose Emma. "No. Me and *him*." "Really?" Now Emma is awake.

"You going to?"

"I donno."

As moms throughout the Bible Belt lurch to their feet in search of a little fresh air, the two girls solemnly analyze the pros and cons of such an adventure. Finally, thankfully, Jennie's fuzzy thinking comes into focus. "I made my decision," she tells Emma. "What is it?" "*Yes.*" "Wow."

Well, semiwow. What ensues is an entirely predictable pastiche of French bedroom (or Romper Room) farce: all comic alibis and coy intrigues, the would-be lovers thwarted by an untimely intrusion—but not before a perfectly wonderful, and gorgeously written, little exchange between Jennie and Jason, alone in Jason's house and suddenly awkward over their preliminary slices of pizza.

"You eat more than any girl I've ever known," Jason assures Jennie, adding hastily, "I mean that in the best possible sense." Pause. "I love you." Another pause. Jennie: "I love you, too—so where'd your parents go?" "To my aunt's house—she has a pool—do you really?" "Yeah—we had a pond—do *you* really?" "Yeah." They kiss. Jason: "Chlorine makes my eyes burn."

Jason's mother bursts in a couple of minutes later—the pair have just settled gingerly on a fold-out couch—and Jennie's "decision" remains neatly, conveniently theoretical. But the show's creators are not content to dispose of the issue itself so tidily. There ensues a final confrontation on the matter between Jennie and Allie. Distilled and epigrammatic as the writing must be for television, Curtin and the young actress Allison Smith still manage to convey a painted, raw-nerved authenticity that elevates the episode (and the series) well above mere chocolate-chip escapism.

"As a young woman of 17," begins the clearly rattled Allie, "you'll probably do what you like." "Mom—" begins Jennie. "you'll *probably* do what you like," Allie barrels on, "but before you do what you like I want you to listen to me for five minutes with an open mind.

"I believe," Allie continues, "that when sex is part of something bigger—when it's part of caring and lending support and understanding as well as pleasure—it's wonderful. But when it's . . . peer pressure or glands, it can teach you some things that aren't true: that you're not special enough to wait for someone special.

"I don't believe in Mister Right. But I believe in waiting till it's right."

Jennie: "So you want me to wait."

Allie: "Definitely, yes."

Jennie: "But you do agree, the choice is mine."

Jennie: "What if I decide to do it?"

Allie: "If you think you are mature enough to make love, I want you to make love maturely"—she sighs—"*go to the doctor, talk to him about birth control and have him send me the bill.*" She reflects. "No. Send the bill to your father." Fade. Credits.

That, I submit, is a remarkable—a seminal—piece of television writing. If *The Cosby Show* affirms Republican obliviousness to unseemly social choices, *Kate & Allie* appears to have placed itself defiantly in the camp of the San Francisco Democrats.

Not only has the deeply freighted issue of teenage premarital sex been *raised* here, it has been *adjudicated*—on the side of those famous bugaboos of conservative dogma, moral relativism and situational ethics, and with a conspicuous absence of recourse to scriptural guidance.

Whether Allie's advice to her daughter was the "right" advice, and whether a major television network, with all its emblematic power to define social norms, has the right to advance such advice under the rubric of entertainment—these are interesting questions. The fact is that just such questions, of sex and responsibility and parental guidance, are being thrashed out in millions of American households by people—black and white—whose groping uncertainties are more nearly mirrored by the *Kate & Allie* menagerie than by the suave and sweatered Huxtables.

Kate & Allie may be slick, but it is at least trying to peel away some layers between its characters and reality—while *Cosby*, up there in cable-knit heaven, seems content to go on pulling the wool over its own eyes.

A Most Uncommon
Common Man

Roseanne's *funny, sure, but she's no workingman's
Barr and hers is no feminist manifesto*

Roseanne Barr—if you haven't caught her on ABC's *Roseanne,* think of Donna Reed fattened up for veal, or Betty Boop
on steroids—is one of the biggest things on television these
days.

Why is Roseanne so big? Well, I'll tell you. Roseanne's so
big because, because . . . because Roseanne's *real.* Roseanne's
honest. Roseanne's *revolutionary.* Roseanne's a *distinctive voice,
rare on network TV.* And Roseanne's even *wondrously free of big-
otry.* ("One of Roseanne's coffee-break chums is a black woman,
and nobody makes a big deal about it," breathes *The New York
Times,* understandably awestruck at witnessing this greatest
leap forward in the civil-rights movement since Rosa Parks
moved to the front of the bus.)

And what is the object of Roseanne's hyper-reality, her ultra-honesty, her distinction, her revolutionariness? Why, it's the working class! Blue-collar America! Those slicers-of-life, those time-punchers in plastics plants, those endearingly tacky bowlers and beer swillers, those eaters of Cheetos (at least five separate admiring reviews of *Roseanne* have mentioned the Cheetos, as if they were so many syllables of authentic dialogue in a Flannery O'Connor short story).

Network television is off on another of its infrequent field trips to descry and limn the Common Man. The Common Man has been descried before by network television—and torn limn from limn in many cases—virtually since the medium opened for business. Jackie Gleason created the TV version of Chester A. Riley, the First Hard Hat, when *The Life of Riley* made its debut in October 1949, then surrendered the role to William Bendix. A few years later, Gleason worked out the persona as bus driver Ralph Kramden on the legendary *Honeymooners*. Since then, the Common Man has been variously lampooned (*The Beverly Hillbillies*, *The Dukes of Hazzard*); treated as a kind of American id *(All in the Family)*; fanfared (*Skag*); and, finally, in the corrosive late 1980s, propped up and used as a kind of gag writers' punching bag (the odious *Married . . . With Children*, currently running on the Fox network).

This time round, ABC and the production team that packages *The Cosby Show* have decided that the Common Man is a 36-year-old, five-foot-four, 215-pound Jewish woman from Salt Lake City who toured on the stand-up circuit for years cracking wise about her contempt for her husband's sex habits and who now portrays a vaguely ambi-ethnic cracker lumpenprole living, with her equally overstuffed husband and three tele-perfect tele-children, in—go figure—Illinois.

A real authentic cross-sectioning of typical American life, wouldn't you say?

That kind of big. The show is not only a hit (Common Man breakthroughs on this scale can never be merely hits), it's a statement. An oracle. A searingly probing look at American life as it is lived by *real people*.

"An honest portrayal of blue-collar family life," says *Time*, which adds that Roseanne's zingers (much is made of Roseanne's zingers'; they rank up there with the Cheetos as objects of iconic fascination) "teach *us* a lesson." *USA Weekend*, that tireless beacon of social realism, tracked down a publicist for the AFL-CIO, who assured the reporter that "Roseanne does a great job of capturing what a working mother is all about. She connects with reality by showing glamour is lost real soon." (Wow. That's the kind of reality that just drives the State Department nuts when it gets leaked into the mass media.)

Even Ms. Barr herself has become inflamed with visions of a Larger-Than-Cheetos Purpose in *Roseanne*. When one of the tele-kids chirps, "Mother, can I ride my bike?" and Roseanne zings back, "Yeah, ride in *real heavy traffic*," that's not just some ordinary escapist gag you're hearing, pal—that's feminism!

Yeah! No lie! May Geraldo bust my nose! Swear on a stack of Oprah! It's been in all the newsmags! You have heard of the proverbial 600-pound gorilla? Well, the producers of *Roseanne* have found themselves dealing with . . . the . . . *215-pound feminist*, and any behind-the-scenes attempts to "tone down" her, uh, her *message* have activated the woman's considerable temper, even leading to the forced resignation of the show's executive producer. (I've caught a few of Ms. Barr's stand-up performances on the cable channels' comedy showcases, where control of material is about as burdensome an issue as the prospect of a meteor shower. I have never been able to discern a feminist "message" in her work that might conceivably invite toning down, unless you count her protracted demonstration of her friends' nose-picking habits; but then, feminism has taken some subtle turns since the Equal Rights Amendment was finally killed.)

———

Why not let's Velcro ourselves to the camera lens, so to speak, and zoom on inside Roseanne and Dan's household and take us a real close squint at some of this distinctive, honest, revolutionary realism that *Roseanne* is always dishing out on behalf of the ordinary, average, blue-collar Common Man?

Here is husband Dan (John Goodman) talking on the kitchen phone. Dan looks worried. Dan is out of a job. (Dan is often out of a job; his chronic joblessness is a running motif on the series.)

Roseanne reassures him on her way to the stove: "You are gonna get the very next job that comes along!" Dan tries a little joke: "Over at the Blue Flamingo, they're hiring topless dancers." Roseanne shoots him a lewd glance out of the sides of her slitted eyes: "I'll put a dollar in yer G-string." Dan jiggles his potbelly: "Go find your purse."

There ensues a brief freeze in the action to allow for what has become a kind of visual signature on *Roseanne*: matched close-ups of the post-zinger *cleansing grin*. First, Roseanne gives a cleansing grin. Then Dan gives one. The cleansing grin is like aerosol disinfectant on this program; it sanitizes—let's say it Cosbyizes—Ms. Barr's industrial-strength cable-comic whimsy for the more tepid palates of Mom and Pop Primetime. ("Cute?" roars Roseanne. "I bet his parents are *brother and sister!*" CLEANSING GRIN! CLEANSING GRIN!)

Jackie, Roseanne's sister (played by the adept Chicago actress Laurie Metcalf), sashays in. Friction develops. Jackie's presence irritates the normally affable Dan. In fact, it Cheetos him off pretty good, if you want to know the goddamned truth about it. Dan, we begin to perceive, is a ball of enraged gristle waiting to explode. Hey, the man's out of a job. Some distinctive honesty, some Common Man *reality*, seems festering at the edges here, and sure enough, it erupts: "What's *bothering* me, Jackie," Dan suddenly roars, "is that you're over here all the time!" "Well, Dan," rejoins Jackie, *"if you had a job*, you wouldn't notice so much!"

Ooooooooooooooh, goes the scandalized sound track, and we are in Tension City. No cleansing grins this time; a long, murderous stare from Dan, who then heaves his bulk up, flashes his ivory tusks, curls his trunk menacingly and lumbers out of the room, slamming the door. Commercial break. It looks like a moment of truth for the Common Man.

Not on your Cheetos. The essential neutralizing falsity of this program begins to take hold as soon as the action resumes. The locus of concern starts to shift.

We find Roseanne scolding Jackie in her flawless Common Man patois: "You always manage to say the most perfectly wrongest thing at the most perfectly wrongest time!" A plausible enough complaint—but now the dramatic, the comedic center of the plot is no longer Dan and his job crisis. It's Jackie and her manners. The issue: Should Jackie apologize to Dan for her sarcastic zinger or should she not?

"He's been on my case ever since I came in the door," Jackie pouts, establishing the false symmetry that will carry this episode out of harm's way to its conclusion. (The motivation for Dan's petulance—terror at the prospect of poverty, a very real and present prospect for a good part of Common Man America—becomes a wisp of smoke; just another device to move the zingers along.)

A tele-moppet enters. "Are Dad and Jackie really mad at each other?" she wants to know. "No," drawls Roseanne. "They fight for the same reason you and Darlene fight. To torture me." Zingo! Cleansing grin! The pre-commercial tension fades a little further into oblivion.

The episode plays itself out with Roseanne in the center. She's the arbiter between Dan and Jackie, the peacemaker. "She's over here all the time 'cause she's my sister," she explains to Dan as his great ears flap fitfully. Then, to hands-on-hips Jackie: "He don't mean nothin'; he's just blowin' off steam." The final scene has Roseanne and Jackie playfully dumping old unemployed Dan off the living-room couch, where he has fallen asleep watching a late movie on TV. The question of whether Dan will find work—the issue that pretended, at the outset, to define this program's plot—has simply ceased to exist.

Let us say this for Roseanne Barr: She delivers a nifty punch line. And in the current cable-comic bestiary of screamers, sneerers, haters, verbal crotch flashers, neofascist race-baiters and the other apostles of anal-retention-as-art who are desecrating the legacy of insurrectionary American humor, she has some distinction—she at least knows how to read. (You can pick up traces of Ann Beattie in her bummed-out persona; there's a little Bobbie Ann Mason in the dialect, a little Francine Prose lampooning the brand names.)

Let us say further that *Roseanne* is in many ways an above-average network sitcom. With the accomplished John Goodman, as well as Laurie Metcalf, in the cast, Ms. Barr is the least polished actor among the principals—and she has her own tons-of-fun patina of charm. (She is in some respects a female John Candy; maybe the two should team together for *The Candy-Barr Show*. Hey, it's only a concept.)

Roseanne Barr, and her series, would be easier to take if everyone concerned would just grind out the honest, Cosbyized, standard-issue disposable zingers and stop pretending to evoke the Common Man. Because the Common Man is the last thing this shrewd and savvy little piece of Left Coast merchandising knows or cares about.

Dan's unemployment-as-shtick is fine evidence of the show's callousness. If you think that the *Roseanne* writers have performed some kind of public service simply by *noting the issue* of unemployment—taking the topic as far as the parameters of visual art allow—then you really need to look up a little masterpiece of independent work called *Silver Valley*.

Silver Valley is a study of an actual American family, desiccated by unemployment in a played-out mining town in Idaho. It was made in 1983 by the team of Michel Negroponte, Peggy

Stern and Mark Erder; it has since won grand prizes and special-merit awards in France and the United States, has been featured on television and in festivals throughout Europe and recently ran on a cable-television series I was involved with called *Spirit of Place*. Later this year [1989] it will be made available to PBS stations.

Silver Valley features an out-of-work dad, an opinionated mom, some kids and a menagerie of relatives, just like on *Roseanne*. Here the similarity stops. There are no zingers in *Silver Valley*. The dad—an unforgettable man named Jerry— doesn't trade cleansing grins with his wife; he goes around town scavenging Dumpsters for refundable soda cans, muttering, "Thank you, God and Jesus," after each harvest.

There are no indulgent wisecracks about hiring out as a topless dancer. One young woman in the family, desperate for cash, actually does enter a seminude Jell-O–wrestling contest down at the local bar; her ensuing humiliation, as observed by Negroponte's camera, is about as bathetic as anything ever recorded regarding the American Common Man.

The family in *Silver Valley* is a fairly close real-life counterpart of the family in *Roseanne*. The difference is that here, the unemployment issue does not dissolve into a comedy of manners. The *Silver Valley* family is, basically, doomed.

Real is what you would call *Silver Valley*. Honest. Distinctive. Revolutionary, were it ever to gain the mass exposure routinely accorded confections such as *Roseanne*.

I'm not suggesting here that the nice people who write, produce and act in *Roseanne* should stop doing comedy and start doing social realism. I am suggesting that they face up to their inherent, inescapable compromises and stop selling themselves as surrogates for the gritty get-down world of working-class America. That may be a tall order, given the eagerness of an increasingly fatuous pop-cult critical press. But it would be very, oh . . . big of them.

DABNEY COLEMAN, WORLD'S GREATEST, UH, JERK

The man who offended you as Buffalo Bill will really piss you off as sportswriter Slap Maxwell

Dabney Coleman as Slap Maxwell takes a fist that liquefies his jaw and crushes him against a hotel-room wall, but he comes up talking, talking. He's not going to press charges here, he reassures his assailant; he's got a deadline to meet; he's willing to continue the interview and let bygones be bygones. Regaining his professional aplomb almost at once, he inquires of his subject, a large professional golfer in lime-green pants: *When did you first realize you were gay?*

This earns him a body toss into the corridor. Coleman/Maxwell calls through the slamming door: *I tellya what. If this is a bad time, I could come back later.* Slithering on all fours now toward whatever grim balm awaits creatures of his reticulation, he encounters an exemplary pair of nyloned legs on their way to the very door through which he has just been ejected. Clearly the opportunity for some Dostoyevskian epiphany is at hand, and Slap/Dabney's deeper human instincts do not fail him: He suggests to the blonde beauty that she is a man in drag.

We're traipsing on familiar slime here, we connoisseurs of the uncouth. For many viewers, this genial bit of stage business will be nothing more than their introduction (and possibly their adieu) to a new fall ABC comedy called *The Slap Maxwell Story*. Slap is a sportswriter. As the more perceptive among this mass will quickly notice, he is a sportswriter of the distinctly post–Oscar Madison stripe: Jack Klugman's Oscar may have been a slob, but he never claimed he was denied a Pulitzer Prize because the committee was soft on Communism.

But we hard cases—we know better than to pay attention to the title. We know it's not the label, the outer packaging, that counts; it's the rotten, corrosive human sensibility deep down inside. Those of us who still proudly bear the singe marks of the short-lived *Buffalo Bill* on our retinas recognize that *Slap* is really the latest reincarnation of that seminal figure in American television comedy, that embodiment of all that is praiseworthy, nay, *sacred*, in the urban ethos of the late 1980s— the Asshole.

And we know that Dabney Coleman, who interpreted—*inhabited*—the role of Bill Bittinger with such memorable grossness on NBC is the only actor who could possibly do injustice to the part.

Dabney Coleman may well be the greatest asshole in the history of television.

I'm not just saying this to be nice. I echo the esteem of the industry. Writer-producer Jay Tarses, who should know, agrees. "He can play assholes like nobody else," gushes Tarses. "It's like rolling off a log for him." One can almost envision the words engraved on a special Emmy statuette: "CAN PLAY ASSHOLES LIKE NOBODY ELSE." There is nothing in show business quite as meaningful as the honest adulation of one's peers.

Truly, Coleman's unique gifts set him apart. Carl Reiner,

Harvey Korman and the others who came before him are like choir boys before his sulfurous luster. Consider the Coleman-ian face itself: that pasty tundra of caved-in flesh with its de-monic little black knot of tics screwed into the center—the bulletproof eyebrows, the eyes like a con man's glance of rec-ognition, the Watergate-criminal mustache. This is less a comic scalawag than some post-nuclear mass of pure survival; this is a life-form that will outlast the cockroaches.

The visionary who animates this extraordinary physical plant—the divine afflatus, as it were—is Tarses. Tarses created Slap Maxwell from the spare parts of Buffalo Bill, his prototype character who introduced high-test assholery to mom-and-pop prime time in 1983 and then paid the price in the ratings. Coleman's darkly witty caricature of a glory-bloated small-time talk-show host trapped in Buffalo, New York—Ted Baxter reduced to pure human orifice—lasted one season on NBC before the shrieks of decent citizens forced programming chief Brandon Tartikoff to heave a torch into the monster's circuitry.

Tarses is blandly fatalistic about that cancellation. "People were so repulsed by Buffalo Bill's character that they actively switched channels," he owns up with the deadpan evenness of Lieutenant Colonel Oliver North admitting that he deceived Congress. "A *lot* of people were terrified by this guy. He walked on people's heads. To my way of thinking, though, there was a lot of vulnerability to this guy. He was like a cobra, though. . . ."

But . . . er . . . at the risk of spoiling a good joke, one sort of burns to wonder . . . *why*?

Why this sudden, and still very incipient, sitcom boomlet for humor built around basically unsympathetic lead characters? Buffalo and Slap are the most interesting to date, but there have been others: Peter Boyle, dangerously funny as the burned-out cop on the take in last year's now-you-see-it, now-you-don't *Joe Bash*; the ineffable *Tortellis*; the coarsely written armpit-scratching couple in Fox's *Married . . . With Children.* One might even include the title character of Jay Tarses's own surprise hit from last summer, NBC's *The Days and Nights of Molly Dodd.* As portrayed by the proctologically unimpeachable Blair Brown, Molly could hardly be accused of being your standard cookie-cuter asshole—in this case, it was the world about her that seemed wedged between the Buns of Desolation. Early on, Tarses's story line had Molly, the ultimate New York single-woman-as-terminal-victim, quite unambiguously losing . . . her . . . mind. I laughed so hard I could barely open the Valium.

But . . . *why?*

There's something chillingly neutral at the core of this new sensibility. Tarses and his competitors have reduced Norman Lear's socially and politically grounded anger, so stunning and novel just a decade or so ago, to an utterly value-free kind of random—almost passive—*appetite.* It has even detached itself from the strutting, assertive brand of para-right-wing comedy that for a while laid claim to the 1980s: the victim-bashing snottiness of Eddie Murphy, Joan Rivers and the MTV-addled cutouts of all those HBO and Cinemax comedy specials.

The Buffalo/Maxwell paradigm is different. It doesn't attack so much as it *lies in wait.* A cobra, eh? That's not a bad image. One is often dazzled by the writing in the Coleman vehicles; it's compressed and richly rooted in character, as befits Tarses's own stand-up-comedian background (he was half of the Patchett and Tarses team of the late 1960s).

Witness this exchange between Slap Maxwell and his editor, who is in the process of trying to fire him.

"You can't fire me."

"Of course I can. That's exactly what I'm doing."

"We go back twenty years."

"Twenty-two."

"Before they started callin' 'em condoms."

"Even before that."

"I'm godfather to your daughter."

"My son."

"Whatever. The kid was a baby. I couldn't tell. How's he doin'?"

"He's got a lotta zits."

"Just like his mom. How old is he now?"

And so on. Witty. Line for line, some of the sharpest and deadliest writing on the tube. But—where's the motivation? How and why and where do we engage these comically awful characters, and why do we want to immerse ourselves in their vileness week after week? (All right, all right, as I write these words my favorite ball team, the Mets, is disintegrating into a cauldron of seething, scraped egos. The right fielder skips a couple of games and cuts a rap record; both the center fielders want to be traded; the star pitcher is accused—by an unnamed front-office source—of being on snow all of last season. These are the veritable Assholes on Parade; these are the Bad News Bears From Hell. Do I turn them off? No. I can't wait for the next telecast to see what horrible things they've said about and done to one another. So maybe I've answered my own question.)

Don't ask Jay Tarses. Like the characters he creates, Tarses appears to be entirely detached from impetus, from cause and effect. Ask him where the Buffalo/Maxwell model comes from, he'll tell you about his Baltimore roots—the work ethic, the Colts and the Orioles, not a ton of money. . . .

Huh? This sound like diner country, and in fact a pal of Tarses's, Barry Levinson, wrote exactly that; he wrote *Diner.* As Tarses will tell you. But the gentle ruefulness, even the brief, impulsive cruelties, of that luminous movie is so far from the gestalt of Dabney Coleman's inspired seediness. . . .

"Actually I'd like to return to the motivation question," says the character "Martin Amis" in Martin Amis's *Money,* a novel whose hilarious, nightmarish vision has certain resonances with *Slap Maxwell.* "It seems to me it's an idea taken from art, not from life, not from twentieth-century life. Nowadays motivation comes from inside the head, not from outside. It's neurotic, in other words. . . ."

That strikes one as a fairly shrewd observation, or at least as good a stab as any to account for Western culture as we are presently encrusted with it.

If indeed the American sitcom hero has progressed—or regressed—from the benign Eisenhower rationality of Robert Young to the Reagan-ridden neurosis of Dabney Coleman, well, what the hell: We can at least settle back in our bunkers and know there'll be some major giggles en route to the void.

Or, as (the married) Slap Maxwell puts it to his girlfriend, Judy (whom he's just compared not to a summer's day but to an expensive call girl), "We do get into some snappy repartee, don't we? Kinda hip, kinda sassy. . . ."

Kinda.

V

News, Weather and Sports

As I type these notes, the world is in a paroxysm of political change—the most profound change since the Bolshevik Revolution. The Berlin Wall has been breached; the Communist governments in East Germany and Poland, Czechoslovakia and Romania are in disintegration; those of Bulgaria and Yugoslavia are at risk. The Leninist monolith totters in the Soviet Union. China hangs in the balance. The Pentagon has announced that it would ground the airborne command fleet, which for three decades remained perpetually aloft against the moment of nuclear war.

It is an extraordinary time in the annals of information, and in the need for information. New heroes and heroines are advancing toward their places in history. The destinies of 400 million Europeans, and perhaps of the planet itself, are in revision. As I type these notes, for instance, Vaclav Havel, a remarkable playwright who suffered for years in prison because of his ideas, and who wrote letters of luminous affirmation and hope to his wife, has become president of Czechoslovakia.

As I type these notes, the December 1989 edition of *Life* magazine lies on the desk beside me. On the cover, in formal photographic portraiture, is the standing torso and smiling face of an American public figure, dressed in a black suit with gold accessories. The backdrop, a canvas displaying cherubim and seraphim, heightens the aura of statesmanship. And the caption, set in elegiac type, white against the darker field, tears at the jangled consciousness:

OUR LOSS, HER DREAM

What? The mind gropes for a context. Images come hurtling up: the martyred JFK, the martyred Reverend Martin Luther King, Jr., the martyred Bobby. *Life* covers, every one! Has someone else been shot, at this hair-trigger juncture in geopolitical affairs?

No. This is no eulogy for a fallen leader. This is just *Life's* way of reminding us that Jane Pauley is leaving *The Today Show* after thirteen years, to appear in prime time instead.

Thus the grinning skull of what was once known as TV news.

A distinction is necessary here. This is not intended as an assault on Jane Pauley. I knew Jane Pauley. I nearly *worked* once with Jane Pauley. (Deborah, you're no Jane Pauley.) The point here is to consider the star-spangled idiocy of proportion that elevates a morning anchorperson, *any* morning anchorperson, to the status of Deposed Head of State—simply because she's switching work shifts.

But *that's the way it is.* (Sorry, Walter.) Amid the general abolition of reality that marked the video Eighties, the new managers of TV news—those elegant Snopeses—led the way: partly by the way they chose to cover stories, partly by the continuing story they allowed their news divisions to become. This was, after all, a decade that began with Dan Rather dressing up like a peasant to get into Afghanistan, and ended with professional actors dressing up like Abbie Hoffman to get onto *Saturday Night With Connie Chung*.

Well before Jane Pauley's soap-opera sandbagging by her stainless-steel nemesis Deborah (Gorgeous People Have Rights Too!) Norville, it was all coming unglued. The whole experiment with TV as public journal/public trust—an experiment compromised by corporate and show-business considerations from the very outset—was collapsing in bathos.

Worse, it seemed to be dragging the best traditions of typographic journalism along with it. We will examine *USA Today*, in its print and video incarnations (fine distinction) later in this section. But the irony of Jane Pauley's canonization on the cover of *Life* should not pass unnoticed: here was the magazine that half a century ago elevated visual journalism—images linked to elegant prose—to a valued and useful aesthetic. (In that same issue, there is a small inset photograph of a young man in World War II combat fatigues. This is John Hersey, the former *Life* correspondent and one of the founding fathers of twentieth-century American nonfiction.) In certain ways, *Life* was the forebear of television news. It was also one of the new medium's earliest casualties; it vanished from Time, Inc.'s rolls for years, and lately has reappeared as a kind of ceremonial monthly.

The bathos seemed weirdly centered on CBS News, where a new cadre of executives, trained in the cosmetic values of local-station news, gained power. There were the continuing catastrophes of Dan Rather: Rather's abduction in a Chicago taxicab; Rather's mugging on Park Avenue by assailants unknown; Rather's six-minute hiatus from the CBS Evening News set; Rather's mugging on the CBS set by assailant George Bush (leading to the Big Question of 1988: "Did the Bush camp bushwhack Rather, rather than the Rather camp bushwhack Bush?"). Rather, like Pauley, was a fundamentally decent individual—ardent, even—but caught up in a misbegotten star system that inevitably diminished him.

There was the bathos of CBS News and the William Westmoreland libel suit. There was CBS News and Miss Bathos herself, Phyllis George, famously encouraging an accused rapist and his victim to hug before the commercial break. There was the hot-ticket retooling of the newsmagazine format (*West 57th, 48 Hours*), and the mothballing of the venerated *CBS Reports*.

Much of this squalid, ungainly behavior stemmed from forces beyond the control of the visible performers (though the visible performers were by no means always in opposition). The Eighties were the decade of the corporate takeover, a phenomenon that afflicted each of the three major networks, with chaotic results in their news divisions. The new corporate overlords, men without the vaguest regard for the public-interest obligations of the systems they'd inherited, lost no time stripping them down to skeleton strength and sanctioning an unprecedented blurring of journalistic and show-business values.

And so the decade closed with Diane Sawyer's defection from CBS to ABC, where she joined Sam Donaldson on a newsmagazine set before a studio audience. It closed with the arrival, as senior executive producer of *The Today Show*, of a man who previously had held a similar title at *Entertainment Tonight*. It closed with two news-division programs—*Yesterday, Today and Tomorrow*, on NBC, and *Saturday Night With Connie Chung*, on CBS, incorporating dramatic re-enactments of news and historical events. (ABC News, a cutting-edge leader in audience-building glitz since Roone Arledge moved from Sports to the News presidency in the mid-1970s, completed the circle: it permitted dramatic re-enactments on its regular network newscast, *World News Tonight*. In November 1989 *World News* pulled past the CBS Evening News for the first time in years.)

This wholesale realignment of the boundaries between fact

and fantasy, perhaps the most insidious example of television's self-marketed "reality," will remain a legacy of the 1980s for years—perhaps until a war or natural disaster forces a cutback in rehearsal time.

To the particulars, then:

"Shock of the News" places the new, self-referencing gloss of TV news and public affairs—CBS's *West 57th* most prominently—in the context of the postmodernist idiom, a handy idiom indeed for the rearrangement of reality.

"Dan Rather Loses the Frequency" examines a short-lived, radical extension of that idiom: TV news as micro-data. (The program failed after this column was published; Gannett retooled it, reintroduced it, and it failed again. Yet micro-data itself remains an economically compelling strategy; its essential features are increasingly visible within the networks' 60-second newsbreaks, in early-morning news summaries and within local-station newscasts. Its time as a national form will come round again.

In "Womb With Ado," we meet a Boston anchorwoman who, like many of the Eighties network stars, became her own best story: Her announced decision to have a baby out of wedlock turned into the most overweaning—as it were—news story in the city for several weeks. And in "The Boob Tube," we get down to the root system of TV news as nonfiction entertainment in the person of one smart local-news cookie from Arizona whose more calculated efforts to wean herself from the small-time turned out to be a big bust.

"The Right's Tough" is a visit with that scourge of creeping détente-ism, Bob Novak, perhaps the ultimate Washington-insider talk-show star. Through him we see how the genre he helped make famous has been infected with the pyrotechnics of Morton Downey and Tabloid TV.

As to the weather: since I wrote "Hurricane Willard and Other Blowhards," the weather itself has surfaced as a news story of literally life-and-death proportions: as the 1980s ended, a growing body of responsible scientists testified before Congress and in other public forums that chemicals and industrial wastes have conclusively and irreparably harmed the environment: The ozone layer has been ripped open, global temperatures are rising and nature itself has been unwittingly engineered out of its natural state.

Since a fried planet would likely spell (among other things) the end of hundred-year-olds' birthday parties and other events of compelling interest to Willard Scott, one might have expected the TV news weathercast to open itself up a bit and serve as an occasional forum for such information and debate. (Particularly since the degree of public consciousness could directly affect the degree of the earth's heating in decades to come.) Maybe I've missed something, but in the era of "the death of nature," the TV weathercast has continued to be just as deeply mired in escapist buffoonery as the news itself. Have a sunny day, Willard—y'hear?

Finally, we venture briefly into the world of tele-sports with two pieces. "Love That Bob" is an amiable look—by my standards, anyway—at Bob Costas, a cerebral and witty young sportscaster who retains a deep respect for the legacies of his craft. (Costas has since branched into the postmidnight talk-show format—*Later With Bob Costas*—with considerable success.) "The Seat of Power" brings us back into the surreal world of the Gannett Company, as we visit a TV sports columnist for *USA Today* whose opinions may actually affect the look and the cast of characters in network sports programming. In the inverted world of 1980s media, that made him a kind of sage.

Dan Rather Loses
the Frequency

USA Today: The Television Show *will launch
an era in which no news is bad news*

The Nanoids are coming. The Nanoids are *here*. It is too late
to stop the Nanoids.

Here is what we know: We know the target date and beachhead of the first major Nanoid video assault wave—September 12 [1988] at Rosslyn, Virginia, the key redoubt of the
Gannett communications empire, as it happens—and we know
the USA cities that have been targeted to receive their electronic rays; they are 118 in number.

We know that soon afterward there will be more Nanoids;
many more. We can accurately predict that before long Nanoid culture will be general not only in the USA but in the
developed nations of the West, and doubtless one day around
the globe.

We know the likely effect of this widening Nanoid invasion:

the dissolution (heretofore deemed impossible by leading USA physicists and the presidents of CBS, ABC and NBC News) of the 500-year-old typographic media and the 50-year-old video media as discrete, incompatible communications modes. We now understand that the two will merge. Fuse. Agglutinate. In fact, the process has begun to mature in the print world.

We know all of this, but we are powerless to blunt the Nanoid advance. Indeed, the very word "we" has been subverted of precise meaning. The seeds of Nanoidism have long since been implanted among tens of millions of the populace.

There is but one rational course of action for the as-yet un-Nanoided. And that is to prepare. Prepare for the Dawn of the Epoch of Nanoid News.

Nanoid: dwarfish, from *nano-*, combination form (from Greek *nanos*, dwarf), one billionth (10-^9) part of.

They haven't reduced the news to a billionth part yet. Not yet. They are working on it. Give them time. This is only the Dawn.

"We're gonna get up to forty stories into some of our programs," says Steve Friedman. Friedman is the executive producer of *USA Today: The Television Show*, which will begin its minimalist revision of video news on September 12. The syndicated program will be a half hour in length, five nights a week. This means twenty-two minutes for news (a half hour minus commercials) per show. Given Friedman's plans for a five-minute lead story, he will have about seventeen minutes left for his remaining thirty-nine news items. Thirty-nine items in seventeen minutes comes out to an average of twenty-six seconds per item.

Consider that until now, the prevailing standards of over-compression in television news were the "minute-thirty" story and the twenty-story count within a newscast.

Friedman offers his new figures not as a tear-choked confession but as a boast. This is, after all, the essence of Nanoidism: *the quantum,* "the smallest maneuverable broadcast bit," as scholar Michael Sorkin puts it. Nanoidism is the purification of every tendency in mass communications since the invention of the telegraph: the transcendence (Sorkin again) of interest and investment in sequence. *Flow* as ultimate aim.

Obviously, Steve Friedman is an extremely high ranking Nanoid. Yet not quite the supreme, not exactly the exalted. The former executive producer of the might *Today* show on NBC is but Third Nanoid in the new order.

Nanoid Two is Grant Tinker, whose GTG Entertainment is the production arm of the new Gannett program.

Nanoid One, the only earthling who will now or forever be worthy of the title, is, of course, Al Neuharth, the founder of the original *USA Today: The Newspaper.* Neuharth took his inspiration for *USA Today* from television. Now his minions in charge of *USA Today: The Television Show* are taking their organizational concept from Neuharth's newspaper.

Trying to imagine a television news show based on a newspaper based on television is like trying to imagine infinity. It is like trying to hold no thoughts in your head at the same time.

So why are we seeing this Dawn of the Nanoids? Why this new wave of technological gene-splicing that is forging a hybrid form out of those discrepant entities, video and print? And make no mistake, the trend is upon us: This fall will bring a new half-hour weekday newscast from *The Christian Science Monitor.* Already *The Wall Street Journal* has breached the early-morning fringe hours via syndicated TV. Time Inc. is exploring a video format vis-à-vis Cable News Network. The Associated Press (*the Associated Press!*) is conferring with Conus, the satellite-linkup outfit.

The answer, quite obviously, is economics. The Age of Video has rendered the cost structure of giant publishing organizations—anybody here remember *afternoon newspapers?*—lethally obsolete. The communications history of the past fifteen years has been written (read: broadcast) in the convulsive efforts of newspapers, magazines and even books to identify with the usurper: to tart themselves up in the lurid makeup of video (Brevity! Color! Personalities! Surface! Baby-talk prose!) in the hopes of coaxing back a few of their stampeding former customers. Very tawdry show.

Nanoid News promises at last to reverse this hemorrhage. Think of videodollars actually flowing *back into* a print empire, instead of seeping away! In fact—and here is the truly diabolic power of the Nanoids—the likely victims of their empire-in-progress on television will not be magazines or newspapers.

The likely victims will be the recent predators of print themselves: the television networks.

"The network newses are encumbered with the *scar tissue* of Murrow," Steve Friedman is saying. "They have the *scar tissue* of being the news 'of record.' They have everybody on their backs carping at 'em for not being *thorough* enough.

"I don't have that, because I already know all these people, these Journalists with a capital *J*, are gonna *hate* my show.

"But you know what?" Friedman shows some teeth and leans forward over his desk in his office above midtown Manhattan, a smallish and deceptively boy-faced man in spectacles, tieless, gripping his trademark scuffed baseball across the seams, hefting it, revving up for the brushback:

"You gotta go beyond people who think linear. People who think that when they print something, somebody reads it. This program will be done BY people who were born and raised on television FOR people who were born and raised on television!"

It is a classic Nanoid preemptive strike: a sneering swipe at TV news's one canonized figure of conscience, a glancing blow at typographic thought, capped by the war whoop of the liberating populist.

USA Today: The Television Show is in a position to do some nasty bodywork on the gasping heavyweights in the network news divisions. And Steve Friedman—though he affects choirboy innocence at the very notion—knows it. His glistening, opulent, smooth-as-a-suppository program will be broadcast head-to-head with one or more net/newscasts in most cities. (In Los Angeles and New York, *USA Today* will run on CBS-owned stations, knocking Dan Rather himself out of his accustomed 7 P.M. time slot.) Nor will it fade quickly from the scene if early ratings are slow: GTG has extracted an unprecedented (for a new program) two-year commitment from nearly every station that has contracted to run the show. Nanoid Nirvana!

Now the bad news.

Come September, the three major networks will be looking into an economic abyss. The chill prospect of a business turndown, which always follows the high-revenue, high-spending orgy of an election-Olympics year, will have begun seeping into the bean-counters' bones.

People meters are showing that aggregate net/news audiences are down by at least 3 percent since last fall, being bled by a variety of sources: the surging Cable News Network; the new parajournalism programs in syndication; game shows that counterprogram the nightly news; big-deal local newscasts; even public television, with its robust following for *The MacNeil/Lehrer NewsHour*.

Just a little here and a little there, but it adds up. It especially adds up when one factors in the dismal ratings for the networks' prime-time news specials on primary-election nights last spring—and when one considers that the new corporate stewards of the news divisions have shown no hesitation in the past to staunch such bleeding by amputation: the quick hacking away of damaged parts.

"We're entering an era of cheap news," says one network professional who decodes the economic signals of the industry, "and even after the cutbacks, the networks are locked into a cost structure that doesn't fit the world of 1988. Their news budgets are in the $300 million range. They've spent so much on the elections. They have so many vice-presidents. They have so many computer graphics. They spend so many millions on opinion polling.

"I think the network presidents and CEOs are looking around for ways to cut. If *USA Today* gets numbers comparable to the networks' with something that looks like a news program but runs on the cheap, it's going to have a tremendous impact on the nightly news."

"Runs on the cheap"? How about *USA Today*'s sleek $40 million operating budget for the first year? How about a scanty editorial staff of seventy (including just ten on-air personalities) to cover the entire *world*? How about Friedman's insouciant—well, *Nanoid*—attitude toward the duties of capital-*J* Journalism?

"Our code is, if we can't do it better or different, we don't do it," he says. "We don't have to show you that thirty seconds from the Persian Gulf—with the ship coming down, and the viewer saying, 'Mabel, is that a Kuwait flag? Is that one of ours?' We don't have to do that."

What *USA Today* will do in lieu of such scar-tissue stuff is a great deal of pure Nanoid journalism: that is, journalism generated by public-opinion polling and depicted via computer-generated graphics. It will be this sort of laser data, flashed across the screen in mere seconds' time, that will make up the bulk of those forty "stories" per show.

But didn't someone just make the point that opinion polls and computer graphics are exactly the sort of high-cost glitz that has the net/news divisions in economic trouble? Correct. But, you see, the networks aren't doing it the *Nanoid* way.

For one thing, Friedman's show will have access to the massive *existing* opinion-poll apparatus that already gluts so much of *USA Today: The Newspaper*. This is where the amortization benefits of the new mixed media begin to kick in.

For another—and here Steve Friedman starts turning positively seminarish—his computer graphics will not be just any computer graphics. They will amount, in their splendor, to a reinvention of the wheel.

"We're going to do three-dimensional graphics on TV," says Friedman. "We think it will enhance the newspaper, because people identify the paper with graphics, and it will enhance us. Because we're not gonna do graphics the way the networks now do them, which is to basically waste time. They show *and* tell you. 'The stock market went down a little more than a point today, in active trading.' Then they do a bumper that reads 'Down 1.3, 200 Million Shares.' *That's wasting time.* Our graphics are going to move, they're going to come atcha. And they're gonna be self-sufficient."

Nanoid. Friedman pops a cassette into his VCR and pushes a button. The screen flickers, and the promotional pilot for *USA Today: The Television Show* comes on. The opening animation shows the familiar *USA Today* newspaper vending box—which is designed, as everyone knows, to resemble a television screen—sending out a latticework of eerie white rays that cause passersby to stop in their tracks, poleaxed, mesmerized. Very Nanoidish. Then the rays sort of deliver us into the *USA Today* anchor desk, or command center—a vast rectangle of a glass table around which the four anchors sit, dwarfed by several gigantic video screens that hang above them.

"I'm Edie Magnus," comes the voice of Edie Magnus, who will anchor the news section. (The program will replicate *USA Today*'s four sections—News, Money, Sports and Life—each with a separate anchor: Magnus, Kenneth Walker, Bill Macatee and Robin Young, respectively.) "Across the USA tonight, the question is: 'Do love and marriage still go together like a horse and carriage?' Twenty thousand people answered a *USA Today* survey and told us their intimate secrets about sex, passion and love."

"It's not my problem that the networks are so lockstep, so similar," says Steve Friedman. "My problem is to try and do something else. To look, feel, sound and *be* different from those programs. But, yes. If we're successful, some of the stuff we do will start to show up on the network news.

"The first thing that will happen is, they will try to look like us. The second thing is, they will try to take our tone. And the *third* thing is, you will start to see *every* print organization saying, 'The way we can help ourselves is by doing a television show.' I think *that* is more an effect that we're gonna have than on the network news."

What an exciting possibility—as John Dean once remarked to Richard Nixon. In the silken prophylaxis of the GTG corporate offices, where all the disputations and horrors and mendacities of the modern world seem to dissolve into a computer graphic, the coming merger of print and video can sound as sumptuously inevitable as a splash of bitters in the gin.

But there are others—"Journalists with a capital *J*," in Friedman's formulation—who do not share the complacent glow.

The communications scholar Herbert Schiller (*The Mind Managers*) has issued a call for the presidential candidates to include the "information crisis" as an issue in this year's election campaign. "The seeming cultural diversity provided by thousands of newspapers, magazines, radio stations and TV channels is a mirage," Schiller wrote recently, "which conceals the fact that most of them are owned by giant media combines. Concentrated ownership . . . calls into question the basic assumptions of democratic government.

"If the communications system that informs us is itself out of alignment—providing us an inadequate picture of reality— we are in deep trouble."

We *are* in deep trouble. The Nanoids are coming. The Nanoids are here.

Womb with Ado

An anchorwoman's pregnancy raises questions of
responsibility, privacy and our choice of heroes

Liz Walker is one hell of an anchor. I say that without sarcasm, without fear of contradiction and without firsthand authority, having never observed the woman in the act of
anchoring; that is to say, in her anchorial mode, or in the full-
ness of her anchoressence.

Liz Walker makes one half of a million dollars every year to
perform the ablutions of the anchorperson (to be technically
correct, she is a co-anchorperson, or co-anchor) for WBZ-TV
in Boston. Boston is a big city. It is in fact a major city, or
major market. Ergo, it may be presumed that the people who
run WBZ do not consider themselves "stuck" with Liz Walker
as anchor, or co-anchor: If they wished, they could find lots
of other young women—"talent"—who would willingly assume the co-anchorpersonal mode, don't you see, for half a

313

million simoleons per annum. As a last resort, WBZ could solicit for the position out of town. Post notices. "SITUATION AVAILABLE." That sort of thing.

So let us accept it as a given that this Liz Walker person is somebody who can deliver the goods when it comes to being an anchor.

Let us make one further observation—again, without the slightest trace of irony: Anchoring is hard work. No, it is damned near impossible work. Like a lot of other skills peculiar to the twentieth century—the moonwalk, carpet bombing and the topspin backhand come immediately to mind—anchoring calls forth functions and neural responses previously unstressed in the human evolutionary chain.

The television news anchor must—for starters—be adept at reciting aloud from a vast, seemingly endless waterfall of scrolled type as it swims rapidly past on a small visual screen, the TelePrompTer, while pretending to make intimate eye and vocal contact with an invisible auditor. (You think it's easy? I've watched experienced TV journalists freeze into tongue-tied silence in the midst of their deliveries; they later reported, in shock, that the individual words and sentences melted together into a horrible sort of alphabet soup.) Frequently the type is smudged, or crossed out and re-edited in a wax-penciled scrawl or hopelessly misspelled. Or the 'PrompTer operator gets lost in his copy of *Soldier of Fortune*.

Sometimes the TelePrompTer scroll sticks. Or the wrong copy comes up. Or an unfamiliar foreign word appears. (I will never forget the stricken look that crossed the face of a New York local news anchor—I think he actually rose halfway out of his anchor chair—the first time he saw the word "Shiite" ascend into his narration field.)

News anchors must endure all this while keeping in mind such considerations as pace (their reading of lines per second must be predictable when narrating a story with a preedited sound track), transition (the art of signaling a change of emphasis, or the introduction of a new thought, by the slightest operatic shift of octave or tone) and facial expression (no grinning while announcing the latest airline disaster). All of this while the booth director's voice fills the anchorial earpiece with demented screaming. Not to mention maintaining good grooming. This is what one means by functions not previously stressed in the human evolutionary chain.

All of which futuristic functions Liz Walker unquestionably possesses. At issue with Ms. Walker, however, is her demonstrated command of functions that go pretty far back in the human evolutionary chain.

Last spring, the unmarried Ms. Walker was suddenly taken pregnant. She announced this fact to the Boston news media. She also announced that she planned to have the baby, and that the identity of the father was nobody's business but her own. And now a look at the weekend weather.

Well. Excuuuuse me. Excuuuuuse *Boston*. At once, and for months thereafter, Liz Walker was no longer your average everyday 36-year-old black six-foot Congregational minister's daughter from Little Rock earning $500,000 a year in the cradle city of Yankee rectitude.

Now she was something special. Now she was, by God, a Role Model. Now she was the de rigueur topic for newspaper columns, radio call-in shows, sociologists, child psychiatrists and a good percentage of Boston public opinion. Liz Walker, anchor, was being weighed.

What follows here is not founded on any conversation with Liz Walker; she stopped giving interviews within days after her morals and leadership responsibilities became topics of civic referendum. What follows is not a continuation of the debate over whether she was right or wrong, or whether her decision was "destructive," as Washington columnist Carl Rowan declared, in light of the "national social tragedy" of unwed mothers.

What follows is a slightly puzzled and wary speculation on why, beyond a certain point of humane concern, anybody should care.

Why, in the summer of Donna Rice and Tammy Faye Bakker and Jessica Hahn—in the third decade of moral relativism's reign, of "Personal Choice" as the People's Choice— why Liz Walker? Why should some anchorwoman in Boston throw a city, half the eastern seaboard and the cream of American punditry into a prolonged scene from *The Scarlet Letter*?

What the hell is it, in other words, that Americans expect from their anchorpeople?

Having acknowledged the technical difficulties of the anchoring life, let us now be a little brutal: It ain't brain surgery. More to the point, it very often ain't journalism. Or any other ism that depends on opinion, scholarship or some sort of intellectual risk. (Hey, somebody else *writes* that stuff, you know.) And while network anchors frequently wield some editorial influence in their newscasts' content, such participation is quite the exception at the local level. Liz Walker's academic degree, it is instructive to note, is in theater and speech.

Anchors, to put it most bluntly, are typically authority figures without authority: richly rewarded for performing skills high in visibility, low (or nonexistent) in content.

A little historical perspective here. Anchors have existed in the television continuum only since the 1952 political conventions. In the heat of competition against NBC and its polished commentator Bill Henry (yes, the very same, the legendary *Bill Henry*), CBS thought to organize its convention coverage around the editorial and dramatic focus of the lesser-known upstart Walter Cronkite. Cronkite may have lacked Henry's experience as a pundit, but even then, there was star quality in that pencil mustache.

CBS decided that the old-fashioned radio word "commentator" was inadequate to express the grandeur, the sweep of Cronkite's mission. He would be the human conduit through which every current of intelligence must pass before it reached the viewing public. He would be the *anchor*. The term did what anchors are supposed to do; it stuck.

Cronkite went on to be known as the Most Trusted Man in America. His name was mentioned on vice-presidential possible-candidate lists. His on-air opposition to the Vietnam War in the late Sixties helped pressure President Lyndon Johnson toward seeking a settlement. He even played himself on an episode of *The Mary Tyler Moore Show*.

Walter Cronkite cannot be written off as just another pretty face. But thirty-five years after he invented the anchoring profession, his video children have gained an iconic power in the idol-worshiping American consciousness that even Cronkite has found appalling.

When Jesse Helms smirked of thirsting to "be Dan Rather's boss," he was shrewdly playing upon this popular enthrallment. When a freshly hired local anchor literally dropped from the skies into his new station—via helicopter—and intoned, after springing to earth in a blue sequined jumpsuit, "Thus begins the assault upon the Miami market!" (this actually happened), he was not-so-innocently internalizing the same mythology.

Point being, it *is* a myth. News anchors have long since joined the pantheon of the cowboy and the private eye as the only indigenous American folkloric characters. Marketed, promoted and advertised relentlessly over two decades by their stations as pure personalities, recruited increasingly from the overlapping demimondes of dramatic arts, fashion and what might be termed the Anchor Underground (knock twice and tell 'em Sherlee Barish sent you), protected hermetically from the icky grunt work of news gathering, local news anchors are the perfect fulfillments of that Media Age elite, the Famous who are famous for being Famous.

Small wonder, then, that when the theater-and-speech specialist Liz Walker announced her unwedlocked pregnancy, half
of Boston began feeling labor pains.

(The city of Boston, it should be noted, has compiled a rather
rich tradition in the anchor as public curiosity. Boston, after
all, was the video home of Anchorboy. Back in 1970, WNAC
hired a 17-year-old kid named Jay Scott, sent out airbrushed
glossies of his sensuous countenance and put him on the air
with the promotional trappings that would later come to be
associated with androgynous rock stars. The resulting onslaught of ridicule from Boston critics and feature writers
eventually drove Scott from the air; his career as an anchor
was destroyed before he was old enough to run for public
office.)

So, the question: Is there any better way to do this? A more
rational way to present television news to the American public? One that preserves the medium's inescapable appetite for
Star Power and yet slices through a layer of journalistically
irrelevant and distracting, not to say costly, personality? Is there
a format that takes into account the new economic realities of
television news, one that could redistribute those anchorial
millions back into the news-gathering infrastructure (producers, beat reporters, researchers), where they are truly, desperately needed?

Maybe there is. Maybe, in part, the prototype has already
been glimpsed, on two CBS newsmagazines: years ago on *60
Minutes*, and more recently on the beleaguered and doggedly
hip *West 57th*.

The correspondents on these two programs introduce their
own stories, thus functioning as a sort of rotating anchor ensemble. The device has promise. No one would question that
West 57th reporters have Star Power; they damned near fry the
retinas with it. And yet there is that ineluctable sense that the
personality has at least gone out there and brushed up against
the subject matter, has earned the legitimacy of his or her nar-

ration through an experience more demanding and more visceral than that of reading from a smudged TelePrompTer.

I recognize a few obvious objections to this proposal: one, that we are comparing weekly news*magazines* with daily news*casts*, and two, that this may seem cruelly aimed at Liz Walker at an extremely vulnerable period in her life. (And in Yuletide season at that, one hardly need add.)

To take the second point first: I have no doubt that Ms. Walker, like many of her contemporaries in the local-anchor ranks, possesses the intelligence, the drive and the camera experience to generate excellent video journalism. As to the first point, it seems almost irrelevant, given the rapidly shifting economics and technologies and competitive demands of television news as it approaches the 1990s. In several smaller cities, correspondents are expected to double as camera operators and even as their own producers. (The networks themselves are hungrily pressing the unions to permit these multiple functions for their own correspondents.) In television life as in television art, Ted Baxter is giving way to Max Headroom.

Given this fluidity of format, the anchorless television news show could well be a breakthrough for the news director daring enough to try it: in economics, in ratings, in critical acclaim—hell, maybe even in journalism.

This would *truly* begin the assault on the Miami—and the Boston, and the New York and the Oklahoma City—market. And Liz Walker, bless her, might escape from the pages of *The Scarlet Letter*.

Shock of the News

CBS's West 57th, *which more than anything is about its own new look, is the latest example of TV's postmodern tendencies*

A few years ago television couldn't even spell "postmodernist." And now it *is* one.

In fact, video has always had a little postmodernism in its circuits. Maybe it has taken TV these forty years to shed enough of its inherited forms from radio and the movies—let's call them "romantic"—and reveal its essential mode, which happens to be quite similar to the mode that writers and musicians and painters and sculptors have been adopting with geometric rapidity for the last, oh, say, forty years.

Whatever the process, it seems increasingly clear that a new clustering of video traits and attitudes and editing styles, perceived as chic when they broke the surface (with music videos) a few years back, are adding up to something quite a bit more substantial than mere chic: the medium's first indigenous voice, to be precise. And that voice may well be post-modern at its very essence.

Consider postmodernism's defining characteristics: anti-narrative, self-reflexive, preoccupied with performance over content; fascinated with bourgeois kitsch as a sort of moral principle; resistant to mundane grounding in objective reality, in life as it is lived in the world. Sound familiar? Tom Pynchon, meet Tom Selleck. Gabriel García Márquez, meet Geraldo Rivera.

I know. Admirers of Pynchon and Márquez, or John Barth or Stanley Elkin, may find all this a shade preposterous: equating *any* content transmitted on advertiser-supported mass media with the deliberately esoteric, not to say insurrectionary, output of artists who aren't screwing around with audience flow or bimodal skews. Well, I have an answer for that: *Stanley Elkin never misses a segment of* Entertainment Tonight. You see? It's all connected.

Look, postmodernism has come to the TV. No question. The question is, Is it for everybody? Mom, Dad, the kids, Hugh Downs—*everybody?* Can this gorgeous but tricky idiom satisfy whatever remains of television's responsibility to clarify, make distinctions, affirm values? What happens when the antirationalist, the antirealist, the antibourgeois become the idiom for broadcasting to children? When they find a habitat in docudrama? The news?

Does the fact that all of this has happened already bother, or gratify, anyone?

Television has dabbled—however unconsciously—in post-modern attitudes for at least half its life. Perhaps the father of the form in videoland is Roone Arledge, who in the early Sixties—out of pure necessity—implanted the notion that ABC Sports's coverage of a sporting event was more significant than the event itself. (Remember Acapulco cliff diving on *Wide World of Sports?* Remember Howard Cosell, the William Gass, as it were, of sportscasters?) In 1970, *Monday Night Football's* open-

321

ing-credit sequence expressed the mode rather boldly: Instead of the traditional clips of athletes in action—the subject of the text—Arledge's graphics people created a montage of action *within the ABC Sports control room*, the text commenting on itself. After that, it was but a short step to the Olympics as ABC miniseries.

Meanwhile, local-news TV reporters were starting to become value-free performers in the stories they covered: lending a picturesque hand with the sandbags during a flood, sitting down to dinner with a laid-off steelworker and his family. The news team was the news; the stories were props for performance. Here again, competitive necessity, not some reverence for an emerging cultural aesthetic, dictated the shift—but the resulting idiom was postmodern at its very vitals.

The creators of *Entertainment Tonight* watched all of this very closely—and invented a postmodern category of performance news that was indistinguishable from its performance conduit.

The glossy Chanel commercials, with their European-inspired disposal of language (woman in sunglasses reclines beside swimming pool; shadow of jet airplane passes over her; primal male torso swims toward her . . .), helped consolidate another postmodern trait—tableau, stripped of explicit meaning, as the replacement for narrative persuasion. Several of MTV's early directors either came from those commercial-auteur groups or were influenced by their emphasis on nonverbal, extranarrative design.

And then MTV went to Florida and put on this really cunning little badge. . . .

With the advent of *Miami Vice* and its imitators, the subversion of text became a mode of big-network prime-time drama. The thing now was to let the audience in on the joke—there are no stories anymore, no tales left to tell, nothing is at stake. Performance is its own content—performance as tableau, or series of tableaux, not as a rising (and dramatically narrowing) logic of causes and effects.

But by then, of course, the secret had long since spread—
to television news.

ABC's 20/20 has for several years owned the postmodern sensibility in network journalism. Under executive producer Av
Westin, a programmer who is in certain respects the Roone
Arledge of the Eighties, 20/20 quickly, albeit subtly, revised
the essential contract between a newsmagazine show and its
audience. That new contract turned out to be oddly similar to
Monday Night Football's. It stipulated that 20/20 was not to be
consumed as a program about news—but as a program about
being about news. Tableau, the self-reflex, the emphasis on
its own process—these were hallmarks of the 20/20 style. (An
Av Westin invention called the "Moment of Crisis," for example, allowed the show's producers to coax actual partici-
pants in real-life upheavals to dramatically re-create, for the
camera, their behavior leading up to the event—a palpable
introduction of artificiality into the story.)

And there is another hallmark of 20/20, one that has its
analogy in the postmodern author's intrusion of his own commentating voice into the narrative text—to ensure that the
reader never forgets that the text is artificial, a device, always
subservient to the performance involved in writing the text.

That final hallmark may be described, in strictly academic
terms, as Geraldo Rivera.

Until he sulked off the show late last year, Rivera seldom
merely narrated a 20/20 story or reported it—he acted in it.
He played a character named "Geraldo Rivera," a correspondent for a network newsmagazine show who was always finding out what it was like to be smack-dab in the middle of the
story he was covering. It may have been a staged pursuit of a
Caribbean drug-running airplane by actual drug-enforcement
officials—with Geraldo playing "Geraldo" playing " 'Geraldo,' " a handsome drug smuggler who ends up sprinting
across the tarmac of a landing strip, hair billowing, only to be
cornered by the law. Or it may have been a piece about "Ger-

aldo" going off to Spain to run with the bulls in Pamplona, skinning his knee and falling to the ground as the 20/20 camera catches his spiraling descent in a series of freeze-frames.

The dismaying thing is 20/20 can claim some of the most talented behind-the-scenes people—producers, writers, video editors—in all of television news. The show's journalistic instincts are frequently intelligent. But too often on 20/20, it's the idiom—not the medium—that's the message.

More recently, the postmodern style has expanded to CBS News. Its exponent is *West 57th*. *West 57th* is the Manhattan Project of CBS's news division; it underwent several test detonations on the air last summer, and now is scheduled to be deployed in actual combat. A newsmagazine tailored explicitly to the sensibilities of a young, video-literate audience, the show adapts postmodern aspects of a different sort than 20/20. Its repertory cast of young, hip correspondents does not dominate the stories it covers in the way Rivera does (although the techniques of "reporter involvement" are certainly present, as in the long, studied cutaway shots of them listening, smiling, empathizing). *West 57th* is about another kind of "aboutness." In its more controlled moments—that is, in pieces that don't involve celebrity interviews, which so far have been strained and cloying—*West 57th* is about a redefinition of narrative for strictly video purposes.

Consider a report by John Ferrugia last summer on the topic of PCP—angel dust—and its prevalence on Washington, D.C., streets. After the obligatory introduction by Ferrugia in the CBS control room (Hi, Roone!), the soundtrack shifted to the percussive beat of—yes!—a rock tune titled, as it happened, "Angel Dust."

"This song hit the charts in the past eight months," Ferrugia noted in the pared-down, captioning language that is a *West 57th* trademark. "PCP has been number one in Washington for the past three years." A minute later Ferrugia added,

"PCP is a businessman's dream. Low inventory—high return."

A PCP peddler—his status vis-à-vis the law was left unstated—appeared onscreen in silhouette. "Why is Washington a center?" Ferrugia asked in a reasonable sort of way. "Okay," said the peddler. "First, the market is there. Second, the expertise is there. Third, you have access to the chemicals."

Aha. Then there was some footage and a little dry narration suggesting how easy it was to get into the PCP business—all one needed was a basement and an eighth-grade understanding of chemistry. Only then, back in the interview setting, did Ferrugia bring up what in earlier times might have been the thematic underpinning of the whole piece.

"Were you ever aware," he asked the silhouetted peddler, "when you were a cooker, what PCP did to people?" "Yup," said the subject.

"Didn't bother you."

"Nope."

"Why?"

"I figured people knew what they were gettin' into. . . ."

End of subject. No journalistic ambushes, no histrionics, no third degree. The next scene *did* show a PCP addict in a hospital emergency room, trying to bite through the metal restraining bar of his stretcher. One might imagine a connection between that scene and the previous one if one wished; no such connections were stressed. The abiding mood of the PCP story, like that of most *West 57th* pieces, was savvy but cool; plugged in yet uninvolved. The visual images searingly evoked an American netherworld (*West 57th* is fascinated by netherworlds, as are many music videos) but were remote from its final meaning or consequences.

As for narrative—well, as the term is generally used, to describe the act of *telling a story, in detail*, it wasn't there. Nor will it be there in future *West 57th* pieces. (Senior producer

Tom Yellin has said that his ideal narrative style is that of Fred Wiseman, the documentarian who uses no narrative at all, but that since it's impossible to do a segment in which the essential action happens on camera, some captioning is necessary.)

Instead of narrative, *West 57th* offers tableaux—a sequence of images and sounds, materials out of which the viewer may assemble his or her own narrative. Those materials are edited purposefully—"people knew what they were gettin' into," followed by a crazed victim trying to chew through steel—but ultimately *West 57th* is a show about its own new style, its own new look, its own performance: about, in other words, its postmodern sensibilities. The program's producers insist they are beaming to an audience that is more intelligent than generally conceded and also highly attuned to video's nonverbal codes and rhythms.

If they are right, television's first truly indigenous idiom is now universal—sports, commercials, music, prime-time entertainment, news. If they are wrong—if viewers are not making those connections, completing the narrative, supplying their own aesthetic and moral conclusions—then maybe it's necessary to conclude that *clarity* is the truly indigenous idiom for any mode of journalism.

. . . And Now,
a Nanosecond
for the News

As local radio news erodes, so does a bit of our social glue. And nobody will hear its obituary

Local news on the radio is an endangered program form; it could be extinct within a few years. That information may not move you to drape a sackcloth over your silicon chips or whip off your Walkman for a moment of respectful silence. Perhaps reports on hospital admissions in Possum Corners are, well, a touch outside your personal matrix of meaningful electronic-input option patterns. Perhaps you are a good deal more curious, at this moment, about why a piece on local *radio* is appearing in a column normally devoted to national *television*.

It is necessary, this month, to journey beyond such atomizing categories as "radio" and "television" and into more unifying ether. It is necessary to think at least briefly about *airwaves*—that lovely, poetic archaism—and their ancient, largely violated power to induce myth.

It is on the airwaves that the decline of local news on radio commingles with, say, the rise of satellite-distributed infotainment tonight and every night from Paramount Television. It is on the airwaves that the consequences of this commingling enhance or diminish—however marginally—America's grasp of its past, its continuing national story.

As for the immediate facts of the case—just how fast local radio news is declining, or what the decline means in statistical terms (total hours of news lost, total number of reporters and news directors thrown out of work, total ratings points gained as a result)—not much is known. But the decline is indisputable. A recent issue of *Electronic Media*, that admirable trade publication, surveyed the trend, concluded that "local news may soon become the exception on radio, instead of the rule," and offered four main reasons for the decline:

- the growing costs of running a local news department
- increased competition among FM music stations, which feel local news costs them listeners
- the federal government's recent deregulation of radio
- the rise of national and state networks able to "replace" local news departments.

Growing costs, I suppose, we can all relate to. (All of us except the Pentagon; perhaps we should turn radio news over to Mr. Weinberger. Then again, perhaps not.) The last three reasons, though, point to deeply troubling dynamics—not just in radio news, nor even just in radio, but throughout the runaway, self-gratifying leviathan known as the broadcast industry.

FM stations feel that local news costs them listeners? That's not much of a testimonial to the statesmanship, or citizenship, of FM management, or to the free-market model for broadcast competition. Even fast-food franchise owners are obliged to provide receptacles for their customers' trash so that the community will not be defaced. In broadcasting, the trash is cycled directly *into* the community without restriction; it's the nutrients that are hermetically disposed of.

Deregulation has abetted the decline of radio news? Then deregulation would seem to be the reverse image of Prohibition. It has given license (as it were) to broadcasters' narrowest and greediest instincts and has worked against the public interest; it has failed in its merits and should be rolled back.

National and state networks are "replacing" local news departments? This rationale, while on its surface a plausible justification for local news's banishment, is in fact the most offensive and depressing indictment of the trend.

It is an exquisite paradox that in this so-called information society we inhabit, in this "data age" of ours, so much of the information and data (at least that which is distributed through mass-media channels) is redundant. All those *Newsbriefs* and *Newsbreaks* and *News-on-the-Hours* (and, yes, all those *Evening Newses* and *Nightly Newses* and *World News Tonights*). All those sanitized, Gannett-ized, market-researched, tightly packaged, full-color little slabs of factoidal boilerplate that have sprouted podlike in local communities and devoured the identity of the indigenous daily paper. All those city magazines—oh, don't get me started on the city magazines. The point is, it's now excruciatingly possible for the citizen of Galena, Illinois, to have access to exactly the same quotidian information as the citizen of Washington, or Detroit, or Los Angeles. Perhaps at least one of those citizens deserves—needs—more. Perhaps that citizen is the citizen of Galena. Which brings us to the point I raised at the beginning, the question of airwaves and myth. The loss to American communities that accompanies the decline of radio news cannot be measured strictly in terms of "public interest" or "right to know" or similar civic standards. Something deeper, more private, is at stake—something maybe more precious, when it's all counted up.

A few days after I read the *Electronic Media* report, I picked up the telephone and called KHMO, one of the two radio stations in Hannibal, Missouri, my hometown. My call was a whim. It had been a generation since I knew anyone at KHMO. I asked

329

for the news director. A man who identified himself as Jon Hanvelt came on the line. Hanvelt's voice sounded curiously distracted, almost petulant.

I told Hanvelt who I was and asked him whether he had heard of this alleged trend in radio to do away with local news.

The line went silent for so long that I thought Hanvelt had put the phone down for some reason and walked away. Then there came a cold little chuckle.

"It's funny you should call today," Hanvelt said.

Hanvelt told me that just that morning he had received orders to cut back on his station's local newscasts. Up until then he had had fifteen spots, eleven running three and a half minutes. The new directive required him to pare ten of those down to a minute.

"That means we're basically a headline service," he said. "By policy, we're saying less and less about less and less. It's the perception of ownership that we should get back to the pabulum as quickly as possible."

The "ownership" that Hanvelt mentioned—like so much ownership in radio and television—is absentee. KHMO is controlled by a concern in Springfield, Missouri, a large and distant city. The concern is pleased to call itself Mark Twain Media. Undoubtedly, the title lacks conscious irony. The specifics of Mark Twain's success—a seminal bequest to world literature founded on material harvested from the local life in Hannibal, the local *stories*—may not have figured in the owners' . . . perceptions.

I asked Jon Hanvelt to give me an idea of some of the stories on his news budget for that day. There was the sound of papers being riffled; Hanvelt read: "Road crews at work on a snowbound county route . . . dismissal of Hannibal public-school children because of failures in the heating system . . . the weather in northwest Missouri and how the melting snow might be expected to affect driving . . . some obituaries."

Nothing special. Just the stuff that people needed to know in order to live their lives. Just connective tissue.

"We stay away from Happy Talk," Jon Hanvelt said.

It would be a mistake to conclude that the demise of radio news is merely an affliction that attacks small, isolated stations. There are some piquant casualties in the larger markets, as they are called. WIND-AM in Chicago—Chicago, one of the great local-news arenas of the Western world—lost its news director and city-hall reporter to layoffs. WIND is a Group W station, part of Westinghouse, as is KDKA in Pittsburgh— which also lost its news director, whose duties were then heaped upon the program director. Aficionados of trivia may recall KDKA as America's first radio station, which started in 1920. It was at KDKA, on August 5, 1921, that a daytime foreman named Harold Arlin invented play-by-play broadcasting by hauling a carbon microphone and power generator into Forbes Field and describing a Pirates-Phillies game—ah, but that was before Adult Contemporary.

It's not that these despoilers, these strip miners of localism, are *unaware* of its charms, mind you. They are not *oblivious* to the public's wish to *perceive* localism in their media, or at least an illusion of localism. And give them credit, by God. They are trying to satisfy that need. They have created fake localism.

Take the case of the Satellite Music Network, a three-year-old programming service with headquarters in Dallas. SMN links up with a communications satellite to flood about 500 radio stations around the country with a choice of four centrally programmed music formats. Each format (rock, country, Adult Contemporary, Middle of the Road) is cleverly and purposely packaged to suggest that it is originating from the local stations.

Satellite Music's jocks, situated in Dallas and outside Chicago, are live on the air with their patter between music cuts—

except for certain five-second "drop-ins" throughout the day, in which computer technology activates their prerecorded voices with messages specific for each market.

"The affiliate station writes the copy and our jocks record it," explains an SMN functionary. "When it's time to go to a drop-in, the jock fires off a control function that produces a contact closure at each station and activates an automation machine. So you hear the jock give the local call letters, the name of the town, some reference to something local.

"It creates a sense of intimacy. Listeners love it. They send cookies to our jocks the same as if they lived right in town."

And what, finally, does all of this have to do with myth? I think it is this: News about a community is more than the sum of its data. It is an affirmation that the data matter; that the people who live in a community and the things that happen to them have an inherent legitimacy, even a grandeur of sorts, that does not need ratification by *Real People*. Local news is a testament that towns and smaller cities are more than simply spectators to the manufactured pertinencies of the coastal media centers.

Some years ago, I was traveling back to Hannibal by car for the funeral of my Aunt Rose, a kind and sickly woman who died young of a heart attack. Aunt Rose had no particular identity outside the family, so far as it would have occurred to any of us; she was . . . Aunt Rose. Someone in the car switched on the radio, and an announcer's voice began, "Funeral services for a well-known Hannibal woman—"

That moment is lodged in my memory as vividly as the news of the death of John F. Kennedy, as is the associative memory—a rise in the two-lane highway, a fine rain on pasture. For that moment, on the airwaves, Aunt Rose was a figure of myth.

"When news breaks out, we break in!" the local radio newsmen used to say. And: "More news, more often!" And: "You're never more than twenty-four minutes away from news!" I used to find those slogans a shade grandiose. I don't think that anymore.

What I think is that a country that cannot spare three and a half goddamn minutes to be apprised of its snowy roads and its school boards and its mayors and parades, a country that will not suffer those who would read, on the airwaves, the names of its local dead, is a country at war with its history and its soul. It is a country that deserves no less a punishment than to be informed, continually, repeatedly, about the lifestyles of its rich and famous.

THE BOOB TUBE

*Any thought of journalism creeping into
local news has been a real bust*

April may be the cruelest month, as T. S. Elliot Weston remarked wryly to Michael in that famous episode of *wasteland-
something*—but June can be a bummer too. Take TV journalism.
(Please.)

It was this past June, at almost exactly the time we were
beginning to witness those incredible televised images of
democratic defiance in Beijing (think of that lone citizen, bare
of weaponry, arm upraised, halting a column of advancing
Chinese Army tanks), that local-television news in America
gave off several little spasms of anarchy from within its own
murky province. In this case, the tanks had all the good lines.
The operative images here were of Dave Marash's bared teeth,
Mike Schneider's bare escape, Tom Brook's bared soul and
Shelly Jamison's bared breasts.

Let us—as Ms. Jamison might put it—take things from the top. David Marash is quitting. Dave Marash is quite likely *the* most legitimate local-television newsman in the nation. Rumpled, balding, bearded, Marash was actually the *first* stripper in TV-news history: A decade ago in New York City, he stubbornly appeared on-air in shirt sleeves, sans the anchorman's uniform suit jacket. Marash put in twenty-two years anchoring and reporting in New York and Washington, D.C., including a three-year stint (1978–80) with ABC News's *20/20*. He's won seven Emmys. He has an Overseas Press Club award, a New York Press Club citation. He is a graduate, in English literature and film, of Williams College and Rutgers University, where he taught briefly. He is a distinguished veteran of assignments in West Germany, Nicaragua, the Middle East, Spain.

And he is outta here. It was in June that Dave Marash told his employers at WRC, the NBC-owned station in Washington, that they would have to find themselves another (anchor) boy.

He didn't bother to prettify his reasons. "I think it's a tragedy," he fumed for the record, "that television news, which really is 'the people's news,' should be abdicating more and more of its responsibilities as a watchdog of government and society."

When I called Marash a few days later to ask him to amplify on this, he told me he had had all he could take of witnessing the WRC news management spike his ideas for local stories. Marash's ideas had included coverage of the critical problem of truancy in Washington-area schools and of the changing pattern of D.C.'s AIDS victims. What he saw getting on the air instead was what he described as "anecdotal stories— shootings, stickups, fender benders—all presented as daily factoids.

"What's missing," Marash said, "is what I call 'systemic journalism.' That's part of the legacy of Ronald Reagan—his success in creating the 'mindless-government' point of view.

335

Television news largely accepted that view and stopped giving any idea of the magnitude of the task that government faces."

But if Ronald Reagan left his legacy, so have the new corporate masters of TV news. Robert Wright, CEO of NBC, is a premier example. His penny-pinching policies have earned him the anger and contempt of serious journalists throughout the NBC system. "What's driving this avoidance," as Marash put it, "is nothing more than cheapness. If you're going to get beyond the anecdotal factoid of the news, you've got to set a reporter loose for days at a time, but local-news budgets can't allow for that. They're constrained these days. Why? Because General Electric ran up a lot of debt in acquiring NBC, and they want to liquidate that debt, partly by pruning their local-news operations."

Marash will continue his role as host of *Science Journal*, on PBS, and will look for opportunities to produce documentaries.

Mike Schneider was a little luckier—he escaped with his shirt, as it were. Schneider is (was) a young local-news anchorman with a very respectable career record in Miami, Pittsburgh, Buffalo and New York City. Last May, Schneider—a presentable-enough chap, by most human standards—was kicked off the air at WCBS in New York. His bosses there did not question Schneider's journalistic credentials. But they questioned whether he had that, um, well, you know, *chemistry* we've all come to except from local newshunks. The ratings seemed to indicate otherwise. And so the higher-ups vaporized him and hired a face named Ernie Anastos, who had made Yuppie hearts go pitty-pat on a competing station for years 'n' years.

What's interesting about this story is that Schneider, the local-news reject, was picked up by a *network*. ABC News, not exactly a Trappist monastery when it comes to cosmetics, decided that the lad could be trusted not to stampede cattle or frighten small children on its airwaves, so it hired him to re-place Forrest Sawyer on its *World News This Morning.*

Maybe it isn't really chemistry the local stations are looking for. Maybe it's genetic engineering.

Next we come to the case of an anguished British reporter named Tom Brook, who last June paid a visit to my Vermont aerie in a kind of hair shirt. Brook was on a personal and reportorial odyssey, seeking to purge his conscience of his brush with local-TV news, American-style.

Brook is a free-lance reporter for the BBC and other outlets in England, a sensitive and intelligent man. In December 1988, Brook found himself amid a herd of newspeople at Kennedy Airport—a hunting party, whose quarry were the surviving relatives and friends of passengers on Pan Am Flight 103, which had crashed in Scotland en route to New York from London.

What Brook saw that night—and participated in—came to haunt him. Last spring he began putting together a unique documentary of his reflections, and those of other journalists who had been a part of that scene, and of several victims of their tender inquiries.

"At some point there, it hit me that what I was doing was wrong," Brook told me. "But I couldn't just then understand *exactly why* it was wrong."

He let me see a videotape that made it quite clear to him why it was wrong. The tape was an excerpt from a local-TV newscast—from Syracuse, as it happened, where many of the crash victims had attended college.

The cut showed a woman writhing on the airport floor. (The woman, as it later turned out, had a name: Janine Boulanger.) She had just at that moment learned that her daughter was among the dead. As video and still photographs crowded in around her—hunters closing in on a wounded animal—Mrs. Boulanger released a wail that will forever echo in my memory. Typography cannot reproduce the depth of the despair of that wail, and so I will simply note the words here:

"My baby!"

A moment later the local co-anchor team, a well-groomed, well-jawlined man and a well-coiffed blonde woman, appeared onscreen. They did not bother to confer an identity upon the wailing mother. The blonde woman said that they would be back with more after this.

Tom Brook had already sought out Mrs. Boulanger for his documentary. She had likened the experience—the shock of grief, the merciless lenses—to being violated. Now Brook wanted to know if I, as a critic, would be willing to answer a few questions on-camera for him and his crew. He handed me a long list he'd written out. One of the questions was as follows:

"News producers I have talked to say they decided to use the pictures of the woman on the floor screaming because it brought home the full horror of the tragedy. Do you agree?"

Our final little spasm of June comes courtesy of the former Phoenix newswoman Shelly Jamison. Ms. Jamison made do with no shirt at all and served, if nothing else, to remind us in her briefly famous appearance in *Playboy* magazine that June is National Dairy Month.

She also reminds us of the priorities. There are about 20,000 people employed in TV journalism in this country, and not all of them are out to save the world, sugar. We have just met three rather starry-eyed exceptions. Shelly Jamison represents the others—the realists, today's clear-eyed aspirants—who perceive television news in the Eighties for what it has, perhaps inevitably, become. Ms. Jamison herself articulated it best when I spoke to her by telephone. "I said, 'Television news—now there's an accessible field,' " she recalled. " 'It has theatrics to it.' "

(Are you listening, Mrs. Boulanger? Does this help explain anything?)

Shelly Jamison was practically computer programmed for TV news. A 1984 graduate of—so help me—the Walter Cronkite

School of Journalism and Telecommunications at Arizona State University, she is also the stepdaughter of Phoenix anchorman Phil Allen. She is also blonde and possessed of, let's face it, a set of gazongas the aggregate size of Connie Chung. As she winningly put it to the *Playboy* copywriter, "I'm a product . . . a package."

The package was hired off the assembly line by KTSP in Phoenix. And then a strange thing happened: She did not become an overnight star. The management at KTSP actually expected her to work. Okay, work she did. Behind the scenes. She produced the noon news. Once in a while she got on-camera—news briefs, mainly. And Shelly Jamison stewed. "I began to feel powerless" is how she put it to me. "It was clear that I could go somewhere else, grow in the field, become the next whoever—Diane Sawyer. But I didn't want to climb from one market to the next."

So instead she climbed into the pages of *Playboy*. (Her husband, a Phoenix fireman, had sent in nude photos of her.) She kept her posing a secret until the issue appeared—going so far as to conceal the affiliation of the photographer who came to snap her (clothed) with the KTSP news set as a backdrop. Then she triumphantly told her bosses to take her job and shove it and sallied forth to claim her rightful place in the cosmos.

She dove into the demimonde of programs designed to amplify and legitimize precisely her vision of American public life: *USA Today on TV, A Current Affair, Larry King Live* and the fountainhead, *Entertainment Tonight*—a program, she let slip several times, she wouldn't mind hosting when she finished her tour.

But then damned if another strange thing didn't happen. The system went down! Jamison *still* did not become a star!

"Right now there are no acting jobs forthcoming," she pouted from back home in Phoenix about a week after her tour had ended. It wasn't that she lacked a strategy. "I tried to figure out, What can I do to maximize the potential of being on the

Playboy-magazine cover?" she explained. "I decided to sit back and wait. I assumed whatever happened would be in the entertainment type of industry. But people don't look on me as an actress."

It's hard to think why not. Meanwhile, the month of June edged toward sere summer; somewhere, a cultural revolution failed, the tanks rolled, and a bright promise of some sort was squandered. I forget exactly which country it was.

THE RIGHT'S TOUGH

"The Press is the living Jury of the Nation."
— JAMES GORDON BENNETT, 1830

"We get very little mail on the column today. We get an enormous amount of mail on the television show."
— ROBERT D. NOVAK, 1989

There you have it. The imperial period of political punditry as a pillar of the print press is kaput.

After one hundred sixty years, the Jury is *out*—out at the studio. The Jurors have scraped the tobacco flecks off their lapels, bought some red ties, signed with ICM, self-applied their Max Factor No. 2 and become Broadcast Barons of the Beltway. Hey, now they *mail in* their syndicated pieces . . . en route to their ensemble shots on *McLaughlin, Crossfire, Washington Week in Review, This Week With David Brinkley, The MacNeil/ Lehrer NewsHour, The Capital Gang.*

And God knows how many others before this piece goes to

press. As the 1990s begin, it is no longer the Sunday op-ed essay that frames political discourse or political agenda—such as they are—in the nation. It's the one-line assault gag on the weekend Washington-insider TV talkshow.

The implications are fascinating—and frightening. Given the overheated sensibilities of television in the Nineties, what sort of "discourse" is likely to break through amid the hell storm of new format pitches now flying about PBS, CNN and other potential carriers?

("I am telling you, the stuff that comes in here on proposals," declared a CNN source, "the kind of stuff I hear on the street—everybody wants to have a political talkshow! There are pilots that are crashing into each other! Everybody is looking to put a new twist, a new angle on it.")

Not Martin Agronsky stuff, you can be sure. Agronsky, the founder of video poli-chat, whose *Agronsky & Co.* ran from 1970 to 1987, was a gentle, deliberate man who actually valued sequential thought.

No. The prototype personality is far likelier to be one of the pioneers of prime-time polemic: that perennial pundit-as-pitbull, that rightwing rajah of riposte and ridicule, the old Prince of Darkness himself, Robert Novak.

"I have—and I hope this doesn't sound boasting—I've developed a certain cult following," the irrecoverably rumpled and sleepy-eyed Novak is intoning deep inside the Beltway one Saturday morning—not in his newspaper-syndicate office, but in his CNN-bureau digs, just off the studio where his rowdy roundtable, *The Capital Gang*, will commence its latest unpleasantness in about 10 hours.

"Is it because I snarl and bite?" The saturnine Novakean lip twitches in what is meant, possibly, as a smile. "Maybe some of that. Maybe a lot of that. Maybe most of that. But I think there are some people who are, even subliminally, getting some of the things I'm saying. The substance, the issues. I think that with all the pyrotechnics, I convey ideas on television for a broad audience—particularly in this nonreading, nonlinear society."

Let's face it—Robert Novak is hardly the Arsenio Hall of video punditry. No overnight glitterbug, he. In rest homes and sun cities across America, in fact, he is famous mainly as the posterior half of that far-right death squad of syndicated columns, Evans & Novak. The two first pooled their bylines in the year of John F. Kennedy's assassination, and have appeared in tandem on CNN as well. To poli-vid junkies of the 1980s, Novak was something quite different: a TV mega-star, Jumpin' Jack Slash, one of the raging inmates on the notorious PBS asylum known as *The McLaughlin Group.* (Few fans from either era recall that Novak has been doing television, locally and nationally, nearly as long as he has been established in print.)

His political convictions are dead serious. "I read *Witness,* by Whittaker Chambers, when I was in the army in the early 1950s," he says, referring to the bible of anticommunist true believers. "That had a huge impact on my life. I've read the book at least five times since then, and in the most recent edition I have a foreword. The whole history of mankind has been blighted by the heavy hand of government, and the twentieth century has been the century of government at its most oppressive."

But the world has since turned and Novak, as we shall see, has lost a beloved enemy. Still, even as his print career fades, Novak is rising toward his crest as the reigning symbol of the *fait-accompli* shift, from typography to TV, of authority in American political opinion. And of all its implications.

It has been more than two years since Novak flew over the cuckoo's nest that was *The McLaughlin Group.* During that stint he had thrown himself into a legendary series of vicious on-air shouting matches with the show's fulminating host, John "the Taxpayer" McLaughlin, and with his horn-rimmed fellow panelist Morton Kondracke. Quickly and without apology, Novak moved to CNN and created what in situation comedy is known as a "spinoff": *The Capital Gang*, he announced with injured dignity, was going to bring a little *decorum* to this business of ideological throat slashing.

The analogy between *McLaughlin* and a sitcom does not particularly faze Novak. In fact it comes from him. "Jack Germond was the tough guy in the bar," he says, ticking off the panelists. "Kondracke was the earnest younger brother. I was the mean son of a bitch, and John was this authoritarian figure."

Then a more telling image pops into his mind.

"It was like a stock-car race," he concedes. "People would tune in and wait for something really *bad* to happen. *Really* bad. And sometimes it did. Real animosity. Out-of-control, personal animosity. It got to be personal, between me and John. It helped the ratings, and the popularity, but it began to detract from the show."

(To give Novak his due, McLaughlin does seem to have developed an overweening sweet tooth for raw vitriol. On his new program on the cable channel CNBC, Big Mac can be seen nightly flinging his enormous chassis back and forth about the set, towering over a terrified guest like some enraged Daddy Warbucks. It's as if the poltergeist of Morton Downey Jr. mistook McLaughlin's vast midsection for an empty soundstage and settled in.)

By comparison to its model, at least, *The Gang* is less psychopathic. Like *McLaughlin*, it is built around the requisite panel of regulars, all of them as familiar to viewers as certain faces in the Florentine Court must have been to the Medicis.

Looming as host—"host" seems a surreally delicate description, somehow—is Pat Buchanan. ("A *New York Post* editorial writer recently attacked Pat as a medievalist. Pat would not necessarily consider that an insult," Novak observes fondly.) Then there is the cuddly former Democratic consultant Mark

Shields. ("Mark is an old-fashioned liberal. Yet he's an intelligent man, in my opinion".) Next there is the ubiquitous presence whom this viewer, at least, has come to think of as Al Hunt-of-*The Wall Street Journal.* ("Interesting figure. His role is as the centrist, but he often comes over to Shields's left. I think his heart really burns for the homeless and poor.") Finally, there is Novak himself—who is one of the show's producers—and a weekly guest from the world of politics.

And what sort of measured political discourse arises from this mix? Well, there was the night the Gang paid its last respects to the recently deceased Claude Pepper, the longtime congressman and champion of the elderly. "Claude Pepper's politics did a lot of damage to this country," noted Novak in his tenderly moving epitaph. "He wanted to make us a gerontocracy."

And there is the program's polemic highlight, the Outrage of the Week (for some weird reason I can't help recalling the old TV stock-car-racing staple of my youth, the Crack-up of the Week), in which the panelists get to sound off on what *really* sticks in their craw. One week Novak fumed that the departing Surgeon General, C. Everett Koop, "thinks he's the Nursemaid General!"

What I really want to know from Robert Novak this morning in his office is whether the old print journalist in him is disturbed by the new directions in which television is taking political punditry—directions mapped, in no small part, by Novak himself. For instance: Was there a causal link between the verbal kung-fu developed on *The McLaughlin Group* (and refined on *The Capital Gang*) and the 1980s preoccupation with "scoring a knockout" as the sole criterion for judging a presidential or vice-presidential debate?

Novak flutters his heavy lids, gives a little shrug. "Sure," he says. "Sure. It's a creation of television, obviously."

But is he entirely comfortable with it? Again, the shrug.

"Yeah. I mean, I'm aware enough of its cosmetic nature and that it isn't a serious discussion in the sense of—" he raises his eyes to the ceiling and sighs.

"Look. I remember, in my mind's eye, when I was a young kid growing up in Joliet, Illinois, listening to the *University of Chicago Round Table* on the radio. And they would have these long . . . takeouts. Well, you can't do that for very long on television. I mean, that's a no-no. And so you have to get everything down to a bite-sized morsel. *You can't go into the second paragraph, is one way of putting it in print terms.*"

No second paragraph? *Zut alors.* I have known Robert Novak to be a world-class fatalist, but this seems new ground. After all, however lampooned has been his column with Rowland Evans ("Errors and No Facts," has been one popular epithet), he is the coauthor of several serious and well-regarded books on American politics. The second paragraph, one might think, would hold at least a residual reverence for him.

But then, print has evolved. Even *television* has evolved. It has evolved into a kind of pure arena. And Novak, the consummate cynic, has evolved along with it. He recalls one of the seminal moments in his education as a television animal. It occurred on the very eve of his efflorescence into stardom on *The McLaughlin Group.* His guru was none other than Phil Donahue.

"Rollie and I were doing the talkshow circuit for our last book, in 1981," Novak says, "and we went to Chicago to do *Donahue.* He sat down with us before the show and said, 'I want to tell you guys, *this is not* Good Morning, Seattle. *We're in the entertainment business. And we don't want those sets clicking off!*' " Novak lowers his eyes and smiles at the memory. "And it was a helluva show," he says after a moment. "I'll tell ya, when the host tells you that you don't want to fall on your face—it gets the adrenaline flowing."

For Novak, the adrenaline has never stopped. Nor has the awareness of what the medium demands. "Have you seen McLaughlin's new show?" he asks. "Without making a value judgement, I will say that it's a hybrid of the *Geraldo-Donahue* format with a somewhat more serious subject matter. I think you're going to see a lot more of these permutations.

"The thing is, that's just the wave of the future. You've got to accept it. I still consider myself, in my own mind, a print journalist. I've got a column running Monday on the capital-gains vote. How long have I been writing that column? For 20 years, in a way. And it may take literally hours to write and edit. And yet something I say off the top of my head, impromptu, on television generates a lot more attention.

"I know very well in this world that I'm thought of almost entirely as a television personality," Novak adds. "That's how people greet me in airports. That's how I get out beyond the Beltway."

My conversation with Robert Novak took place several weeks before certain interesting events occurred out beyond the Beltway—namely, the collapse of Communist governments in Eastern and Central Europe. When the dust had settled in East Germany and Czechoslovakia and Romania and Poland, I telephoned the Prince of Darkness to see how badly he was taking this disintegration of all he'd loved to hate. I found him in an unexpectedly thoughtful, almost (for Novak) elegiac mood.

"You've asked me a very embarrassing question," he conceded. "I'm not gonna tell you I am not stunned, because I had thought that two things in this life were nigh onto impossible. One was a modern police state being overthrown by citizens. The other was a Communist government reverting to a non-Communist one."

How did he account for it?

"I think what happened," Novak said, "was that I underestimated the value of ideas, of religious faith and of democracy as against police power and the instruments of the totalitarian state. I'm not ready to say the Cold War is over. I want to see how this all plays itself out. And I don't feel any need to apologize for the beliefs I've held: The people I've been in contention with have never seen all this as a struggle between light and darkness, East and West.

"The revision of my view—and of Whittaker Chambers's view, if he were alive—is perhaps in an underestimation of the human spirit, perhaps even the *divine* inspiration of the human spirit."

Yikes. For a wild moment I wondered whether the outbreak of light had unhinged the Prince of Darkness—had begun to move him away from Pat Buchanan, say, and toward Pat Robertson.

His next remark quieted my fears. "If Communism goes," he went on, with some of the old malicious glee back in his voice, "I've still got the U.S. House of Representatives."

Hurricane Willard
and Other Blowhards

*A frenetic few from the buffoon school remain, but
today's new wing-tipped weathermen are cool, cool, cool*

There's been a change in the weather. At least in the weather
as presented on television. Can you believe how earnest TV
weathermen have become these days—how technocentric, how
upscale, how *wing-tipped* about it all? Is it possible we're experiencing a long-range cycle of Republican weather?

Don't mention Willard Scott to me. I know all about Willard
Scott. I'll get to Willard Scott, as they say in TV weatherland,
a bit later on in this half hour.

Right now, let's go to the satellite map and track some major fronts moving along the East Coast and out into the plains
states.

John Coleman has flowed westward from New York to Chicago (WMAQ) and has been downgraded to (heh-heh) a topical storm. Frank Field, a low-pressure system if ever there

was one, has shifted slightly to fill Coleman's old spot at WCBS in New York. No change likely for Steve Baskerville at *CBS Morning News* or Dave Murray at ABC's *Good Morning America*.

Why does one single out these four TV weathermen for scrutiny when there are several others (many of them Willard Scott) who are more flamboyant, just as famous and equally vital to the ratings fortunes of their local stations or networks?

George Fischbeck comes to mind—Fischbeck of the hyperfrenetic, arm-waving delivery at KABC in Los Angeles. Now, Los Angeles is not a city whose weather might be expected to justify a lot of arm waving unless one is in the final throes of a thermal inversion. Nonetheless, audience surveys have shown that in L.A. Fischbeck leads all TV newspeople in popularity and credibility.

We exclude Fischbeck from TV weather's Big Four because the times, frankly, have passed him by. (I'll get to Willard in a minute. Really.) Fischbeck is a vestige from the recent, but utterly defunct, past—a sulfidic past that also includes such still-practicing eccentrics as headstanding, ear-shattering Lloyd Lindsay Young (late of Idaho and San Francisco, now at a local station in New York); good-ole-boy Warren Culbertson, now doing radio in Dallas; plus a gaggle of former beauty queens, good-lookin' surfer guys, puppet-wielding poltroons and at least one podiatrist (Dave Eiser, who recently hotfooted it from Chicago to Dallas).

This wild-eyed menagerie, part of television's last link with its manic-amateur origins, is being phased out—in favor of the TV weatherman as bureaucrat. As NASA technician. As, hell, John Houseman for Smith Barney.

The shift has something to do with the medium's ongoing passion for high-tech iconography: the weatherman as technician at the center of a computerized weather-accessing module is all the rage these days. (Watching a weatherman in the studio is a little like being in the presence of a madman: He babbles on about highs, lows and fronts while pointing to a blank green or blue wall. The weather map itself is superimposed electronically from the control room.)

The change has something to do with the vogue for data saturation spurred by *USA Today*'s daily full-color national weather map (which took its inspiration from TV weather in the first place). But pin the blame mostly on the TV news's suddenly fashionable posture of doughty seriousness.

The key word here is *posture*: The newly earnest weathermen are not giving their audiences very much that is different *in content* from what Terry Burhans used to provide in Baton Rouge with his rinky-tink piano, *singing* the weather.

What the new, no-nonsense weathermen *do* is lend an air of legitimacy to the newscast—the factoid-drenched kind of legitimacy that in the past five years has all but usurped "Happy Talk" as TV news's most exploitable gimmick.

And that fact—or factoid—is loaded with irony. Because fifteen years ago it was the television weatherman who *embodied* television's profitable, albeit demeaning, plunge into the Happy Talk era.

Consider John Coleman. Today, except for an occasional gurgling retrogression, he is the very model of the modern weather general. Tweedy, corporately corpulent in late middle age, he recently returned to local television news in Chicago, the city of his first great fame, after seven years as a national presence (on *Good Morning America*) and even as a weather entrepreneur (founder and first president of The Weather Channel, a nationwide cable service).

What starry-eyed children would never guess, gathered at Coleman's cathodic knee every suppertime, is that this same grandfatherly presence used to be the very avatar of act-silly, cut-off-your-necktie, buck-and-wing weathercasting, the point man for the original Happy Talk "Eyewitless" news team at WLS in Chicago.

But let us give Coleman his due. Let us declare the statute of limitations expired on his wild-and-crazy weather past. He is unquestionably a symbolic figure in the evolution of his craft:

His decision to organize The Weather Channel was a symptom of an explosion in the cottage industry of companies that generate weather data for the mass media; data that now vastly expand upon the relatively prosaic forecasts offered by the National Weather Service.

Companies such as the Boston-area Weather Services International, emboldened by the cash flow from clients such as Coleman, have lately designed elaborate, computer-based access systems—available to any station or newspaper on a contractual basis—that allow for "real-time" weather information (satellite pictures, for example) instead of mere predictions. Its sister group, Weather Services Corporation, generates the raw data for that *USA Today* weather map.

Then there is Frank Field. How to explain Frank Field to one who has never seen him? For despite a number of morning network appearances over his twenty-five professional years, he is primarily a local man in New York. Well, if weather were music, Frank Field would be Perry Como. Frank Field *looks* like weather (a cumulus cloud in horn-rims would be a way of putting it). He named one of his kids after weather, and now Storm Field is a weatherman himself, making, oh, upward of $400,000 per. Dad, meanwhile, calls down about $750,000. He wrote a goddamn *book* about weather. And he . . . is . . . dignified about it.

He is a veritable maître d' of weather, and during the dark days and darker nights of Happy Talk in New York local television, Field stood alone—hands folded respectably at the weather map—lending that je ne sais quoi of sanity as eyeballs rolled and snickers snorted all around him. Today, reborn at age 61 as a national personality on *CBS Morning News*, Field is in the unlikely role of new-wave auteur: A generation of tweedy, professorial, no-nonsense types has entered the, er, field, paying homage to Frank's majestic dignity.

Dave Murray (of *Good Morning America*) and Steve Baskerville (who may be sharing airtime with Field on *CBS Morning News*) are among the most conspicuous protégés of this new, subdued motif. Each man's on-air style is defined more by a complex, intense and semi-improvisational relationship to a succession of electronic graphics than to personal theater. They may not haul down the kind of ransom that Frank Field commands—about $250,000 would be a generous estimate—but they are strategically vital to the success of their respective shows.

All of which raises a paradoxical question: What are television viewers learning each day about the weather—and how much of that knowledge do they retain?

The volume of facts per second on a television weathercast may be denser than anything else on the tube save commercials. If one were to hold a gun to the head of the Average Viewer (a fantasy that sweetens the dreams of many an executive producer) and demand a disgorgement of, say, *half* the data transmitted in the weathercast just ended, could the Average Viewer deliver the goods? (Bear in mind, as you ponder the question, that a New York radio station recently polled passersby on the street as to the number of hours in a day; an interesting percentage guessed twelve, several more pleaded nolo contendre and one victim responded, "Sorry, I'm not from here.")

Network executives don't know the answer, either—to the weather question, that is. "CBS doesn't do research on the impact of weathercasting," says Jon Katz, executive producer of *CBS Morning News*. "Personally, I find it hard to believe that people don't just open the door or look out the window. That's what I do. But conventional wisdom about the weatherman is so deep that it's not even open to discussion. If I walked into a conference room and said, 'Let's not have a weatherman,' they'd throw me through the wall."

CBS doesn't have to do its own research. Studies by major

consulting organizations have shown consistently that the weather is at or near the top of TV-news watchers' priorities and fascinations.

"Weather and pets are among the few truly universal subjects in this fragmented, specialized universe of information that we deal with," says Katz. "So the weatherman fulfills that mythic 'family' function on a show. In terms of our technical, internal needs, he also provides a transition point between news topics; he gives the anchors someone to talk with—he really is, in many ways, the humanizing statement for the newscast."

The "humanizing" burden that weathercasters carry may explain one interesting lapse in their daily output of data: They almost never do any *real journalism* about the weather. In-depth stories about drought patterns affecting agriculture's future? Severe winter cycles as compared with the past? Acid rain movement? The likelihood of a greenhouse effect and its implications for human life? Forget it—or turn to one of a handfull of weather-conscious newspapers in this country such as *The Boston Globe* or *The Christian Science Monitor*.

In the end, it becomes clear that television covers weather exactly as it covers its other favorite topics, fires and murders: as episodic, discontinuous, transiently interesting phenomena; not as revealing integers that make up ongoing patterns of behavior. Mark Twain, who reputedly quipped, "Everybody talks about the weather but nobody does anything about it," would have made a boffo prognosticator.

All of which somehow brings us to Willard Scott.

Gee, he's terrific. He really is.

LOVE THAT BOB

NBC sportscaster Bob Costas is perfectly attuned to the pulse of a television generation, but his values remain rooted in a more innocent age

What's this? The crafty chieftains of NBC Sports mapping out plans to commit yet another Super Bowl telecast against the decent citizens of Videoville?

And not just an ordinary million-dollar, twenty-five-camera, six-hour, *garden variety* Super Bowl telecast—but (gasp) a Twentieth Anniversary telecast? The dread Double X's? The perfect occasion for perpetrating a pageant of such preternatural pomposity upon the people that once the actual game starts, its very *periods* may be remembered as the Roman, the Seleucidan, the Sidonian and the Syro-Macedonian?

Too true. Too, too true.

It looks like a job for—*Bob Costas, Kid Sportscaster!*

You know Costas: the cherubic and vaguely unpredictable host of NBC's *NFL '85*—he may open a segment dressed as a

355

gangster and order a vanilla egg cream, easy on the seltzer, from a bartender before sliding into the weekend's matchups. Come spring he's the ace baseball play-by-play man whose off-the-wall quips to his sidekicks have become, let us say, a curiosity of the network sportscasting industry. ("Stay tuned after the game for *I Dream of Jeannie 15 Years Later*," he advised his audience during the baseball play-offs last fall—then did a quick take at what he'd just read and added, "So *bag* those plans for the World Series.")

This is the sort of loose cannon the chieftains of NBC Sports have unleashed upon Super Bowl XX.

"I have never seen a Super Bowl show that wasn't at least mildly embarrassing," Costas is saying over a luncheon of chicken-noodle soup and milk at Rockefeller Center. Yes, fans, chicken-noodle soup and milk. And turned out, mind you, in a cashmere diamond-patterned pullover sweater and horn-rims, the straight–guy–in–*Animal House* look—the Kid's alter identity when he is not riding the NBC airwaves on autumn Sunday afternoons with his beblazered *NFL '85* sidekicks, Pete Axthelm and Ahmad Rashad, or on summer Saturdays doing baseball with Tony ("Zany is my middle name") Kubek.

"I happen to think that the Super Bowl is not as endearing a part of Americana as, say, the World Series is," Costas continues. "The World Series is something television transmits; it was already an institution. The Super Bowl is something television *created*.

"I mean, football and God, football and patriotism expressed through militarism. It deserves to be parodied more than embraced."

Yowee! Tart language, coming from a 33-year-old junior member of the NBC sports announcers' ranks, a five-foot-seven-inch, 145-pound civilian in the jockcaster jungle, and an aspirant who understands very well that as host of NBC's two-hour pregame show on Super Bowl XX Sunday, he has an enormous professional opportunity. A *lot* of veteran announcers wouldn't mind being in Costas's shoes on Super Sunday—even if Costas's shoes would probably pinch most of them a little.

Yet here is the designee himself, looking ahead to his role with all the giddy euphoria of a Reagan appointee to a regulatory commission.

"This will be the most watched performance of my career," Costas concedes, taking a swig of his milk. "But I'd say that it's more important to me professionally than personally. First and foremost, I still want to become a great baseball play-by-play announcer. That has always been my greatest goal in sportscasting, and it always will be."

He pauses in mid–chicken noodle to reflect on the implications of what he has been saying.

"Look, don't get me wrong—I like football, believe me. But *within reason*. I think that during most Super Bowl telecasts a feeling begins to grow among the viewers, a feeling of—'Hey, kick the ball already, and let's *enjoy* ourselves.' "

To really know Bob Costas—one of the more interesting young practitioners of sportscasting—is to understand this is no Howard Cosell manqué speaking. Studied contempt for his subject matter is not Costas's style. If anything, he is a throwback (the horn-rims, the argyle sweater, the choirboy face are *perfect*—all he lacks is knickers) to the broadcast sensibilities of half a century ago, to an enchanted and pre-Cosellean time when the airwaves still crackled with mystery and promise, and sportscasting remained, in spirit at least, very much within the province of the Kid.

Perhaps "throwback" is a little too simplistic. Bob Costas is in fact a complicated mixture of the old-fashioned and the avant-garde. He can seem stunningly innocent one minute, shrewd and market-savvy the next. These polarities, however, are linked by a common (and uncommon) passion: Costas's undeniable reverence for *broadcasting*.

His main complaint against Super Bowl telecasts—the pregame shows in particular—expresses his ambition for the cutting edge: Costas just thinks they aren't much *fun*. His ideas for how to make them fun derive from idioms a little hipper than hard-core Jockspeak: *Saturday Night Live* and *Late Night With David Letterman*, a couple of comedy formats that speak deeply to Costas's soul—so deeply that he has tried to integrate them into his persona as host of *NFL '85* and even as a network play-by-play man.

It was Costas who first picked upon Letterman's running gag vis-à-vis the light-hitting Kansas City shortstop with the funny name. Buddy Biancalana. Last October, Costas told his NBC baseball audience that Letterman has started a Buddy Biancalana hit countdown.

"And since Biancalana has fifty-six career hits, he's better than 4,100 behind the Georgia Peach," Costas deadpanned.

That riff was quoted a few days later in a TV Sports column in *The New York Times*, which registered only tepid amusement. Even less amused with Costas's antics was *The Village Voice*, which noted a similar put-on with the acid sarcasm, "Costas, ever the boyish prankster. . . ."

These prim-lipped reactions left Costas bruised and chagrined—and they peeled away, for at least one luncheon, the cocky veneer covering the essential lad, the spontaneous Kid Broadcaster of a vanished era.

"The entire premise of the *Voice* piece was grossly unfair," Costas insists now as the noodle soup cools. "Its basic message was 'Here's an empty-headed sports guy who only loves to clown.'

"People who pay attention to my work understand the humor *in its context*. They know that no one prepares harder—especially for a baseball telecast—and that no one loves or cares more about a game than I do.

"One thing that works against me is that I don't like to say mundane sportscaster things. You have to make a decision at some point in your career. Are you going to locate a vanilla-middle with your audience and lob all your stuff into that middle? I can do that. If you want to sit here and discuss baseball without cracking a smile, I can do that as well as anybody. *Better* than anybody. But I'm reaching for an audience that loves sports *and* loves the language, loves the sense of community that sports engenders."

There are elements in that self-analysis that do seem to hint at a sensibility borrowed from the Great-Vanilla-Loather-and-Language-Lover himself. Howard Cosell's graceful valedictory to sportscasting—crowned by the gallant bouquets strewn throughout his memoir, *I Never Played the Game*—was a recent matter of public enthrallment. Would not the teensiest particle of Cosell's great Jeddi spirit live on in the Costas generation?

Costas smiles into his cold chicken-noodle soup.

"I heard once, indirectly, about his reaction to me," he says quietly. "Ax [Pete Axthelm] asked him to do an interview on a show I was hosting, and Cosell said, 'I'm supposed to sit for fifteen minutes for a show hosted by a child who rhapsodizes about the infield-fly rule?'

"What happened with Cosell at the end," Costas continues in a measured voice, "was a shame. In terms of public perception, he undid much of the good that had accumulated in his career.

"The very status he so deeply craves would have been his if he'd left well enough alone. If he had been more gracious— if he'd been a less bitter, a less tormented man—history would have taken care of him."

Costas shrugs, either at Cosell or at his cold chicken-noodle soup, which the waitress is impatiently eyeing to clear away.

Bob Costas came to network television four years ago from a far purer venue for the sportscaster's art—the radio airwaves. He began calling pro basketball games at age 22 for KMOX, the behemoth CBS radio station in St. Louis. He still returns during pauses in his NBC TV assignments to conduct open-line sports conversations, a practice that allows him to pay homage to radio and a chance to work at the textual edges of his craft.

He arrived at NBC with a Kid Broadcaster's notion of priorities and possibilities. In a universe whose star system was built on NFL football telecasts, he expressed a preference for baseball. When he was invited in 1982 to replace Bryant Gumbel as host of the NFL pregame show, an obvious stepping-stone to glory, he shocked everyone by declining. "If you asked me would I rather be the most famous TV host in the world," he said at the time, "or capture the poetry of a double off the Green Monster in Fenway Park—there is no question that I would prefer the latter."

Two years later, Costas finally accepted the pregame host's job—but characteristically, he has resisted the competitive ferocity that goes with the territory.

"You would not believe the warfare that goes on between our show and *The NFL Today* on CBS," he says. "A lot of it is meanspirited on both sides. I have not contributed. I have tried to smooth it.

"Our executive producer takes potshots at them, calling them tired and boring. They take the smug approach toward us: They say we've gone in the direction of Happy Talk. This is the part of the television business I don't like. I'm a broadcasting freak. I'm not a corporate warrior."

It is his very status as a broadcasting freak—his consciousness of announcers' styles and nuances is virtually lifelong—that accounts for Costas's enthrallment with David Letterman.

"He's got a whole . . ." Costas makes circles with his hands; words fail him. "He's got a whole *head* full of the little snippets and the frames of reference that a whole TV generation grew up hearing," Costas says finally, "and a sense of how wonderfully empty-headed they all were. Phrases from old TV shows that are like *mantras*. He just pulls them out and throws them into other contexts, and they're just as funny as hell.

His whole show is an ongoing joke about the pretenses of television."

And then the Kid Sportscaster changes his mood again. David Letterman may be fine for smuggling onto Super Bowl pregame telecasts—but darn it, *There's serious work to be done!*

"The reason why Howard Cosell was able to make so much of himself as the only serious sports journalist on television," Costas suddenly insists, "is that ABC was the only network to give a *forum* to a serious journalist. There are lots of guys at the networks, in magazines, on newspapers, whose credentials are every bit as good—*better than*—Howard's. And God knows, the stories, the issues are there to do.

"I would *love* to have thirty minutes, twenty minutes a week of plain, simple studio time so that I could sit down with a guest and explore, in a journalistic way, the issues and the accountability stories that flow from the world of sports."

Judging from his radio work on KMOX, which is seldom less than superb, the Kid Sportscaster could indeed handle such a role.

In the meantime, however, it would be prudent for him to finish his milk.

THE SEAT OF POWER

USA Today's *Rudy Martzke likes to watch . . . and the sports world can't help but pay attention*

It is game time in America, Sunday afternoon in all the households of the present tense, and in the perfect suburbs the screens are flicking on. PRO SPORTS ON TV APPEALS TO US! Let's zoom in a little tighter.

"See, I got the early shit typed inna machine. I try to type it up by 12:30, when the pregame shows start."

We are . . . someplace, a place more median than most mortals dare dream of: a neighborhood that wasn't a neighborhood a generation ago; cedar-sided dwelling units, passive solar; the two cars; the mall just down the tollway. Two major markets in the frequency spectrum.

"I was called by ESPN this mornin', sayin', 'Watch this if you watch anything. . . .'"

We are in the living room of Everyfan, the living statistical mean of every armchair jock in America. Rudy Martzke, the TV-sports columnist for *USA Today*, puts his socked feet up on the coffee table, crosses his arms and scowls expectantly at his $2,500 forty-five-inch Mitsubishi. ("I popped for it. Tax write-off.") On the carpet below the set a fluffy cat twists onto its back, paws up, like in a Booth cartoon.

As if to oblige Martzke, the Mitsubishi screen bulges with men in blue blazers. Rudy digital-clicks them to hell and gone; they are replaced by more men in blue blazers. Suddenly Martzke grows tense and alert. He has spotted something significant.

"Shee . . . *Musburger in glasses!*"

He whipsaws forward, feet on the floor now, and scribbles in ballpoint onto a spiral notepad. This data seems certain to make it into Rudy Martzke's machine.

Rudy Martzke represents a purification, of sorts, in American journalism: a seamless extension of his readers. The one among them who can live out the fantasy of picking up the phone and yelling at the stupid bastards running the telecasts. More to the point, the stupid bastards call *him*. He is the inevitable star columnist for the inevitable periodical of the Television Age. Bigger, given his available pool of 6.3 million scanners, than Evans and Novak, bigger than Lippmann in his prime. His mandate—to cover the pure performance of people covering pure performance—resonates perfectly with the Gannett Corporation's larger ideals. It is hardly surprising—it is perfect, it is inevitable—that in six and a half years Martzke's "Inside Look at TV Sports Programming" has become the second-most-scanned feature of *USA Today*. The only bigger star is the weather map.

Although he writes four times a week, his raison d'être is his Monday-morning wrap-up column critiquing the weekend's innumerable sports broadcasts. Among his categories: Best Production. Hype Award. Best Reporting. Oops Award. Hustle Award. Best Features. Worst Question. Best Analysis.

363

Strongest Comments. Top Fact. All-Cliché Team. And the centerpiece—the dread Dreaded Glitch.

Best Analysis of Rudy Martzke: "The guy wields influence you wouldn't believe," says a senior network sports producer. "Network presidents wonder what he's gonna say. Boards of directors of the networks. Why? Because they can't help themselves. They know people feed him the stuff—PR people, announcers' agents—but he's read inside the industry. He's got incredible power."

The Mitsubishi flickers.

(*Click.*) "Here's another Viking story on CBS. Are they gonna have any racism in it?"

(*Click.*) "See, Costas has got Flutie."

(*Click.*) In Minnesota, a blue-blazered CBS Sports reporter named James Brown is saying, "Players say 'discrimination' is the word." Martzke is not satisfied. He's suspicious that CBS is "catching up" with a similar story aired earlier on ESPN.

Rudy's wife, Phyllis, known to all as the Mouse, comes in from the garage, a sack of groceries in either arm. "I just wanna let you know," she tells Rudy, "I got lunch stuff out on the table."

(*Click.*) Martzke's eyes never leave the Mitsubishi. "Yeah, yeah. One o'clock, okay?"

(*Click.*)

Best Explanation for Rudy's Power: "You don't read Rudy for his taste," says a programmer. "You don't read him for his accuracy. Everybody understands what he does is about 50 percent accurate—he doesn't watch everything that gets in his column; people call him and tell him. That's why he's powerful. Because he is the only columnist, on a broad, national scale, who allows the TV industry to talk to itself."

Martzke narrows his eyes at Dick Butkus on CBS.

"See, he can't do it. What they've done—I've already written this—they decided, Let's keep Butkus down to a damn minimum so he won't screw up. Christ, he rambled on for forty-five minutes. *What did he say?*"

Rudy is dressed today in a "CAL" Rugby shirt with blue, gold and white stripes, and jeans. Big shoulders. The face of Sluggo at 47.

"I told Brent, I said—I talked to Brent this week onna phone. I said, 'You know why you do a better job than Costas?'— and, by the way, I technically discovered Costas—I told Brent he does a better job 'cause Brent, I believe, does more with less. Irv [Cross] smiles a lot. The viewers are comfortable with that. But Butkus has been a zero replacement for Jimmy the Greek."

Rudy Martzke impacts things. Gary Bender blames Martzke for getting him sacked at CBS. He's credited with boosting Dick Vitale's career as a basketball analyst. He helped hasten Joe Garagiola's departure from NBC. ("Yeah, maybe Joe had lost half a step," says one insider. "The thinking at NBC was, Jeez, if Martzke noticed it, it must be bad.")

In the den where Martzke writes his column: a Sears ergometer Exercycle, several family color photos, a macramé owl, an ironing board with a blue plastic bottle of Spray 'n Starch. On the wall: a color photo of the CBS Sports crew baring its collective ass. The caption: "CBS Sports awards this moon trophy to Rudy Martzke for writing and reviewing destined to go into the anals of television sports reporting."

The phone rings—an electronic trill from the GTE All-American Team Hall of Fame Inaugural Class model. This will be the first of several calls Martzke will receive this afternoon from public-relations people at the various network sports departments.

"Okay, okay, yeah, I know, I saw it. Yeah, Vikings. See, my prediction, my feeling is—huh? Oh, lissen. It's already been typed inna machine." Martzke clicks channels as he talks. "Oh, no. Oh, no," he mumbles at the screen. Into the phone: "But you're right, you guys had it first. That's odd, 'cause usually you guys are playin' catch-up."

He puts the telephone down. "Chris LaPlaca, ESPN publicist. He's sayin' CBS looked like they copied 'em."

365

Martzke was a publicist himself once—for a college athletic department, three pro basketball teams. Best Book Title on His Shelf: *Strange but True Basketball Stories*. He was summoned from the Rochester, New York, Gannett paper when *USA Today* got started in 1982—one of those human "loaners" Al Neuharth vacuumed up from around the chain. Martzke stuck. The rest, as they say, is data.

Rudy makes a call. To Mark Carlson, CBS Sports PR. "Okay, here's the deal. ESPN had a feature on that earlier. I'm just wondering if you guys planned. . . . My personal opinion is. . . ."

So far, Martzke has spotted no Dreaded Glitches. But the afternoon is young.

He bounds up two flights of carpeted stairs to make himself a sandwich—white roll, turkey, mayo—from the Mouse's cold cuts before the Redskins-Saints kickoff on CBS. From a pantry shelf, amid cans of baking goods, comes John Madden's shrunken voice: "That's the thing the Skins *wanted* to do. . . ."

"We have four TVs," says the Mouse.

Back downstairs, Martzke grabs the trilling phone again. "I thought it was a great telecast. Except, you know what? Way at the end there was a couple bad camera cuts. Guys getting in the way, you couldn't see the celebration on the mound. Yeah, but that's okay." Kevin Monaghan, NBC Sports. Just checking in.

The Mitsubishi draws his attention. "He's holdin'! *Are you shittin' me?*" Best Adjustment: "I got the ability, no matter where I move—and I've lived in a lotta different towns—to, within three weeks, become a fan of that football team."

He clicks around the dial. Scribbles on his pad. Talks. Best Quote: "The point is, nobody's ever been a better reporter than me. You develop a lotta contacts, you develop yourself newswise. I know I'm not the best writer. Every now and then people say to me, 'Goddamn, that's a pretty nice piece you had, Rudy. I didn't know you could write.''

The phone trills. "Wait, wait, look here, Sandy, you're doing a great PR job on me, okay? . . . Well, then, why didn't you have it in the piece? . . . You know what? That isn't a very good answer. ESPN put it in their piece. I'm tellin' ya—that's how I woulda done it as a producer." Sandy Genelius, CBS Sports.

The Mouse appears, shivering into a raincoat. "I'm outta here for awhile," she tells Rudy.

Where's she going? Martzke shrugs. "Shoppin'. Hit the stores."

A Rudy Quoteline on his impact: "It's not something I ever intended it to be. Yeah, the networks react. They react to the Oops Awards. They take extreme pride in Best Production. But there are people who claim I cost people's jobs. Gary Bender, now at ABC, blames me for gettin' him dropped at CBS. He said to me, 'Rudy, I blame you.' But I was one of several guys who'd written about him makin' mistakes. But I also had some pulses for Gary. Other guys—Dan Jenkins said I'm Brent Musburger's PR agent.

"It's kinda tough to take at times. I get up with a knob in my stomach on Sunday mornings. Just like the head coach or a quarterback. But hey! I look at it this way: I work hard at it. And I am well versed in noticin' things."

Halftime. So far, many small epiphanies, but still no Dreaded Glitch. Rudy makes a call.

"Sandy. Rudy. I got a question. Brent, with the glasses. This is his first time, right? . . . You got my number, if he wants to call."

Rudy hits his den to type his notes into the machine: a Radio Shack TRS-80 Model 100 portable computer. He keeps an ear cocked toward the Mitsubishi in the living room.

Outside the Martzke's picture window, a soft rain, perhaps chemically enhanced, is falling on the perfect suburb. Late in the afternoon, as players in brilliant, shifting uniforms and men in blue blazers flash and disappear on the Mitsubishi's time-present screen, Rudy Martzke's telephone trills again.

"Okay. So he's probably worn 'em once or twice before."

It is almost time for Martzke to type everything else into his machine and send it all off to Gannett headquarters for tomorrow's column. Martzke's concentration as he clicked through the frequencies for more than four hours was truly remarkable, a performance in its own rights. Best . . . Concentration.

Now his day is almost over. And yet it seems his column still lacks a necessary something, that certain je ne sais quoi. . . .

Suddenly Martzke seems to crouch. Almost to *point*. His eyes are on the Mitsubishi. One of the networks is rewinding the videotape of a commercial—*on the air*!

"Lookit this," Martzke barely breathes, and then: *"Lookit this!"* He buries his pen to the hilt in his notepad, making it squeak, making it hurt.

"Fuckin' GLITCH!"

Afterglow

From the study window in my house at the eastern edge of Middlebury, Vermont, I can see the western facade of the Green Mountains, their lunulate peaks rising and dipping seven miles in the distance—like frozen music, as Goethe said of architecture. Ancient in the earth's own time, sculpted by an ice age, this range silences the small shrillnesses of time-present and draws one's attention into its own tremendous performance.

These mountains are inexpressibly satisfying for me to contemplate, as was the Mississippi River from my grandparents' porch on a high hill in Hannibal when I was a child. Mark Twain saw that same Mississippi and that same untended Illinois shore. Robert Frost wrote poetry within my line of sight here. I have hiked with my wife and young sons in these mountains, and spent two happy weeks each summer at the Bread Loaf writers' conference in a high meadow there, and I feel, through them, what Ethan Allen's sharpshooters must have felt, and the Abnaki before them—a fierce proximity to the inviolate.

An item on the "TV Tips" page of my daily Vermont newspaper, on my study desk, catches my eye: "10 P.M., Warner, pay-per-view: THUNDER AND MUD. Jessica Hahn hosts a night of female mud-wrestling and heavy-metal music, which definitely won't soothe the savage breast. . . ."

And the past vanishes; scale flattens out. The Green Mountains are not so inviolate anymore. Jessica Hahn is all in them, has blown out here on the air from Warner and coated them with something as pestilent, as polluted, as resistant to life in its way as the carbon monoxide that blows out on the air from Ohio and falls on these mountains in the rain. Jessica Hahn, and *Lifestyles of the Rich and Famous,* and *Family Feud,* and *A Current Affair* and all the unrelenting rest of it. There is absolutely no surcease from television; no escaping it, no respite, no sanctuary, no deflecting one's eyes from its enervating, anesthetizing, colonizing glare. It has left a thickening residue on the surface of the world.

Turn off the set? Why, yes, but the residue remains: "10 P.M., Warner, pay-per-view: THUNDER AND MUD. . . ." It has adulterated print. It is pouring through the windows of our weakened, ineffectual public schools via Channel One, the video factoid-and-commercial network conjured up by Whittle Communications as an alternative to texts and the interplay of students and teachers.

Its photoemissions have incrassated whatever movable parts remain of our postwar democratic system. Toward the end of 1989, first *Time* magazine and then the political columnist David Broder, writing in *The Washington Post,* noted that the system had damn near stopped functioning. "Is Government Dead?" asked the cover of *Time,* and Broder answered: "In our era of debilitated political parties, Washington is run by 536 individual political entrepreneurs—one president, 100 senators and 435 members of the House—each of whom got here essentially on his own. Each chooses the office he seeks, raises his own money, hires his own pollster and ad-maker and recruits his own volunteers."

And what institution has replaced the political party? What device makes it possible for politicians to run as entrepreneurs, stepping free of their parties' apparatus to reach the voter directly—complete with their own advertising departments and immune from direct rebuttal by their opponents? Television.

Perhaps most unforgivably, television in our time has virulently attacked the very consciousness of a world beyond itself. At a time when scientists and naturalists and thoughtful journalists have forged a steadily intensifying consensus that the end of nature is at hand—that Western society is perilously close to tipping the scales toward an irreversible poisoning and heating of the physical world—television draws its audiences ever further from a consciousness of nature. The interior environment of television—the decontextualized context for its dramas and its music videos and its newscasts and its commercials—is increasingly posturban, synthetic, nocturnal, self-referencingly technological. The world, croons television, is television.

To populate that denatured world, television supplied its own anti-Genesis: the Eighties saw the ascendancy of Max Headroom, The Beast, ALF, Spitting Image (those moving molded-rubber excrescences of politicians and celebrities), the Hollywood Raisins. These and other mutants—I recall at least one supercar with an intelligence equal to that of its hunky young wheelman, not exactly a prodigious leap of credulity, in the scheme of things—became Ur-stars, while Robocop and Jason and Freddy Krueger stalked the cable movie channels. (Freddy Krueger, the razor-clawed phantasm of the *Nightmare* movie cycle, turned up as host of his own late-night syndicated series.)

Television even found a way to dehumanize its images of human beings: through time-lapse edits of videotape, it could

373

drain these forms of their natural human movements and rhythms, reducing them—or elevating them, depending on the point of view—to the status of cybernetic replicants. Rock videos and commercials, especially those aimed at the adolescent market, fell in love with this image.

One giant leap, as they said in a more innocent time, for mankind.

This surge of rampant synthetization, this manufactured sphere of "reality," seemed capable, in the end, of inspiring little else from TV watchers than a kind of pervasive smugness and irony, a sense of permission for detachment from the remote concerns of the world beyond the screen. What was left to fill the void? Continued viewership, consumption and waste—the very cycle that fueled the economic structure of commercial television. In the growing absence of indignation at its brazenness, the newly deregulated medium tuned up the sell: child viewers were subjected to a commercial brainwashing without precedent in human history; for the grown-ups, entire cable channels sprang up (Home Shopping Network) devoted to round-the-clock impulse-buying.

The consequences of consumption and waste—the fouling and heating of the planet, say—had not yet penetrated the regular agendas of the evening newscasts. What some environmentalists saw as the permanent destabilizing of weather did not seem to be something that worried Willard Scott. On television in the 1980s, "the earth," when considered at all, was likely to be thought of as something one mixed with water to form the ingredient for female mud-wrestling.

So what of the future? What are the alternatives? Or, to ask these same questions in slightly less contemporary terms: Is redemption possible?

The simple answer is "no." American commercial television has struck a bargain with the dark gods that is worthy, in some respects, of Greek tragedy. It seems doomed to reach ever outward, at peril of its audiences' satiety, toward new extremes of shock and vulgarity and self-abasement—only to find that those extremes have been absorbed within weeks into the fabric of the commonplace. And so it must reach out again. (Morton Downey may prove to be TV's Sisyphus, although he may not like the sound of the word.)

Television as we know it, in other words, is fated forever to be a victim of its own excess. I cannot conceive of a corrective arising from "the marketplace," nor can I imagine a formula mandated by the government that would not do violence to the principle of free expression, however debased that principle has become in practice. A war or a natural catastrophe — the ultimate California earthquake, say — might restore a little seriousness of purpose to mass communications. But not even I am Draconian enough to hope that those prospects, as Howard Cosell used to put it, will eventuate.

(Besides, I'm not absolutely convinced that a natural catastrophe would do the trick. A couple of days after the 7.1-magnitude event in the Bay Area last October, I overheard a woman at O'Hare Airport in Chicago loudly proclaim herself "sick" of all the TV coverage. That leaves World War III, which, I suppose, would have the advantage of being shorter even than this woman's attention span.)

No, we cannot assume that mainstream television will redeem itself in our lifetimes, nor in any imaginable future before some even more hellish permutation — brain-implanted transistors, say — arises to take its place.

The best we can hope for is the emergence of some countervailing voice, some alternative idiom *within* video, that will illuminate the medium's inherent but mostly forsaken capacity to delight, to deepen, to inform, to ennoble, to re-invoke history, to enchant the senses and engage the political consciousness.

Within this more limited frame of expectations, some real promise is at hand.

Last September a tiny new entity within the endless lists of American television enterprises met in Washington to elect its

375

first board of directors. The entity called itself the Independent Television Service. Its prospects rested on a modest operating budget of $6 million a year for the ensuing three years. Its precarious existence was the culmination of more than 10 years of dogged negotiating between independent film- and videomakers in this country and various congressional bureaucracies for an assured place in the spectrum of public-television programming.

"Independent television" was a notion that flared briefly, and marginally, into the nation's consciousness in the counter-cultural ferment of the early 1970s. It meant what the title implied: television that was "independent" of advertising or corporate budgets, and the mainstream constrictions that went with them.

It was a variation on the concept of the "alternative press"—the vision of ordinary people, in possession of their own television cameras and microphones and editing equipment, going out there into the streets and communes and rock festivals of America, and making TV programs for other ordinary people. Where would this "people's television" be shown? Why, on the many available "access" channels that would open up as soon as the Cable Revolution liberated video from the repressive pig airwaves!

It never really happened. Equipment in those psychedelic days was too big and cumbersome and too expensive for most ordinary people to own, and the much promised "public access" adjunct of the Cable Revolution withered after a few years. And much of what the early experimenters came up with was tendentious and as dull as dishwater anyway. And so, before too long, American independent filmmakers and their new video brethren had to go back to pretty much showing their artistic and journalistic efforts to one another.

And yet the producers—about as politically helpless a group as ever lobbied for public recognition in America—never stopped trying. They turned from "access channels" to a programming conduit that not only reached established audiences, but also was explicitly designed to offer alternatives to commercial-network pap. They turned to public television.

As early as 1978, an organization called the Association of Independent Video and Filmmakers persuaded Congress to require public television to set aside a certain amount of money to fund independent projects.

Two years later the Corporation for Public Broadcasting actually created an ongoing program fund to support independent production. Its guidelines urged producers to "rethink and break through the conventional forms and subjects of broadcasting." That was fine. And then Ronald Reagan got elected President. Suddenly, the locus of "rethinking" and "breaking through" had shifted from the grass roots to the office of Michael Deaver. Reagan's Congress not only slashed the CPB budget (and thus the independents'); it even authorized an advertising "experiment" that would, if consummated, have "privatized" public television on a grand scale.

Independent programming on public TV was generally bruised, restricted and treated as a quasi-subversive force during the Reagan years, although there were notable breakthroughs: In 1982 the Boston station WGBH created the estimable prime-time documentary series *Frontline* with a $5 million CPB grant. *Frontline* has continued to be a public-affairs showcase for independent works. But some existing independent series (*Matters of Life and Death,* for instance) got canceled or severely cut back as public television directed most of its resources to such high-cultural (and politically safe) projects as *American Playhouse* and *Great Performances.*

The independents soldiered on; by now they were gaining the attention of some important Congressional figures, including the chairman of the Senate Communications Subcommittee, Daniel Inouye. Senator Inouye's report on the Public Telecommunications Act of 1988, a massive restructuring measure for public TV, contained the following passage: "Although the CPB has testified that approximately half of its television program funds are allocated to the work of indepen-

377

dent producers, representatives of the independent production community suggest that funds . . . are significantly less. The Congress is not satisfied that the CPB has allocated sufficient funds to smaller individual producers working independently of stations or station consortia . . ."

With that stroke, Inouye's subcommittee proposed the creation of the Independent Television Service, funded by Corporation for Public Broadcasting money. Congress approved it, and Ronald Reagan, in one of his last official acts as President, signed it into law in November 1988.

What all this amounts to is a consummation—with important and sophisticated refinements—of those halcyon "people's television" dreams of the early 1970s. It is a call to arms for anyone in America (or beyond) with a camera, and editing equipment, and a vision of how video might enrich the culture on its own terms, rather than the terms of audience exploitation for the consumption of goods.

"We want to challenge filmmakers and videomakers to produce significant work," said Jeffrey Chester, a central figure in the 10-year ITS struggle, "not only in documentaries, but even in series and magazine shows. We want them to be willing to make mistakes. We want them to be willing to address the journalistic and artistic needs of the nation. We intend to challenge PBS by showing them what public TV might look like if TV were conceived to serve the public interest, not the interests of ratings people and underwriters.

"And we hope to challenge audiences—give them the chance to view works of different styles, made with passion and always with intelligence. We want to broaden the perspectives of audiences; we want to show them as many different points of view and purpose as we can."

Those points of view are out there, in the land, in film and video canisters, waiting to be shown. The independent movement attained its majority in the 1980s. Well out of the mass-public's line of sight—in academia, in the visual-arts centers of New York and California, but also in a thousand smaller enclaves around the United States, videomakers matured and professionalized themselves.

Some of their points of view have already caught the attention of the mainstream: *P.O.V.* (the initials stand, conveniently enough, for "point of view"), an independent nonfiction showcase, premiered in 1988 on PBS and received critical attention throughout the country. Its jarring, disturbing offerings have included "Who Killed Vincent Chin?" a classic video investigation into the murder of an unemployed Detroit autoworker. The video employed *Rashomon*-like interpretations of truth and testimony; it took five years to complete and was nominated for an Academy Award in 1989. Other *P.O.V.* segments have included an examination of the Nicaraguan Sandinistas from the inside, a portrait of a dying young AIDS victim, embattled ministers in Pittsburgh confronting big institutions on behalf of laid-off steelworkers and an extraordinarily shattering probe into the lives of young runaway girls in Boston.

In Chicago, an ambitious new independent series, *The 90s*, began its satellite transmissions last November—transmissions that are being picked up by at least 25 public stations reaching a total of 25 million households. Its executive producer, Tom Weinberg, is a veteran of more than 500 independent works over a 20-year period. *The 90s* presents a fast potpourri of journalism, video art and personal essays that address the political and cultural currents of a changing world.

Nor is public television the only venue for the newly resurgent movement. The Learning Channel, an educational cable channel headquartered in Rosslyn, Virginia, has showcased such independent series as *Spirit of Place*, a collection of nonfiction video essays dealing with people's mythic responses to their native ground. (I served as host for that series.)

Even public-access cable itself—the original dream-concept of the early 1970s—has survived and grown into a strong grassroots presence, with more than a thousand "access centers" across the country. The vestigial porno-peddling channel to the contrary (such as the erstwhile Channel J in New York), most "access" programming is aimed at coverage of local municipal government, although women's groups, labor organizations and even high-school students are strong presences in the movement.

(Cable access still has its battles to fight against the forces of the video big-time. In Pittsburgh not long ago, a popular ongoing series found itself narrowly averting extinction. The series was called *Hershow*; it focused on women's news, women's art and coverage of social and educational issues from women's perspectives. The corporate giant that owned the cable system in Pittsburgh had been complaining to the city government about its burden in financing community-service channels. The corporate giant was Warner-Amex, the distributor of the pay-per-view program THUNDER AND MUD, hosted by Jessica Hahn.)

The camera eye is not, inherently, a malign force in the life of a society—however contrary seems to be the evidence of the Television Age. There was a time, within the living memory of many Americans, when the camera eye generated a tremendous resurgence in literature, in political discussion, in the moral agenda of the nation. The advent of the Leica, the hand-held 35-mm still camera, in the early 1930s, gave photojournalists an unprecedented mobility and quick access to their subject matter; the Spanish Civil War gave many of them a subject. The resulting mass-distributed images of soldiers at the point of death in combat, and of suffering civilians streaming out of ravaged cities, forever changed the content of war journalism and literature: it could no longer be romantic.

At about the same time, the 1930s, other photographers were fanning out into America to record social realism of a different kind. They included such pioneering giants as Walker Evans, Dorothea Lange, Ben Shahn and Russell Lee. Besides their great technical skills—their deep involvement in such matters as composition and light and the geometry of images—these photographers were united by an older concern, one that traced back to Emerson and Whitman: a concern for transcendence. Their photographs affirmed noble ideals. For instance, they dealt seriously with poverty. Evans trained his lenses directly into the faces of suffering sharecroppers and tried to evoke, or at least confer, an unquenchable beauty in those faces: a plea for redemption.

Evans's collaborator in America's seminal work of nonfiction prose and imagery, James Agee, was profoundly stirred by these photographs. Near the beginning of their book, *Let Us Now Praise Famous Men*, Agee the master prose stylist released an unforgettable cry from the heart:

> If I could do it, I'd do no writing at all here. It would be photographs; the rest would be fragments of cloth, bits of cotton, lumps of earth, records of speech, pieces of wood and iron, phials of odors, plates of food and excrement. Booksellers would consider it quite a novelty; critics would murmur, yes, but is it art; and I could trust a majority of you to use it as you would a parlor game.
>
> A piece of the body torn out by the roots might be more to the point.
>
> As it is, though, I'll do what little I can in writing. Only it will be very little. I'm not capable of it; and if I were, you would not go near it at all. For if you did, you would hardly bear to live.

The point of the Television Age—the point of this collection—is not that television is bad. The point is that television, like any medium, is *capable* of great harm, and that as the descendant of the Leica—the minicam—has passed from the hands of Walker Evans's children and into the hands of Television's children, that capability has been grotesquely fulfilled.

The hope—evidenced through the rise of the independent movement—is that the excesses and excrescences of television in the 1980s will not prove to be its lasting legacy: that, as with the history of the still camera, people will eventually begin using it as well as consuming its commercial yield. The integrity of the Green Mountains outside my window, and of all the beauty and coherence that remain in this century and this life, would seem to depend on that.